JAMES SHIRLEY

A Study of Literary Coteries and Patronage in Seventeenth-Century England

Sandra A. Burner
State University of New York

UNIVERSITY PRESS OF AMERICA

Lanham • New York • London

Copyright © 1988 by

University Press of America,® Inc.

4720 Boston Way
Lanham, MD 20706

3 Henrietta Street
London WC2E 8LU England

All rights reserved

Printed in the United States of America

British Cataloging in Publication Information Available

Library of Congress Cataloging-in-Publication Data

Burner, Sandra A., 1936–
James Shirley : a study of literary coteries and
patronage in seventeenth-century England.
Bibliography: p.
Includes index.
1. Shirley, James, 1596–1666. 2. Authors, English—
Early modern, 1500–1700—Biography. 3. Authors and
patrons—England—History—17th century. 4. Theater—
England—History—17th century. 5. England—Intellectual
life—17th century. 6. Authorship—History—17th century. I. Title.
PR3146.B87   1988   822'.4   88–24899
ISBN 0–8191–7200–6 (alk. paper)

All University Press of America books are produced on acid-free paper.
The paper used in this publication meets the minimum requirements of
American National Standard for Information Sciences—Permanence of Paper
for Printed Library Materials, ANSI Z39.48–1984.

To David

*" . . . Yet they never get tired of each other;
they are a couple."*

Acknowledgments

Throughout the research and writing of this book, the help of two friends deserves special thanks: Professor Thomas R. West of Catholic University for his extensive assistance in stylistic matters and organization, and Dr. Wayne H. Phelps, former Director of Planning and Educational Research, West Virginia Board of Regents, who guided me in the organization and direction of my research over a period of many years.

I am also indebted to the assistance and graciousness of many archivists and scholars in England: David M. Rogers of the Bodleian Library; Peter Walne, County Archivist, Hertfordshire County Record Office, along with several members of his staff; Mr. Brown, Archivist of the Drapers' Company, Drapers' Hall; Mr. Dan, the Beadle of the Merchant Taylors' Hall; A. F. Allison, Dept. of Printed Books, The British Museum Library; Elizabeth Poyser, Archivist, Archbishop's House, Westminster Cathedral; Hugh F. Kearney, University of Sussex; H. E. Peek, Keeper of the Archives, and Mary E. Raver, University Archives, University of Cambridge; W. R. Serjeant, County Archivist, Nottinghamshire Record Office; Brigadier Peter Young, The Royal Military Academy, Sandhurst; Mary E. Finch, Assistant Archivist, Lincolnshire Archives Committee; Edward S. Worrall, Essex Recusant Society; Father Howard Docherty, O.F.M., Headmaster, St. Bonaventure's School; Father Hugh Bowler, O.S.B., Douai Abbey; Father John Hugh Aveling, O.S.B., Ampleforth College, York; F. I. Kilvington, Headmaster, St. Albans School; the archivists and staff of the Guildhall Library; Rosemary Rendel, Catholic Record Society; N. Evans and the staff of the Public Record Office; the archivists in the Manuscript and Reading Rooms of the British Museum; L. Collins and the research staff of the Society of Genealogists.

A number of scholars in the United States and Canada, too numerous all to be included here, gave me encouragement and helpful suggestions regarding my research. They include Professor Albert Wertheim, Indiana University; Professor Richard E. Morton, McMaster University; Professor Martin J. Havran, Northwestern University, Professor W. J. Jones, The University of Alberta, and Dr. Donald S. Lawless.

A generous grant, for which I am most grateful, from the New York State/United University Professions Joint Labor-Management Committee, enabled me to complete final revisions.

Finally, I wish to thank my colleagues at Stony Brook, especially my friends who gave me their interest and support in the Office of Undergraduate Studies, and its former Dean, Dr. Robert Marcus, and the librarians and staff of the Melville Library's Office of Interlibrary Loan. Special thanks go to Mary Masciopinto, whose patience and assistance in the final stages of preparation were crucial. I wish also to thank my personal friend, Benjamin Schwartz, for being just that.

Sandra Burner
Nissequogue, New York

CONTENTS

	Introduction ix
Chapter I	The Early Years: 1596—1625 1
Chapter II	The Gray's Inn Circle and the Professional Dramatists 41
Chapter III	The Court Coteries and Court Patronage 85
Chapter IV	Shirley in Ireland, 1636—1640 113
Chapter V	"London is Gone to York": The Newcastle Circle and the Stanley Coterie 139
Chapter VI	The Last Years: 1649—1666 177
	List of Works Frequently Cited 216
	Index 220

INTRODUCTION

This book examines the life of the prolific Caroline dramatist James Shirley (1596-1666) in its connections with two important seventeenth-century literary conventions, coteries and patronage. Shirley's career of playwright and poet, which spans the years from the accession of Charles I to the Great Fire of London, illustrates in microcosm the development of these conventions, and offers a look into the self-consciously sophisticated, literate upper classes that contained them. The study surveys Shirley's patrons and his membership in a number of professional groups; dedications and verses he composed for his own published work and commendatory pieces offered by his acquaintances; his relationships with other English Roman Catholics, particularly in the Court; and the interrelationships among the people he worked with or was dependent on. Newly discovered primary sources add considerably to knowledge of Shirley's place in a complex social structure.

Among the scholarly studies that have illuminated the profession of writer during the last half of the sixteenth century and the first half of the seventeenth, Phoebe Sheavyn's pioneering investigation, published in 1909, outlines changes in patronage and literary production; she also sketches the social strata of writers, distinguishing between amateurs and professionals. The professional writer, she argues, emerged out of the disintegration of a system of patronage at best sporadic by the turn of the century and the assumption by the publishing trade of the role of patron; a royal edict that centered printing and bookselling in London; the shift from schoolteaching or tutoring to working for a printer or publisher as a method of supplementing the writer's income; and the development of considerable rivalry and, at the same time, comraderie among writers, amateur and professional, in the keenly competitive effort to claim the diverse middle class audience and buyers of books or pamphlets.[1]

---

[1]Phoebe Sheavyn, *The Literary Profession in the Elizabethan Age* (1909; rpt. New York, 1964).

A 1959 study by Edwin Miller of the writer of non-dramatic literature during Elizabeth's reign adds to scholarly understanding of this group. Miller notes that most were children of London tradesmen or professionals, many of whom sent their sons to the university. In addition were the amateur writers, most of them from families of higher social position in rural England. The nobleman's often half-hearted bequest, appointment, gift, or offer of room and board to the author gave way in large part to a contract between a publisher and an independent writer. Selling a piece to these new middleman became more profitable than the chancier dedication to a wealthy merchant or nobleman. The economic and social developments during this period, which began in the later years of Elizabeth's reign and came to characterize the time of Charles I, firmly established a middle-class literature for a middle-class audience.[2]

As a means of raising funds, the Stuart kings resorted to selling titles of nobility, thereby creating a new class of gentry. Changes in the mercantile system increased the number of merchants rich enough to buy a title. This also affected what remained of the convention of patronage. A wealthy merchant, for example, who had purchased a knighthood from the Crown might quickly reward a poet or playwright for a literary dedication. Rarely, however, would he provide tangible support for one individual over a long period. This was not a new development, but the combination of a burgeoning printing profession and the creation of a *nouveaux riche* made standard the one-time recompense for a dedication. In the reign of James I few writers had possessed such assurance of sustained patronage as Ben Jonson enjoyed from William Cavendish, then Duke of Newcastle. The custom of dedicating each publication to one or more new potential patrons became established during the Stuart era. The author might profess personal friendship or thanks for earlier support or candidly admit that the dedicatee is known to him only by reputation or title.

---

[2]Edwin Haviland Miller, *The Professional Writer in Elizabethan England* (Cambridge, MA., 1959)

Throughout the reigns of James I and Charles I, the interests and prominence of the Court in dramatic and artistic production steadily increased. The success of a writer became more dependent on pleasing the Court than on securing a nobleman as patron. But the Crown assumed much of the burden of patronage without either adequate financial means or sufficient court appointments to offer authors as recompense for their works. Conventional patronage continued to affect not only the fortunes of individual writers but also the type of literature produced. More often than not during the Caroline period, the Court contained the more influential of patrons. The preeminent arbiters of taste in matters of art and literature were King Charles and Queen Henrietta Maria and their powerful courtier favorites. Even those noblemen with independent wealth and literary talent, such as Newcastle, strove to please the sovereign's taste, usually in hopes of securing a Court appointment. Popularity with the Court might gain a playwright an ambitious patron. Inigo Jones, "Surveyor of the King's Works," emerged the favorite for constructing the important scenery and designs that came to be associated with the masque. Perhaps it was because Newcastle had hired Ben Jonson, out of favor with the Court, to write the entertainments the Duke presented to their Majesties in 1633 and 1634 that the appointment of Newcastle as governor to the Prince of Wales did not come until 1638.

The theatre public during Shirley's ascendancy was more socially cohesive than the lusty mixed crowds that had responded to Shakespeare. It looked for itself in the dramas it attended, looked particularly for standards of wit and elegance that it perceived in its own fashionable existence. It is not uncommon for audiences to wish to be flattered, whether by pleasing imitation of them or by dramas that claim to test their willingness to be judged or intellectually challenged. At times Shirley criticized the superficiality and fads of his audience; at times he complimented its style and mannerisms. His relationship was ambivalent, and an inquiry into his associations within the coteries and literary circles of his time aids in understanding that ambivalence. A number of Caroline plays written during the 1630's reflected the tensions among jostling social classes much as the masque in the closing years of the reign of Charles I served as a vehicle for royal political statement.

Professional Caroline playwrights turned to publishing as a means of augmenting their income. Once a play was no longer in the performing repertoire, the author could hope to profit by selling it to a publisher (with the permission of the acting company for which it was written). Although hard evidence is yet to be found of contractual arrangements between publishers and authors, Shirley's long associations with particular publishers suggests the likelihood.

Increasingly the publisher became the patron, determining what was published by what would sell. The closing of public theatres during the Civil Wars and Interregnum reinforced the importance of the publisher, and the reading public, deprived of its public shows and entertainment, also turned to the readily available quarto or octavo. Newssheets, describing political events and reporting gossip, had to suffice as substitute for bearbaiting or other rough-and-ready entertainment. For the more literate audience, reading plays and masques became the means of recapturing the grandness and style of the earlier Caroline masques and private playhouse drama. Professional writers such as Shirley became highly involved in the publication of their works, overseeing the printing, adding particular prefaces, and strategically dedicating specific pieces. Publishing served the dual purpose of keeping a reputation current and providing an income.

Writers of the Caroline era, whose craft was in the peculiar condition of becoming a profession without the benefits and protections enjoyed by established fraternities such as the trade guilds of London, were turning more and more to membership in various circles and coteries that could give them access to patrons and bring greater literary recognition. A number of fairly well defined groups formed, some as a result of rivalries between amateur writers—university students, Inns of Court men or courtiers—and professional playwrights or poets whose livelihood derived primarily from writing and publishing. Gerald Eades Bentley presumes that these professional dramatists wrote almost exclusively for the commercial theatres, held formal contracts with specific acting companies in particular playhouses, and received salaries in return for fulfilling quotas of plays and other writing for the theatre owners.[3] "Coterie," a word that would not come into common usage until the eighteenth century, will refer here to a small intimate group formed of select members of a circle, which in Shirley's time simply meant "a class or division of society."[4]

Shirley's professional success came in part because of his alliance with five distinct but interconnected groups: the Gray's Inn circle, the Catholic and the Irish Court coteries, the Civil War group under William Cavendish, and the literary people who gathered around the poet and translator Thomas Stanley in the later 1640's. The membership and literary activities of these groups illuminate the development of the drama from 1625 to 1660. During the Interregnum and into the Restoration a sixth circle existed, looser in its membership but still distinct enough to indicate the methods of survival pursued by playwrights, an underground group that survived in the years of suppression of play performances. From among all these friends and associates, a small group is discernible that constituted his own continuing, working coterie of professional dramatists. It is this last group that Bentley's definition of professional writer clarifies.

How many of the literati during the reign of Charles I flirted with Catholicism or converted is far from clear, but the incidence of affiliation with the Roman Church was much publicized. Ambition might argue for conversion to a religion that was in vogue with the Court. But Shirley's embracing the Roman faith appears to have been genuine. And his religion was inseparable from his social and literary associations. Membership in a circle or coterie was rarely strictly literary. That groups which had formed ostensibly for creative writing combined for political and religious reasons as well is most evident in the Court coteries. Similarly, the

---

[3]Gerald Eades Bentley, *The Profession of Dramatist in Shakespeare's Time, 1590-1642* (Princeton, 1971).

[4]*OED,* 3rd ed. (Oxford, 1955).

Newcastle circle, from what an investigation of Shirley's friends of the time would indicate, came together for religious and political as well as literary interests.

From a study of the life of James Shirley emerges a broad perception of the social, professional milieu of Caroline dramatists. No attempt is made to present a critical analysis of Shirley's plays and poems. But the patrons of Shirley and his fellow playwrights, the political and literary circles to which writers belonged, the complex class structures that were open to Shirley and his colleagues provided the fictional subjects and the fashionable standards of taste to which seventeenth-century dramatists responded, with the greater or lesser sensitivity that ultimately establishes a writer's uniqueness and worth.

I

The Early Years: 1596-1625

James Shirley was a Londoner by birth. He did not have to discover the city that was to provide him the fashionable audience and the narrowed, mannered theatre of the time of Charles I. He would spend some years outside London— studying at Cambridge and possibly at Oxford, writing plays in Dublin when plague closed the London theatres, actively assisting the Royalists in the Midlands during the early Civil War years, and traveling abroad at least once. But he always returned to the city where he had been raised and was to die, the London that sustained him as playwright, poet, and scholar.

At the end of the sixteenth century, when Shirley was born, the old city of London within the ancient walls was a half-mile wide and slightly over a mile long. The populace already was seeping outside these boundaries: within the area now called "Greater London," with a population then of 200,000, lay various small boroughs and liberties, as well as the walled city. Moorfields, bordering the London wall north of the city center, was a rural seat of a lower class of money lenders. Spitalfields, farther to the northeast, was only a village with a parish church. Clerkenwell, the northwest section just outside the walls, had become by the early seventeenth century the favorite neighborhood of the aristocracy. Directly west of the core city and south of Clerkenwell came Holborn, a residential area with gardens. Westminster, stretching westward from Holborn and Clerkenwell, was under royal and episcopal rule; its nobility and gentry contrasted to the predominantly bourgeois population of the corporate city. It was connected to London by the Strand, a rural avenue dotted with aristocratic "town houses." The Thames River cradled the city on the south and separated it from Southwark or Bridge-Without-Ward, the second most populous section outside of the walls; the theatres and bear-baiting gardens were concentrated here, and patrons reached it by boat or by crossing London Bridge.[1]

The eight-foot thick medieval wall of nearly two miles tightly encircled the old city and suggested much of its character: lean, dark streets winding up and down between crowded low houses framed of oak and tiled above the gables; the overhanging stories, built to give protection from the weather, nearly meeting across the passageways, shutting out air and light. These streets, some of them paved with cobblestones laid in sand and gravel, challenged the pedestrian or rider. In the center or on the sides was a common gutter for the garbage and debris that was haphazardly washed away by rain or cleared by scavengers, who swept it to river banks to rot. Baskets, barrels, and stools obstructed all traffic: the easiest way to get any distance within London was by means of the river. Every street was packed with people; tradesmen's boys stood at the shop doors shouting "What is't ye lack, ladies?" while workmen with carts cluttered any open space. The London shopkeeper held his business on the ground floor of the building and lived on the upper floors with his numerous children, some servants, and perhaps a few apprentices. Most houses were three or four stories high. Behind the shop on the ground floor were a kitchen and sometimes a small room. The second and third stories in a typical house contained two rooms each; often a dining room was on the second floor. The top floor might hold two small garrets. Houses were narrow, about 16 feet wide and 29 feet deep.[2]

Almost every block had its church. Its importance was economic and social as well as religious. Hearth taxes, levies for the parish poor, legal records of baptisms, marriage and death entries—all were the works of the church. At the beginning of the century more than one hundred churches were in the city; over eighty would be destroyed by the Great Fire of 1666.[3]

The parish register for one of these, St. Mary Woolchurch, Haw, records the baptism of James Shirley on September 7, 1596.[4] Precisely in the center of the old city, the church area included the site of Shirley's birth. One of Shirley's sons told Anthony à Wood, an early chronicler of the seventeenth century, that the dramatist's birthplace was "where the Stocks market now is"— so called because a stocks for public offenders had once been at the site.[5] Several major streets—Poultry, Cornhill, Lombard, Threadneedle—converged at the spot, and some of the names indicate the range of goods sold at this market in a neighborhood where commerce, crowds, and smells must have been at their thickest.[6]

It was in this pulsing district that Shirley was to spend his early years. The birth records of his sisters Ellen in 1598 and Elizabeth in 1599, and a death entry in 1606 for a third sister, Mary, reveal that St. Mary Woolchurch continued to be the home parish of the Shirleys.[7]

The family had lived there for some time. Shirley's grandfather, William, was probably the William Shirley who married Marie Newton on November 11, 1561, in the nearby church of St. Mary le Bow.[8] As early as 1564-65 he was living in a house belonging to the parish of Woolchurch and paying rent of £4 a year; in addition, he paid 13/4d. for a little house or "tenement" adjoining. The following year he contributed also for "good Wiff Wilson['s] house" in the amount of 5s. and for each year until his death in 1593 William Shirley's name appears among the churchwardens' rent listings.[9] In the Woolchurch register are numerous birth and death entries for William's children: Thomas, baptized on April 25, 1565; an unnamed child buried on November 30, 1566; and the dramatist's father, James, baptized on January 18, 1568. The births of two girls also are entered, Brigit in 1569 and Elizabeth in 1571; neither survived infancy.[10] During this time William's name was placed in the churchwardens' accounts for paying 6/8d. to have ground broken for burial of his maid.[11]

Beginning in 1571, William Shirley, along with several others in the parish, was involved in a court case about his rented house. Brought by Thomas Jenkinson, who claimed various lands from the church, the suit began in the Lord Mayor's court and was subsequently removed to the Exchequer. Shirley's fees were paid with church funds, and the episode may have enhanced his standing in the church. In 1577, at any rate, he won election to the post of churchwarden. During the next decade his signature went down regularly among those approving the accounts.[12]

William Shirley called himself "citizen and draper of London."[13] As early as 1364 the drapers had been granted a monopoly for the retail sale of cloth; in time these merchants came to sell nearly everything.[14] John Stow in his *Survey of London* notes that the drapers were located in Candlewick and Watling Streets, an area merging into the Stocks Market about one hundred yards north.[15] An item for January 22, 1561, in the Minutes and Records of the Drapers' Company, reports that William Shirley entered into the freedom of the company through apprenticeship to John Dissell [Dycell]. This indicates that as early as 1554, on the estimate of the usual seven-year apprenticeship, Shirley's grandfather was in London. Curiously, though, William Shirley does not appear in the Drapers' rather detailed apprentice lists, although others are entered under the mastership of Dissell. Prior to William's appearance, no Shirleys were noted in the company records.[16]

Under the date of October 26, 1586, when Thomas Shirley was 21, he was entered in the Freedom List as "filius Shorley, Willmus per redempcoem"—that is, free by redemption. Yet in the Wardens' Accounts Thomas is listed as paying 3/4d. for being "made free by patriomon" [sic].[17] It seems likely that the Freedom List is in error and that Thomas was given freedom through his father rather than by purchase; James, the dramatist's father, is entered the 20th of February, 1594, on the Freedom List as "Filius

Sherley, Willmus per patrimonium." James also appears in the Wardens' Accounts as paying 3/4d., the standard fee then for receiving freedom by patrimony.[18] James senior was 26 years old; his father had died the year before and it is probable that Thomas also was dead, for church and guild records indicate that James carried on his father's house lease and business.

The nature of the elder James Shirley's association with the Drapers is revealed in the company's "Quarterage" and "Bindings" books. Quarterage rates were charged to members for various activities of the company such as dinners, entertainments for royalty, charities, and miscellaneous expenses.[19] For each year from 1605, when the quarterage account began, through 1613, payment is recorded for "Sherley James Stockes." Another entry, reading "Shorley James Woolchurch," shows payment from 1605 through 1616. Above the notation for 1616 is written "Katherine Shorley his widowe," and an entry for 1617 in a separate quarterage book reads "Widdow Sherley of James Sherley by Woolchurch 1616"[20]—the elder James was buried at St. Mary Woolchurch on June 2, 1617.[21] Apparently Katherine paid the previous year's fees in 1617. A book that records "bindings"—records of boys bound or apprenticed to tradesmen—reports that on July 30, 1617, Roger Highewaye was bound to Katherine Shirley for eight years. Another bindings book, noting that Roger is son of Thomas Highewaye, cordwainer, describes Katherine Shirley as a free-woman and late wife of James, "A haber of small wares by the Stocks."[22] In the early seventeenth century, a haberdasher was the proprietor of a small notions shop selling items ranging from gentlemen's hats to fans to books.[23] Shirley's father, then, had apparently operated a small shop, possibly set up in 1594 when he received his freedom or perhaps inherited at his father William's death a year earlier.

More about Shirley's mother is revealed in the dramatist's own license to marry in 1618. Katherine Shirley's name is given as "Catherine Chatwyn als. Sharley" of the parish of St. Botolph Without Aldgate in London.[24] This disclosure that she had acquired a new married name within a year of her husband's death and that she had some connection with the parish of St. Botolph, which was east of London just outside the walls, suggests that Roger Highewaye's function may have been to manage the business and free her for a move. Yet there is no record of her in that parish.[25] A burial entry of May 26, 1627, is for a "Katheryne Chetwyn, widow" in St. James, Clerkenwell, a parish near to St. Andrew's, Holborn, where the younger James resided about that time.[26] But no real connection between this widow and Shirley's mother can be found.

So Shirley was of sturdy business stock. That does not exclude the possibility of gentry lineage also: William could have been a second son of a gentle family sent to London for apprenticeship, as were many youths of that condition.[27] The playwright apparently sat for a portrait, now in the possession of the Bodleian Library at Oxford University, that is graced by the arms of the House of Ettington, the Shirleys of Warwick.[28] An engraving copied from this portrait appeared in a little book, published in 1659, containing two masques by Shirley. The engraving, dated 1658, clearly shows the arms of an offshoot of the Warwick Shirleys, the Shirleys of Wiston and West Grinstead in Sussex, but "differenced with a crescent," which denotes a second son.[29] E. P. Shirley's *Stemmata Shirleiana* (1873) does not place the dramatist among the Shirleys of Sussex or Warwickshire; but the genealogist presumably had no acquaintance with the Woolchurch Shirleys, and therefore had no occasion to search for a William Shirley.[30]

There were gentle William Shirleys of that time among whom could have been the dramatist's grandfather. One of them is mentioned in the will of "Thomas Sherley, gent. of Clementes Inne, London." All of Thomas' property is left to a brother William, who was named executor in the will entered in probate in London on October 23, 1565—soon after James's grandfather began to rent his fairly expansive dwelling from the Woolchurch parish. Most of Thomas Sherley's lands were situated in Sturminster Newton, County Dorset.[31] According to E. P. Shirley, one family of Shirleys in Dorset bore the arms belonging to the House of Ettington, which the dramatist claimed in the Bodleian portrait; the family had lived at Bagbere in the parish of Sturminster Newton since the time of Henry VIII.[32] But it cannot be certain that the William who executed Thomas Shirley's will was the citizen and draper of London.

Other possible gentle connection could be to the dramatist Henry Shirley (d. 1627), of the Sussex family that bore the arms portrayed so plainly in the 1658 engraving of James Shirley. Some scholars have presumed a blood relation between the two Shirleys because they were playwrights of the same period, and because their lives did curiously intertwine, but E. P. Shirley's thorough pedigree of Henry shows no connection.[33] The dedication in 1632 of James Shirley's play, *The Changes,* is "To the Right Honourable the Lady Dorothy Shirley." She was Dorothy Devereux, married in 1615 to Sir Henry Shirley—unrelated to the dramatist Henry Shirley—of Staunton in Leicestershire; he was of the Warwick Shirleys, whose arms are carried in the Bodleian portrait of James.[34] But it is probable that had there been a blood relationship, James would have addressed her husband, who was still living at the time.

It is at best a speculative matter. Shirley's use of differing arms—if indeed he supervised the engraving at all—perhaps suggests that he had no right to bear them. Yet perfectly legitimate means were available to him for the assumption of high estate. In designating both William Shirley and the elder James as "Mr." the Woolchurch parish records may have been following the common practice of assigning the honors of gentry to men of substance and position. For the same reason, Shirley would not have been presumptuous in signing himself "Gent"; and had he applied for a Patent of Armorial Bearings, he would have received one simply because he was from a substantial mercantile family.[35]

The "citizen and draper" of London who was James Shirley's grandfather had been a figure of considerable status. Mr. William Sherley [Sharlie, Shorley] appears frequently in the Woolchurch Churchwardens' Accounts, which note his rent payment, the burial of a friend's son, and repairs to his house and to property near it. A comparison of rent payments for his house with those for other church-owned property suggests a substantial dwelling. When William died, his son James paid fees for burial in the "crosse alley [aisle?] by the fount," for the paving of the grave, and for the tolling of the "great bell."[36] Beginning in 1593, James continued to rent the house from the parish at an annual rate of £6/13/4d.; later he was granted a twenty-one year lease to begin "Ladie Daie 1611" at a rent totaling £10 in addition to a fee of £20 for the lease.[37] Whether James the dramatist as eldest son and child "inherited" the lease is unclear, for the entries stop abruptly in 1616, then skip to 1627 and then again to 1637; no Shirleys are listed under rent receipts. What is certain is that James Shirley grew up amidst mercantile prosperity of the sort that at times became the object of the playwright's sophisticated mockery.

Perhaps it was Shirley's early education that started him toward more fastidious tastes. At the age of twelve, in 1608, he was enrolled in the fourth form at the Merchant Taylors' School. The first record of Shirley as student there appears in the book of Probations for the school under the date of December 11, 1608; here the dramatist's month of birth is given, September 1596, and the date of his entry in the fourth form, October 4, 1608. The students in the school at this time totaled 213 with 103 admitted as free scholars, 10 entered for 2/2d. per quarter, and 100 enrolled for 5d. per quarter. The Court Minute books of the Merchant Taylors' Company generally give the names of boys admitted and note whether they are free or paying scholars, but no record of Shirley's admittance is included. Two years after his entrance to the school, James stood first in the fifth form.[38] Probation records that show the relative standing of students are missing for 1612; the entries for 1613 and later give no trace of Shirley, and we may assume with Alexander Dyce, Shirley's first editor (1833), that on June 11, 1612, the annual election day, Shirley left the school, for that day was the normal time of departure for upper form boys.[39]

Standing about three hundred yards southeast of the Stocks Market on Suffolk Lane (now Cannon Street), which turns up Candlewick Street, Merchant Taylors' School was one of at least four fine schools of the time. The school, founded in 1561, had been made famous by several headmasters, of whom the first, Richard Mulcaster, Edmund Spenser's teacher there, is the best known. Despite Mulcaster's pioneering efforts to teach and speak English in the school, Latin remained the core of the curriculum;

pupils translated Latin into English, wrote verses in Latin, and even debated in that tongue; and they studied classical authors, including Ovid, Donatus, Cicero, Caeser, and Virgil.[40] During Shirley's stay the grammarian William Hayne was master; he remained until 1624, serving more than twenty-four years. In Shirley's fourth form, according to the "Books and Exercises" listed in the school's probation book, the boys were reading both Cicero and Virgil.[41] Later in his life, after the close of the theatres, Shirley himself wrote and published Latin grammars.

The eldest son of a family having something like gentlemanly status could select his career, while one without such parentage could at best hope for an apprenticeship with a tradesman. The noble or gentle youth might begin by becoming a professional soldier, hoping to gain courtly attention and thereby a lucrative royal post. A stay at the Inns of Court in London could prepare him for royal appointment to the bench. Attendance at one of the two universities, Oxford and Cambridge, was for boys of some means perhaps the most frequently traveled road to a career. Often the student entered a university without officially enrolling and left without taking a degree. He could, however, earn his A.B., go on to ordination, and secure a living at some parish—the more influential his family, the easier the duties and the more profitable.

It was beneficial to Shirley as a scholar and teacher that education even of the aristocracy now consisted less commonly of tutoring at home, having become more a process of communal education for all merchant sons, gentry, and nobility. Stratification continued, however, certain schools becoming noted for their concentration of gentry and aristocracy, mostly in and around London. One of the best known was that run by Thomas Farnaby in the parish of St. Giles, Cripplegate, during the reign of Charles I. In this Caroline period Oxford became the choice of the peerage. These young aristocrats lived in separate quarters with private tutors and servants. The aim of most of them was to acquire a broad cultural background through wide reading and application of the arts, along with the study of polite manners and conversation, in preparation for diplomatic or administrative service to the sovereign. On the other hand, students from the professional and mercantile classes, along with the younger sons of gentry, studied to acquire a degree so they could enter either an academic or a clerical career.[42] Shirley belongs in this latter group.

Children of the aristocracy also often went to another "university," the Inns of Court, where while studying law they could learn to become gentlemen attached to the Court. The sons of the professional and mercantile classes followed the same course, more frequently completing their studies and being called to the bar.

Another avenue available to the nobility was travel abroad. Here the skills necessary to serve the King were best acquired, for students learned foreign languages, studied political systems and the martial arts, and acquired formal training in fencing, horsemanship, dancing, and music. The ideal courtier became a man of war and learning, a statesman, a polished cavalier, a virtuoso.[43]

Since the last half of the sixteenth century the increase in aristocratic matriculation, along with the spread of humanism, had been turning the universities from a theological to a secular curriculum. The curriculum was changed in Elizabeth's reign to reflect the new humanism. No specific religious education was offered to those planning to enter the Anglican church. Individual tutors added many extracurricular courses to accommodate noble gentlemen expected to sit in Parliament, manage their estates, and prepare themselves for service to the Crown. The study of history and literature of the times and of modern languages such as French and Italian were included.[44] Beginning in 1613, a young man studying at Cambridge and preparing to enter the church had to subscribe to the three Articles in the 36th Canon, which imposed the oath of supremacy, the Book of Common Prayer, and the 39 Articles. Yet there were exceptions. At Oxford, for example, a student under 16 years of age who matriculated was not required to subscribe to the 39 Articles.[45]

Most boys from Merchant Taylors' School who went on to the university attended St. John's, Oxford, and later entered the Anglican priesthood. That Shirley eventually chose a clerical career, then, was typical enough.[46] But his activities from the time he left grammar school, probably in 1612, until April 1615, when he matriculated at Katherine Hall, Cambridge, deviated somewhat from the usual pattern. J. P. Feil has discovered a deposition in Chancery given by Shirley on March 16, 1616, showing that he had been a servant to a scrivener named Thomas Frith.[47] Family influence may have secured the position, for Thomas Frith's brother William, although he worked as a scrivener, was a member of the Drapers' Company, and Thomas Frith's shop, in the Royal Exchange on the side bordering Cornhill Street, was near the Stocks.[48] From all of the testimony in a series of cases concerning Frith, it is clear that, having become bankrupt from lending money on security or bonds, he had been involved in a series of legal suits commencing in September 1614.[49] Shirley testified that he had known Frith for four years and the defendant-victim, John Crookes, for three years or more, and that he had worked for Frith for "two years or thereabouts." At the time of his testimony, the deposition states, Shirley was a student at Katherine Hall, Cambridge. Unless this represents some sudden turn in ambition, he had probably never been an apprentice scrivener. Two others, Thomas Gregorie and Richard Glover, refer to themselves as Frith's apprentices; Shirley never applies the term to himself, and his testimony reveals his ignorance of the scrivener's affairs. Circumstances suggest strongly that Shirley's employment dated from about 1612 to 1614: the fact of his almost certain departure from Merchant Taylors' School in June 1612, when he could have been seeking work; his statement in March 1616 that he had known Frith for about four years; and the occurrence of Frith's bankruptcy sometime after Michaelmas 1614. When Frith's troubles began, Shirley probably lost or left his service and may have gone to the university.[50]

University records show that Shirley attended Cambridge; in Easter term, 1615, he formally matriculated at Katherine Hall as a pensioner—one who pays his own way—and he received the bachelor's degree April 4, 1617.[51] But Anthony à Wood, the earliest recorder of Shirley's life, writes in some detail of the dramatist's life at St. John's, Oxford, before his attendance at Cambridge.[52]

Though there is no record at Oxford of Shirley's presence at the university—the school's registers are largely missing for the time of his likely enrollment—Wood's testimony should not be ignored. He was in some position to know about the Oxford of Shirley's times, for he lived there all his years from his birth in 1632 and could have drawn upon the reminiscences of Oxonians as well as upon records now perhaps lost. He recounts an incident regarding Shirley that is odd enough to encourage speculation about the poet's possible study at Oxford. The historian tells us that William Laud, then head of St. John's College and later Archbishop of Canterbury, ruled Shirley out of a clerical career because of a mole on the scholar's face that would distract his congregation from the sermon.[53] Two engravings of Shirley, one of 1646 appearing in his *Poems* of that year, and that of 1658, show a mole on his left cheekbone, although the Bodleian portrait depicts none.[54]

If Shirley did attend Oxford, it was possibly with the encouragement of the Merchant Taylors' School, which had some considerable association with St. John's College; the Company had the privilege of choosing from among the boys at the school a number of the best students to be supported at St. John's through a scholarship provided by the college's merchant taylor founder, Sir Thomas White. The Court Minutes of the Merchant Taylors' Company reveal numerous references to elections held every St. Barnabas Day in early June to determine what boys would go to St. John's. But Wood's assumption that Shirley went to St. John's upon election (and thus on a scholarship) from the Merchant Taylors' School has nothing to reinforce it. At the Hall there is extant a scrapbook containing records of elections; Shirley's name is not among them.[55] But a boy from the Merchant Taylors' School would be likely to select St. John's College, especially if he had no family precedent that would predispose him to select another.

Normally, study at either university for the A.B. required four years. A specific number of terms was required for the study of grammar, rhetoric, dialectics, arithmetic and music; during three of these years the student was expected to include such subjects as geometry, astronomy, natural and moral philosophy, and metaphysics. Modifications could be made in this program for reasons ranging from epidemics to a change of mind about taking a degree, a course of action that many took advantage of. Dispensations for non-attendance at either university were readily given to those studying for the A.B. or the M.A.; these dispensations could shorten the residency requirement considerably. Dispensations also were given to count terms at another school, and if Shirley spent two terms at Oxford, he could have applied them to an A.B. at Cambridge.[56]

Clerics studying for the M.A. who were fortunate enough to be appointed to a benefice or "living" could leave their church for the greater part of the year, using the revenue from their benefice and assigning their church duties at a much reduced fee to someone not fortunate enough to receive a lucrative appointment. Or a young cleric could lessen the residency requirement by pleading clerical duties. Others not in clerical orders could secure dispensations for residency by reason of lawsuits or residence at another university or the duty of teaching boys in the country. But the statutes concerning residency and the practice of dispensations liberally granted indicate that enforcing residence requirements simply was not possible. Before Shirley entered Cambridge, university practice made it relatively easy to be excused from all residence requirements for the M.A.[57]

Wood does not tell when Shirley was at Oxford, beyond claiming that it was before he went to Cambridge. The period between Frith's bankruptcy in the fall of 1614 and the matriculation at Cambridge in April 1615—a time for which we have no other information—would be about right. Residence of only two terms would surely be long enough for Shirley to feel the influence of Laud, of whom the Earl of Clarendon remarked that he had "...a hasty, sharp way of expressing himself."[58] An incident such as that recorded by Wood could have prompted Shirley to a change of place.

During Laud's tenure at St. John's from 1611 to 1621 Oxford increasingly attracted those with Royalist sympathies, while much Puritan sentiment was abroad at Cambridge. St. John's also was distinguished for the production of dramatic pieces during this time.[59] This, coupled with the popularity of Spanish literature at Oxford,[60] suggests that Shirley may have been deeply influenced during a relatively brief stay by the environment there, judging from the prominence of Spanish themes in his plays. (Of course, the influence of Fletcher and his use of Spanish sources also undoubtedly affected Shirley.) Possibly also the courtly tenor of much of his dramatic work and his later Royalist activity in the Civil Wars had its roots in an impressionable year at Oxford, which was the university favored by the court of James I and his son.

Cambridge concentrated on logic and training in disputation that would serve at legal courts at home and abroad. In general, the scholar learned through lecture, disputation, and declamation. Four public lectures each week covered theology, civil law, medicine, and mathematics, which indicated the professional interests of the students.[61]

Disputations were usually at the center of official academic entertainment. One such event was presented before King James in 1614 when he visited Cambridge after a hunting trip in the area. An incident the following year, when Shirley was a student there, must have interested him considerably. Some Jesuits being transported from a London prison to another in the country were lodged overnight in Cambridge. Many students traveled across the river to see them, and the Jesuits proposed a disputation with the students. The priests offered to argue in the negative on three propositions: "The Protestant Church is the true Church of Christ"; "There is no external and infallible judge in matters of faith"; and "Faith cannot exist without charity, without which, however, Faith is the adequate cause of justification." Eventually these three questions were disputed before the King but without the Jesuits.[62] Although Cambridge remained loyal to the Royalist cause in the later Civil Wars, Emmanuel and Sidney Sussex colleges were strongly Puritan. The Synod of Dort held in Holland stirred up passionate controversy over theological interpretations between Puritans and partisans of the Church of England at Cambridge in 1618-19. Violence flared in the burning of Regent Walk, the main approach to the school. This incident furthered the growing disdain for Anglicanism during the reign of Charles I. The theological issues disputed, however, pitted not Anglican against Puritan so much as Protestantism against Catholicism, and Cambridge appeared to ignore much of the doctrine espoused by the London Court.[63] The controversies Shirley encountered at Cambridge perhaps led to his later conversion to Roman Catholicism.

Whatever Shirley was doing in those months when speculation can place him at Oxford, he was writing in earnest after his matriculation at Katherine Hall, Cambridge. An entry for January 4, 1618, in the Stationers' Register records the grant of permission for publishing of "ECCO and NARCISSUS the 2 vnfortunate Louers written by Jeames Sherley."[64] Not extant now, the piece was probably an earlier version of the "Narcissus" in Shirley's *Poems* of 1646, a poem stylistically distinct from Shirley's typical work of his mature years. Dyce's suggestion that the work was published in 1618 is based upon a manuscript note appearing in a copy of Wood's *Athenae;* "ECCHO, OR THE INFORTUNATE LOVERS, a poem by James Sherley, Cant. in Art. Bacc. Lond. 1618, 8 vo. *Primum hunc Arethusa mihi concede laborem."* Shirley used this same motto when he published his masque *The Triumph of Peace* in 1634.[65]

Of a number of Shirley's friends who studied at Cambridge and are among the early contributors of verses to his publications, the only person who alludes to his years with Shirley at Cambridge is Thomas Bancroft. Bancroft had matriculated as pensioner from St. Katherine's in Easter term 1613, two years before Shirley.[66] Noted chiefly for his epigrams published in two volumes in 1639, he wrote verses to a number of mutual friends, including Thomas Randolph, Thomas May, and John Ford. One of the pieces in the First Book of epigrams is addressed "To Iame[s] Shirley":

> Iames thou and I did spend some precious yeeres
> At Katherine-Hall; since when, we sometimes feele
> In our poetick braines, (as plaine appeares)
>   A whirling tricke, then caught from
>   Katherine's wheele.[67]

There is little in Bancroft's works to indicate any specific influence on Shirley; Book Two of his epigrams concerns traditionally religious subjects. That Bancroft later lived in London is probable, and the two men most likely continued their friendship there. As early as 1625 a Thomas Bancroft was cited in the Middlesex Sessions Rolls as bailiff to George, Bishop of London.[68] In February 1627 one Thomas Bancroft is named as the complainant in a Chancery case involving payment of rent, but no details about him are given in the interrogation.[69]

Other friends who matriculated at Cambridge include Thomas May, who took his A.B. out of Sidney Sussex College in 1613, probably before Shirley arrived at the university.[70] It is more likely that Shirley made May's acquaintance later at Gray's Inn in London, where May was admitted on August 6, 1615.[71] Charles Aleyn also came to Sidney Sussex, but is not recorded as being admitted there until 1618, after Shirley had left.[72] Both Aleyn and May composed commendatory pieces for Shirley; May's appeared with several others in *The Wedding,* published in 1629, and Aleyn's verses are printed with numerous others in 1630 when *The Grateful Servant* was printed.[73] George Hill, who wrote verses for Shirley's *Poems* published in 1646, is a familiar name in the records of both Oxford and Cambridge, but there is no way to determine whether any of the Hills entered is Shirley's associate.[74] One other person, Richard Owen, should be mentioned in connection with possible school friendships. In 1639 Shirley dedicated his play, *The Opportunity,* to Owen and addressed him as captain of the ship that had brought the playwright safely back from Ireland.[75] For July 1609 a Richard Owen is listed as a scholar at Merchant Taylors' School.[76] In this instance as well, the friendship between the two presumably developed either much earlier or much later. The name appears in Oxford University and Inns of Court records as well as in the church registers of parishes near the Inns.[77]

Shirley probably did not meet at either university any of the aristocracy who were to become his patrons. Since most of the sons of nobility kept themselves apart from pensioners or sizars, Shirley's access to influential young men was limited. Although his associations cannot be specifically named, the environment at Cambridge must have had an important effect on the future playwright. The university at least tried to impose standards on the students. They were expected to converse in Latin, Greek, or Hebrew. Card playing and dice were forbidden except for the twelve days at Christmas, and students were banned from taverns, bear fights, and Stourbridge Fair. The entertainment offered to visiting dignitaries included plays as well as formal disputations.[78] The dramas were at times coarse and contained comments on scandals of the time. Possibly Shirley was in residence when *Ignoramus* was presented before James I in March 1615, for only formal matriculation was required prior to taking a degree. *Ignoramus* ridicules the legal profession, presenting the common lawyer as lacking both culture and education, interested only in money.[79]

Such early influences cannot be ignored. The traditions at Oxford and Cambridge were shared by many courtiers and fellow writers who studied at the universities, and Shirley's propensities for Spanish plots, veiled satire, and commentary on incidents involving well known personages, for example, are hardly peculiar to him. What is striking is that despite Shirley's university experiences and later ordination, he maintains in his works almost a studied public indifference to religion. Though attempts have been made to find Catholic references in his plays and poems, little is to be found that is not open to dual interpretation.[80] That fits with the pattern Shirley was to follow in his life, a restraint quite unlike the conduct of the somewhat morose Massinger or the impetuous Davenant.

Records of Shirley at Cambridge end with the entry of an A.B. conferred in 1617. While no notation has been found at either Oxford or Cambridge that Shirley received the M.A. degree, two documents show that he did at least come to be called M.A. and a third delimits the time he possibly received that degree—between 1622 and 1623. The 1623 court records for the Archdeaconry of St. Albans carry a writ of excommunication signed by Shirley as *Presbyter* (priest) on November 10 that designates him *"in artibus magister"* (Master of Arts),[81] and in a subscription oath of 1662 he signed himself M.A.[82] Yet on May 13, 1622, Shirley sat as surrogate in the St. Albans Archdeaconry court and is noted "in artibus bach." Local St. Albans records indicate that Shirley was actively participating in church affairs as early as October 1619, a month after his ordination by the Bishop of London on September 19.[83]

Circumstantial bits of information imply a connection with Cambridge after 1617. On the death of Queen Anne on March 2, 1619, Cambridge students compiled a book of poems called *Lacrymae Cantabrigienses* as a gesture of condolence to the surviving monarch. In one copy on the fly-leaf are inscribed handwritten verses and an epitaph with the note: *"Flens post posuit* Jac. Shirley, *Aul. Cather. in Art. Bac."*[84] The poem begins:

> Oh, let me weep! and, though I censur'd be,
> I'll ad one drop of water to this sea;
> Yet why should this be vain, since that before
> Heaven being full, one star is added more?[85]

The idea of adding tears to a sea of water appears in "Upon the Death of G. [ervase?] M. [arkham?]" in Shirley's *Poems* and also in the Oxford Rawlinson manuscript poem by Shirley, "Upon the Death of King James."[86] But the metaphor is almost too commonplace to prove that Shirley contributed to the Queen Anne volume of poems.

If Shirley did receive the master's degree, he could have readily dispensed with the required three years of residence, since it appears to have been *pro forma* to secure waivers from the statute. The acceptance of a country curacy was the most common reason given for seeking dispensation from residency requirements.[87] Shirley may have petitioned for a dispensation on the basis of his anticipated duties with the St. Albans Grammar School and with the ecclesiastical court in that town.

As early as June 1618, Shirley was readying himself to take Holy Orders. The entry for his marriage in 1618 to Elizabeth Gilmet at St. Albans notes "clarke" after his name;[88] he may have been an elected "Clerk in Convocation" working for the Archdeaconry of St. Albans in its ecclesiastical court, or he could have been a "parish clerk," a special assistant to a priest.[89] Where Shirley assisted in conjectural, but the marriage license lists him as being from St. Albans.[90] Already entered into the life of literature and launched upon a clerical career, Shirley was still the man of mercantile background and association: the Gilmets were a substantial and locally prominent family of drapers, and had provided mayors of St. Albans.[91]

Both Richard and Robert Gilmet served as mayors of the town, Robert in 1612, and Richard in 1607 and 1618. Both also appear for the period from 1605 to 1625 in listings of principal burgesses. The Mayors' Accounts for the Corporation of St. Albans show that Robert Gilmet was a draper, and entries in the Archdeaconry Act Books recording in two separate places James Shirley's marriage license note that the bride-to-be is daughter of Richard Gilmet, draper of St. Albans. Shirley, "gent," and Richard Gilmet posted surety in the amount of £100.[92] It seems likely that after receiving his A.B. Shirley secured a position as clerk in the St. Albans ecclesiastical court and met the daughter of a prominent merchant and town leader.

By 1619 Shirley held some sort of position beyond that of clerk. His ordination record names him "curae" (curate) for Wheathampstead—a parish within the ecclesiastical Diocese of Lincoln but physically only a few miles from St. Albans.[93] Yet the Lincoln diocesan records and the local parish registers for the years 1617 to 1621 carry no mention of Shirley in connection with that parish.[94] One scholar plausibly suggests that he may have had responsibility for the chapel of St. Nicholas at Harpenden, which was under the jurisdiction of the Wheathampstead rector; it was often assigned to the rector's vicar.[95] But Shirley's signature is nowhere to be found in this parish register where the curate's would be—vouching for the accuracy of the entries. And so it is possible that for about two years Shirley was readying himself for holy orders while attached to the archdeaconry of St. Albans and *in absentia* from his "living." Shirley needed an income. On December 27, 1619, two months after his ordination, his first child Marie was baptized at St. Albans Abbey.[96] Perhaps he had another salary before 1621 in addition to a country curacy and clerk's stipend beginning in 1619.

On November 2, 1618, five months after his marriage, Shirley was officially promised the headmastership of the grammar school in St. Albans; Richard Gilmet was mayor that year and Robert Gilmet the school's governor.[97] Shirley was to have the school upon Thomas Gibson's departure. Gibson appears to have left after Michaelmas 1619; but the Book of Accounts for the grammar school shows that a Mr. Steed and his usher Mr. Carr replaced Gibson. Two entries appear for Steed; one in 1619-20 for wages in the amount of £32/13/4d. for the year, and the other in 1620-21 for £8/3/4d. paid in January 1621 for the previous quarter. Under this second reference is an entry for £24/10 "payd to Mr. Sherley & his usher for there [sic] wages for three quarters of a yeere ended at Michaelmas last...."[98] In all, Shirley waited about sixteen months before he assumed the headmastership. Further confirmation of this appears in the Mayors' Accounts for the town. Each year an informal listing was made of the "goods and chattels, plate, leases, writings, bonds, and other things" delivered to the incoming mayor. In 1619-20 the new mayor, John Saunders, received notification about "Mr. Sherles surrender of his Rightes in the schoole." Among the items listed for 1620-21 is "Mr. Shirley surrender of his former right in the Schoole." Finally, the list given to the new mayor, Mr. Thomas Goodridge, in 1621-22 includes "Mr. Sherleys Surrender."[99]

Although officially resigning his interest in the grammar school from 1619 to 1621, Shirley still may have received money for the position during that time. An entry of 1626 in the *Liber Eleccionum* of St. Albans reveals that the practice of selling or renting the office for a private fee had been going on. In August of that year John Harmar, who according to a notation of July 6, 1626, had been chosen headmaster upon the resignation of John Westerman, swore under oath that he had not paid any money or other consideration for the mastership; under the entry is an explanation that the office had been sold contrary to the wishes of the Mayor, the burgesses, and the founder of the school, and a formal oath to be administered to all successive schoolmasters is appended.[100] Albert C. Baugh suggests that Shirley had sold the mastership to Westerman.[101] Another possibility is that Shirley publicly resigned his right and privately contracted with Steed for a percentage of the income between 1619 and 1621. Part of this income included a share in the revenue from two wine taverns in the town; the schoolmaster's share amounted to about £20, and it is possible that Shirley kept this sum.[102]

Much of the time of Shirley's active headmastership can be established with some firmness. No accounts are entered for the years 1621-22 and 1623-24 in the school's Book of Accounts, and Baugh conjectures that Shirley may have taught until January 1625, when John Westerman was entered as master.[103] But the Act Books of the St. Albans Archdeaconry clarify Shirley's status during these years. A citation of November 1621 to all clergy and church officials, calling upon them to attend a Synodal meeting of the Archdeaconry, lists Shirley's name under St. Albans Abbey without the addition of "ludimagister," or schoolmaster, and we therefore cannot learn from this entry alone whether it is as master or as functionary of the church that Shirley was included. But the call to another meeting, possibly a Convocation, to be held at Lambeth in January 1622, lists Shirley as "ludimagister." Twice more Shirley's name appears for these meetings; for the Visitation of May 1623, the note "ab" is by his name, but he was present at the Synodal meeting in October of 1623. For the Visitation held in April 1624, "Mr. Westerman, ludimagister" is entered under St. Albans but with "ab" before his name. We may suppose that in this same month Westerman assumed headmastership of the school, for he subscribes to the Three Articles "mentioned in the 36 Canon." The subscription and signature are in Westerman's own hand. The record of the next meeting, presumably a Synod, again lists "Mr. Johnnes Westerman ludimgr" under St. Albans. No specific date is given, but gatherings of this kind were held in the fall.[104] Shirley's tenure, then, must have ended at term's closing in March 1624, possibly at the Feast of the Annunciation.

The best source on Shirley's activities from 1619 to 1624 is the "Acta" or Act Books of the Archdeaconry of St. Albans. As schoolmaster after 1621 Shirley was often requested to appear at Archdeaconry Visitations and Synods, but even before this he was busy in the administration of the ecclesiastical court. This court officially met every two or three weeks to dispose of minor business, such as the grant of probates, the settlement of disputes, and the issue of excommunication writs. Usually the court was composed of the Archdeacon, his official—possibly a Clerk in Convocation—and the registrar. The Act Books keep close account of their sittings.[105] A notation for October 25, 1619, speaks of "Mr. Jacobo Sherley clero" as hearing testimony in a summary case. For another case he is noted as "Mgr Jacobus Sherley presbyer suffinto." Since his name appears three times in this one court sitting, it is fairly certain Shirley was acting in an official capacity, probably as the Archdeacon's Clerk. In March 1621, when he received a license to teach, he was also made a surrogate, and for October 10, 1621, the official heading reads "cora magtr. Jacobo Sherley Surr." In all, Shirley's name appears in court entries over thirty times.[106]

Shirley could have left St. Albans after Lady Day 1624, for the last record of his presence there is dated February 1624. This record, again concerning business of the Archdeaconry, was for a Convocation called by the Bishop of London in January 1624. The call to convocation gives only the head of each parish church, and Shirley's name does not appear. Another listing, labeled "for election of Clerke for the Convocation 1623 (1624)...." bears the same names but designates those who voted by carrying their signatures opposite to their name. Curiously, this list includes also the signature of "James Shirley," but does not put his name in the prepared column or give his parish.[107] It would appear that Shirley, along with six other priests, voted for a Clerk; although as an ordinary priest he possessed a vote, he apparently had no parish at this time and probably still was teaching at the grammar school. The indication is that Shirley voted for a new Clerk to replace himself as Clerk in Convocation.

Much about Shirley's formative years is discoverable. On one important subject, however, the evidence is sketchy: we can do little more than speculate about Shirley's early friendships—friendships that could have borne greatly upon his intellectual development.

When Shirley published his play *The Wedding* in 1629, one of his friends, Edmond Colles, wrote verses to the playwright. Edmond may have been of a Colles family at St. Albans that Shirley appears to have known. Baugh has found a writ of excommunication dated November 1623 that James Shirley issued in the case of Colles [Cole] v. Warner against two witnesses who had failed to appear and give testimony.[108] H. R. Wilton Hall's "Miscellaneous Papers of the Archdeaconry of St. Albans" give the facts of the case, which concerned a routine dispute over whether a certain parcel of land was free from tithe.[109] The Act Books again fix Shirley's relationship with precision. He was connected as surrogate and his involvement may have been considerable: his name appears frequently in records of the lengthy case. By March 1, 1624, the decree of the court closed the case in favor of Colles.[110] The Colles family of Park Bury, Hertfordshire, attended the parish church of St. Stephens in St. Albans, and Edmond Colles as late as 1655 gave testimony about himself in another court case, declaring his age as forty-five and his parish as St. Stephens.[111] He may have been a student of Shirley's at the St. Albans Grammar School, for he would have been around eleven or twelve when Shirley taught there.

One noble name, that of the Calverts, is possibly associated with Shirley's stay at St. Albans. A piece "Upon a Gentlewoman that died of a Fever," appearing in the *Poems* of 1646, is similar to a poem denoted "Vppon Sr. G: Ca: Ladie: Ep;" in the sheaf of poems that has come to be known as the Rawlinson manuscript. Ray L. Armstrong, the editor of Shirley's poems, convincingly argues that the lady of the two poems is Anne Mynne, wife of Sir George Calvert, later created Lord Baltimore.[112] She died in 1622 at Hertingfordbury, near St. Albans in Hertfordshire. Her husband was at that time Secretary of State, and remained so until his conversion to Roman Catholicism in 1624. Lady Calvert was a staunch Romanist and undoubtedly influenced her husband's later conversion; possibly Shirley knew her and was impressed with her beliefs. It is likely, too, that Shirley was interested in gaining the attention of the Secretary of State:

> Death (that on humaine flesh doth vse to feed)
> With Tyme, and Sickness (two bold Theeues) agreed
> to robb a house, and e're the breake of daye
> to steale the Riches of this Knight awaye,...

The published later version begins:

> Death, Time, and Sickness, had been many a day
> Conspiring this sweet virgin to betray;
> At last impatient, vow'd ere the next sun
> To finish what their malace had begun.

Lord Baltimore died in 1632; perhaps by 1646 Shirley saw no need to identify the lady and revised the poem accordingly.[113]

What is especially interesting is that even in these early years Shirley's aspirations were set to something different from a career of clergyman or schoolmaster. He was probably writing throughout his stay in Hertfordshire, and there is evidence that Shirley had an interest in drama during this time. On July 31, 1620, a case was entered in the Archdeaconry "Acta" involving a woman named Middleton from St. Albans. She "spake words agaynst one Mr. Sherley a minister and preacher sayinge rather and better it were to staye at home than go to church to hear one more fitter to be on a stage playe than in a pulpit and that it were better to reade prayers at home than to heare one fitter to be on a stage playe than in a pulpit and that he use not bowe in the pulpit with other words . . . ." The case appears to have been dismissed on September 18, 1620. No details are given.[114] So Shirley was preaching from time to time, probably in the St. Albans Abbey Church; and his congregation was recipient or victim of his dramatic sensibility.

Shirley's activities during his formative years neatly follow the custom of the prosperous merchant class. His early years at Merchant Taylors' School and subsequent stay at Cambridge and possibly at Oxford suggest that a successful guild member could provide for his son a likely appointment at church or Court. Neither Shirley's education nor his ordination and teaching is unusual for his class and circumstance. Here is a social circle with interlocking rings: a mercantile class reaching for a classical education by means of a school that catered to middle-class sons; a university training with its particular environment and tradition of creative endeavor; an appointment in the church that gave freedom to write and participate in other activities while collecting the stipend or "living"; a schoolmastership that came through marital alliance with the family of a prominent merchant who, in this case, as mayor and town burgess controlled the administration of the school. These early years begin the pattern of alliance that is characteristic of Shirley's adult life, for often his associations become the means to his success.

These traditional beginnings also prepared him well for the changing social and professional status of writers in seventeenth-century England. And elements of Shirley's early experiences appear in his literary work. He knew at first hand, for instance, the life of the independent, middle-class merchant depicted in his plays, sometimes sympathetically, sometimes satirically. An ambivalence towards this group, its values, aspirations, and customs, was to remain with Shirley throughout his career. At the same time he read the classical authors at a school that boasted a tradition of attention to the English language, situated in the thick of London business activity and founded by members of one of the influential guilds of the city. Shirley's ability to juxtapose the idiom of the working tradesmen and apprentices and their comic distortions of classical Latin with the sophisticated and allusive wit of the gentry and nobility was not the product of second-hand learning.

Shirley was ambitious. His work for a scrivener illustrates that despite his family's solid mercantile status they hardly boasted the affluence of the prosperous burger. Yet this early immersion into the quasi-legal and perhaps somewhat nefarious dealings of a scrivener gone under is to appear many times in his plays, reinforced by the years of association with the Inns of Court men. Shirley pursued a route established by his class to the university and priesthood, seemingly directed towards a life of teaching and sermonizing. Presumably Shirley was assured of a long and fruitful headmastership at St. Albans, ushered in through the influence of his wife's politically prominent family. And local records also illustrate that he was firmly ensconced in the ecclesiastical legal business of the archdeaconry of St. Albans. He held no meager income or lowly status during those post-baccalaureate years outside of London.

Had he lived some years earlier, Shirley would have been unable to consider leaving the security of church and school. But the changes in the system of patronage and the development of publishing as an industry enabled him to return to London without a noble patron—but possibly with a position of school usher—to try his luck as writer, perhaps rightly reasoning that teaching could provide an income to support his growing family if he were unsuccessful. The somewhat parochial life of a small village schoolmaster coupled with the sorting out of the religious pecadillos of rural townspeople clearly influenced Shirley's decision to pursue the work of dramatic writer, but they, too, became fodder for his plays.

Notes

[1] This description of London is indebted to Harold Priestley, *London: The Years of Change* (New York, 1966), pp. 40, 44-5; Maurice Ashley, *England in the Seventeenth Century (1603-1714)*, 3rd ed. (Baltimore, 1961), p. 12; P. F. W. Ryan, *Stuart Life and Manners* (London, 1912), pp. 123, 149; and Amy M. Golding, "The London Background of English Comedy, 1600-1642," Diss. New York University 1960, pp. 3, 5.

[2] Walter G. Bell, *The Great Fire of London in 1666* (London, 1923), pp. 2-4, 9, 11-12, 16; St. Paul's Dean and Chapter Estates Survey, 1649-1657, Guildhall Library MS. 11816A, fols. 134-35, 139, 142, 144, 147, 312-14.

[3] Bell, *The Great Fire*, p. 334.

[4] *S. Mary Woolchurch Transcript*, p. 310.

[5] Wood, *Athenae*, III, 737. Arthur H. Nason, the first modern biographer of Shirley, also was the first scholar to use Wood's information to trace the playwright's birth and parentage. *Shirley*, pp. 16-20.

Other recent biographers include Ben Lucow, *James Shirley* (Boston, 1981); Georges Bas, *James Shirley (1596-1666) Dramaturge Carolien*, Thesis Universite de Lille 1973 (Bas subsequently published some articles cited later in this study, adding some biographical details); and Anna Maria Crino, *James Shirley: drammaturgo di corte* (Verona, 1968). See also Ruth K. Zimmer, *James Shirley, A Reference Guide* (Boston, 1980); Albert Wertheim, "James Shirley," in *The Later Jacobean and Caroline Dramatists: A Survey and Bibliography of Recent Studies in English Renaissance Drama*, eds. Terence P. Logan and Denzell S. Smith (Lincoln, 1978), pp. 152-71.

[6] See the map drawn according to the description given by John Stow in his *A Survey of London (1603)*, Intro. and Notes by Charles L. Kingsford (Oxford, 1908). Norman G. Brett-James, *The Growth of Stuart London* (1935; rpt. London, 1973), p. 421.

[7] *S. Mary Woolchurch Transcript*, pp. 310-13, 383-84, 388.

[8] "Weddings 1651," St. Mary le Bow, General Register, 1538-1631, Guildhall MS. 4996, fol. 20. See also the published register edited by W. Bruce Bannerman, Harleian Society, 45 (1915), Part II, "Marriages," 320.

[9] St. Mary Woolchurch Churchwardens' Accounts, 1560-1672, Guildhall MS. 1013/1, fol. 6^V, entries 3 and 4; fol. 8, entry 7. Entries for William Shirley's rent received are on fols. 9^V, 11, 12^V, 14, 16, 23, 26, 27^V and *passim* in the same manuscript.

[10]*S. Mary Woolchurch Transcript,* pp. 308, 310, 347, 379; for William Shirley's other children, see pp. 300-02, 370-72, 378-79. The original register is Guildhall MS. 7644.

[11]Shirley's maid was buried in 1570. Woolchurch Churchwardens' Accounts, Guildhall MS. 1013/1, fol. 16.

[12]The information on the court case appears in Woolchurch Churchwardens' Accounts, Guildhall MS. 1013/1, fols. 20, 21, and 22; on Shirley as churchwarden and draper, fols. 29, 30, 30^V, 32^V, 33.

[13]Woolchurch Churchwardens' Accounts, Guildhall MS. 1013/l, fol. 30^V.

[14]John Bromley, *The Armorial Bearings of the Guilds of London* (Oxford, 1914-22), I, 99; II, 194-95. London was divided into wards of varying sizes; Shirley lived in Walbrooke Ward.

[15]Stow, *Survey of London,* I, 81, 225; II, 139-40.

[16]Minutes and Records of the Drapers' Company, 1557-1560, Drapers' Company MS. (Rep C) +255, fol. 315, at the Drapers' Hall, London. The Shirleys are also listed in Percival Boyd, *Roll of the Drapers' Company of London* (Croydon, 1934), p. 165. Boyd's manuscript notebooks, which are in the Drapers' Hall, list the information to be found about each member and the manuscript sources. See Boyd's notes under John Dissell, and the Wardens' Accounts, 1547-1562, Drapers' Company MS. +148.

[17]Two freedom lists enter both Thomas and James, and both give Thomas freedom by redemption: Freedom List, 1567-1656, Drapers' Company MS. +378, fols. 57, 79; Freedom List, 1567-1658, Drapers' Company MS. +279, fols. 176, 178.

[18]Wardens' Accounts, 1586-87, Drapers' Company MS. +176/25, fol. 6; Wardens' Accounts, 1593, Drapers' Company MS. +176/32, fol. 6^V. Patrimony was the usual method of entry for those whose fathers were already in the company, provided that the sons were born in wedlock after the father took up his freedom. Entry by redemption, on the other hand, was a fee for privileges, and those who entered in this manner were usually unconnected by birth or trade with the company. See A. H. Johnson, *The History of the Worshipful Company of the Drapers of London* (Oxford, 1914), I, 108, 150-51, 158-60.

[19]The whole fellowship of the Drapers' Company met four times a year at Quarter-Days. Johnson, *History of the Drapers,* I, 94, 111; II, 235, 237, 296-97.

[20]Quarterage, 1605-1618, Drapers' Company MS. +261, fols. 241^V-42, 244^V-45. The reference to Katherine Shirley is in Quarterage, 1617-1627, Drapers' Company MS. +259, fols. 240-41.

[21] *S. Mary Woolchurch Transcript,* p. 388.

[22] Bindings, 1603-1658, Drapers' Company MS. A+287, fol. 231; Bindings, 1615-1634, Drapers' Company MS. B+288, arranged by date.

[23] *OED,* s.v. "haberdasher," "quarterage."

[24] Act Book, 1615-1618, XVIII, Archdeaconry of St. Albans, Hertford County Record Office MS. ASA 7/26, fol. 100. Hereafter cited as Hertford MS. On the use of aliases, see Francis Leeson, "Aliases," *The Genealogical Magazine,* 15, No. 14 (June 1968), 594-99.

[25] It may be that the Act Book entry should read "Aldersgate," an area west of the Stocks and close to the Holborn parish where the dramatist later moved. Other Chetwinds were in the Aldersgate parish; the will of a Mary Chetwind late in the century lists it as her own parish. Archdeaconry Court of London, July 24, 1683; original wills, Guildhall Library. No Aldersgate parish register survives for the earlier seventeenth century.

[26] This Katheryne Chetwyn was buried in the South Aisle of the church, which indicates that she had enjoyed some prominence. "Burials, 1551-1665," *St. James Clerkenwell, Parish Register,* ed. Robert Hovenden, Harleian Society, IV (London, 1887), 189.

[27] Anthony R. Wagner in *English Genealogy* (Oxford, 1960) observes that the younger sons of landowners, without landed heritage since lands normally had to pass intact to the eldest son, would become apprentices to trades or go into training for the church or law. Some poor gentlemen married into trade; others might secure an office in government (p. 114).

[28] *Catalogue of Portraits in the Possession of the University, Colleges, City, and County of Oxford,* comp. Mrs. Reginald Lane Poole (Oxford, 1912 and 1926), I (1912), #131, p. 146.

[29] The masques are *Honoria and Mammon* and *The Contention of Ajax and Ulysses for the Armor of Achilles;* the engraving does not appear in all extant copies. See Nason, *Shirley,* pp. 8-14, 150-51, and Dyce, *Works,* I, lviii.

[30] Evelyn Philip Shirley, *Stemmata Shirleiana; or The Annals of the Shirley Family,* 2nd ed. (Westminster, 1873). This book treats the Warwick and Sussex Shirleys in Chapters I and IX. It is tempting to identify the William Shirley of West Grinstead, Sussex, whom E. P. Shirley listed as "living" in 1557, with James Shirley's grandfather (p. 296); he is approximately the right age, has no burial record in the West Grinstead parish, and, according to a Star Chamber case, had an older brother engaged in a London business. But he is listed as dead in 1573 when his mother's

estate was finally administered. See Shirley v. Grevett, Court of Star Chamber, February 2, 1557, Public Record Office (PRO) MS. Sta. Cha. 4/4/34; and Prerogative Court of Canterbury (PCC) Administration Acts, November 6, 1573, fol. 38. Records of the PCC include wills, administrations, and probates which are indexed under name by year. They cover the years 1358-1558 and 1558-1700.

[31] Pro. Will of Thomas Sherley, December 5, 1563, PCC, 28 Morrison. Probate of the will was granted October 25, 1565; see Probate Act Book, 1573, PRO.

[32] E. P. Shirley, *Stemmata Shirleiana,* pp. 333-34.

[33] E. P. Shirley, *Stemmata Shirleiana,* pp. 269-70, and "Who Was Henry Shirley, The Author of 'The Martyr'd Soldier'?" *N & Q,* 1st Ser., 12 (July 14, 1885), 26-27. Wood assumed that Henry was "brother or near kinsman" to James. *Athenae,* II, 262. In "Annals of the Careers of James and Henry Shirley," Frederick G. Fleay suggested that Henry was Shirley's father. *Anglia,* 8 (1855), 414. At least one known play by Henry Shirley survives, *The Martyr'd Soldier,* published posthumously in 1638. See *A Collection of Old English Plays,* ed. A. H. Bullen (London, 1882-85), I.

Henry was killed in 1627 by Sir Edward Bishop, who had been legally directed to pay Henry Shirley £40 a year as part of his inheritance; and James Shirley knew Bishop's wife, Lady Mary, and her sister Lady Diana Curson, daughters of Sir Nicholas Tufton. One of James's poems that appears in manuscript, titled "To th[e] Right Noble sisters The Ladie B: and Ladie Dia: Curs:," was published in his *Poems* (1646), in revised form, with the title "To the H.[onourable] Lady, D.C. at his departure." Scholars have conjectured that the slaying twenty years earlier was the reason Shirley struck out the name of Lady Bishop, who was living in 1646. More likely it is because Shirley's friendship at this time was primarily with her sister that Lady Mary Bishop's name did not reappear. See Ray L. Armstrong, *Poems,* pp. 10 and 94, and his comments on p. 63. The manuscript version is at the Bodleian Library, Oxford, MS. Rawl. Poet. 88. Among those who suggest the killing as the reason for the exclusion of Lady Bishop's name is R. G. Howarth, "Poems," II, 239-41.

[34] The dedication to Lady Dorothy is printed by Dyce, *Works,* II, 271, and Armstrong, *Poems,* p. 10; see also pp. 63-64. Nason corrects Dyce's information on Lady Dorothy's husband and her widowhood. *Shirley,* p. 9, n.4. See also E. P. Shirley, *N & Q,* 5th Ser., 12 (September 6, 1879), 181-83, and *Stemmata Shirleiana,* pp. 106-20. Yet Nason differs from E. P. Shirley on the death date of Sir Henry.

[35] Shirley has been associated with the Shirleys of London who were goldsmiths. According to the pedigree at the College of Arms, William

Shirley and the Woolchurch parish Shirleys have no relationship with this family. The London Visitation of 1633/4 shows the arms claimed by the goldsmith Shirleys at this time; it bears no resemblance to those the dramatist used. Information in a letter to the author, dated January 8, 1969, from A. Colin Cole, Esq., F. S. A., Windsor Herald of Arms; *The Visitation of London,* ed. Joseph Jackson Howard, Harleian Society, 17 (London, 1883), II, 235-36.

[36] On William Shirley's business affairs, see the Woolchurch Churchwardens' Accounts, fols. 47, 47^V, 63^V, 64^V, and 68. Guildhall MS. 1013/1.

[37] For James Shirley, Sr.'s, rents, see fols. 67, 69, 72, 75, 78, 80, 82, 85, 87, 89, 91, 93, 97, 99; the lease notice is on fols. 101^V and 106. Guildhall MS. 1013/1.

[38] *A Register of Scholars Admitted into Merchant Taylors' School, 1562 to 1874,* comp. Charles J. Robinson (London, 1883), I, 60. The Probations book is titled *"Mercatorum Scissorum Liber Probationis,"* 1607-1651, Merchant Taylors' Company MS., Merchant Taylors' Hall, London. Shirley's entry and the school statistics appear on fols. 27, 27^V. Shirley's progress through the sixth form is traceable in fols. 29, 31, 33, 35, 37, 39, 41, 41^V, 45^V, and 47^V. The Court Minute Books were also consulted. Court Minutes Records, V (1601-1611), fol. 439, Merchant Taylors' Co. MS. Shirley stood first on September 11 and December 11, 1610, and on March 11, 1611. *Liber Probationis,* fols. 37, 39, and 41.

[39] Nason, *Shirley,* pp. 20-21, agrees with Dyce, *Works,* I, iv, that Shirley probably left in June 1612. The exact date of Shirley's birth has puzzled scholars. The Woolchurch register records Shirley's baptismal date as September 7, 1596; *S. Mary Woolchurch Transcript,* p. 310. The school's probation records list September 13 several times and September 18 once as his birthdate. *Liber Probationis,* fols. 33, 35, 37, 39, 41, 43^V, 45^V, 47^V. Andrew P. Reimer suggests that the school was using the Gregorian calendar, which was ten days later than the Julian. The "18" that appears once on the school's probation record could have been a scribe's misreading of "13." If we can safely believe the church record that Shirley was baptized on the 7th, we can place his birth date at about the 3rd, for the custom was to baptize four days after birth. Reimer, "A Study of the Life and Works of James Shirley," Diss. University of London 1963, 2 vols., I, 2.

[40] See the map in Stow, *Survey of London.* Other schools were St. Paul's, Westminster, and Christ's Hospital. Howard Staunton, *The Great Schools of England* (London, 1865), p. 217; Lu Emily Pearson, *Elizabethans at Home* (Stanford, 1957), pp. 142-48, 153; Elizabeth Godfrey, *Home Life Under the Stuarts* (London, 1925), pp. 46, 64-65.

⁴¹The *Liber Probationis* lists the masters of the school as well as the books and exercises used in each form; Shirley's curriculum in the fourth form is on fol. 27. Robinson, ed. *Register of Scholars,* p. ix.

⁴²Lawrence Stone, *The Crisis of the Aristocracy, 1558-1641,* (Oxford, 1965), pp. 681-82, 684-90.

⁴³Stone, *Crisis of the Aristocracy,* pp. 690-93.

⁴⁴Mark H. Curtis, *Oxford and Cambridge in Transition, 1558-1642* (Oxford, 1959), pp. 70-73, 122-27, 137-39; Stone, *Crisis of the Aristocracy,* pp. 672-79.

⁴⁵Curtis, *Oxford and Cambridge,* pp. 171-72; Boase and Clark, *Register: Oxford,* II, Pt. I, p. xxiv.

⁴⁶Ryan, *Stuart Life,* p. 173. See also Boase and Clark, *Register: Oxford,* Preface, II, Pt. I (1571-1622); Robinson, ed. *Register of Scholars,* p. ix.

⁴⁷Feil, "James Shirley's Years of Service," *RES,* 8 (1957), 413-16. Shirley's testimony appears in Town Depositions, Court of Chancery, PRO MS. C24/425/20.

⁴⁸William Frith frequently gave testimony stating he was a draper but practiced as a scrivener. Town Depositions, Court of Chancery, PRO MS. C24/444, Pt. I, nos. 8, 44, 50, 53. Frith's shop is mentioned in Town Depositions, Court of Chancery, PRO MS. C24/438/32.

⁴⁹Thomas Frith's activities in the Scriveners' Company can be found in the "Charter and Ordinance Book," which lists a catalogue of freemen (1392-1678). This Guildhall MS. 3721A is a photostat of MS. Bod. Rawl. D. 51. See also "The Common Paper" book of the Company. Guildhall MS. 5370, fol. 61. No mention of Shirley is to be found in these records, but of course they list only those apprentices who became freemen.

⁵⁰Feil concedes that Shirley may have attended Oxford for two terms but suspects he was never there at all. "James Shirley's Years of Service," p. 416.

⁵¹Venn, *Alumni Cantabrigienses,* IV, 67. In the manuscript books located at Cambridge University Shirley's name appears three times: "Matriculations, 1613-1702," under date of April 1615, along with four others from Katherine College (Shirley is listed under the column noting second "convictus"); "Subscriptions, 1613 to 1638," fol. 20 [?] where Shirley in his own hand subscribes to the 39 Articles early in 1617 along with six others from Katherine College; and "Liber Gratiarium E, 1589-1620," fol. 256, the official entry of his admittance to the A.B., "Ex Aula St. Kath." In this last book, Shirley's is the only name entered from Katherine College and the only one in the list with a date by his name, April 4, 1617.

The entire list is headed June 26, 1617, "Ad Festum Baptiste." See also Venn, *Matriculations: Cambridge,* pp. xxiii, 605.

Those scholars who entered as pensioners were generally from well-to-do gentle or middle-class families; entrance and tuition fees differed with status. A fellow commoner, for instance, paid as much as 25s. four times a year, as son of a wealthy nobleman; Shirley probably paid 10 to 15s. quarterly. Alice K. Smith, "The English Country Clergy in the Early Seventeenth Century," Diss. Yale University 1936, p. 153; A. C. Baugh, "Some New Facts About Shirley," *MLR,* 17 (1922), 234.

52Wood, *Athenae,* III, 737.

53Wood, *Athenae,* III, 737.

54See Armstrong, *Poems,* Intro., p. xiii. Armstrong accepts the veracity of Wood's account in its broad outlines, if not in its specific chronology. Nason, while disclaiming Wood as historian and biographer, nevertheless bases his most important discoveries about Shirley's parentage on Wood's outline. *Shirley,* pp. 16-20. Prints of all three Shirley likenesses appear in Nason's *Shirley.*

55See Charles E. Mallet, *A History of the University of Oxford* (New York, 1924), II, 180, 188-89; *Merchant Taylor Fellows of St. John's College Oxford,* comp. Mark J. Simmonds (London, 1930). Simmonds notes that 37 of 50 fellowships at St. John's were to be held by Merchant Taylor boys, who were generally expected to study theology and philosophy (pp. xi-xii). On pp. 16-17 Simmonds lists those Merchant Taylor boys elected to St. John's during 1611-1613 and gives their approximate length of stay at St. John's, but Shirley is not among them. The scrapbook used by Simmonds is a gathering made of all the loose sheets concerning the school; it was put together in this century and is described by Henry L. Hopkinson in his *Report on the Ancient Records in the possession of the Guild of Merchant Taylors* (London? 1915). See some further notations of elections in the Court Minutes, Merchant Taylors' Company MS. V (1601-1611), fols. 245, 303, 327, 403, 439, 515 and *passim.*

56*Manuscripts of E. P. Shirley,* Historical Manuscripts Commission (HMC), 5th R (C1432 of 1876), #138, pp. 368b-369a; Boase and Clark, *Register: Oxford,* II, Pt. I, pp. xxiv, 25.

57Boase and Clark, *Register: Oxford,* II, Pt. I, pp. 68-69; Curtis, *Oxford and Cambridge in Transition,* pp. 96-97.

58*The History of the Rebellion and Civil Wars in England Begun in the Year 1641 by Edward, Earl of Clarendon,* ed. W. Dunn Macray (Oxford, 1888), III (Books VII and VIII), 120-21.

59H. R. Trevor-Roper, *Archbishop Laud, 1573-1645,* 2nd ed. (Hampden, Conn., 1962) pretty much treats Laud in the context of historical events, adding that Laud was "neither an agreeable nor a convivial character" (p. 34); see also John H. Jesse's *Memoirs of the Court of England During the Reign of the Stuarts, Including the Protectorate* (Boston, n.d.), III, 156-74; David Nichol Smith, *Characters from the Histories and Memoirs of the Seventeenth Century* (Oxford, 1918), pp. 97-102. On dramatic production at Oxford during Laud's tenure see Trevor-Roper, *Archbishop Laud,* pp. 34-35.

[60] On the influence of Spanish literature and the Court on Shirley see A. W. Ward's essay, "James Shirley," in *Representative English Comedies,* ed. Charles M. Gayley (New York, 1914), III, 545-62.

[61] William J. Costello, *The Scholastic Curriculum at Early Seventeenth-Century Cambridge* (Cambridge, MA, 1958), pp. 8, 11, 13.

[62] Costello, *The Scholastic Curriculum...Cambridge,* pp. 24, 30-31.

[63] Costello, *The Scholastic Curriculum...Cambridge,* pp. 110, 113, 122, 128; James Bass Mullinger, *A History of the University of Cambridge* (London, 1888), p. 150.

[64] The entry begins "Frances Constable Entred for his Copie vnder the handes of master TAVERNOR and master warden Lownes . . ." and a fee of 6d. is paid. Arber, *Stationers,* III, 286b.

[65] Dyce, *Works,* I, vi. Further commentary on Shirley's poem itself is in Armstrong, *Poems,* pp. 70-73. Shirley's father had died in 1617 and it may be that some of the modest estate enabled him to finance publication. The death was entered in the Woolchurch Parish Register on June 2, 1617. *S. Mary Woolchurch Transcript,* p. 388. The records of the Commissary Court of London note the administration of the estate, putting the property value at £136/10. "Catherine Shirley, relict," probated the will on June 16. Act Book 16, Guildhall MS. 9173A/8, fol. 273^V. When Shirley published his collected *Poems* in 1646, one of his friends, George Buck, wrote verses in praise of "Echo and Narcissus" that refer only to that poem. Perhaps Shirley merely transferred the poem and accompanying verses from an earlier edition. The poem is printed in Armstrong, *Poems,* pp. 19-28.

[66] Bancroft matriculated as pensioner for the Easter term, 1613. Venn, *Alumni Cantabrigienses,* I, 78.

[67] Bancroft, *Two bookes of epigrammes and epitaphs,* 4°, Pr. by I. Oakes for Matthew Walbancke (1639), 13th epigram (Book One). See also Hunter, *Chorus Vatum,* V, pp. 69-70.

[68] Jeaffreson, *Middlesex Records,* II, Goal Delivery Register, January 17, 1625, p. 186.

[69]Town Depositions, Court of Chancery, PRO MS. C24/530, #38. Unfortunately, no mention of Bancroft is given in the interrogation, and the pertinent depositions are missing.

[70]Venn, *Alumni Cantabrigienses,* I, iii, 167; Venn, *Matriculations: Cambridge,* p. 455.

[71]Foster, *Register: Gray's Inn,* fol. 699, p. 137.

[72]Venn, *Alumni Cantabrigienses,* I, 16.

[73]Dyce, *Works,* I, lxix-cv.

[74]A poor scholar (sizar) of that name matriculated from Trinity College, Cambridge, in 1608 and proceeded to the A.B. in 1612. He was ordained deacon at York in March 1614 and priest in September of that year. Venn, *Alumni Cantabrigienses,* I, 370. The name also appears in the Subscription Book for Oxford on June 3, 1614. Boase and Clark, *Register: Oxford,* II, Pt. II, ii, 333. A younger man named George Hill resided at Clifford's Inn in the Inns of Court some years after 1646. He gave testimony on November 23, 1657 in a Chancery court case, calling himself "gent" and stating that he was "aged 29 yeares or thereabouts." Town Depositions, Court of Chancery, PRO MS. C24/815, Pt. 2. In 1646 he would have been 18 years old, possibly just entering one of the Inns of Chancery to prepare for the study of law.

[75]Dyce, *Works,* III, 369.

[76]Robinson, ed. *Register of Scholars,* p. 62.

[77]Oxford records a Richard Owen, admitted A.B. in June 1614 at Jesus College, and licensed M.A. in 1618; he was incorporated from Oxford to the M.A. at Cambridge in 1624. Boase and Clark, *Register: Oxford,* II, Pt. III, Degrees, iii, 329; Venn, *Alumni Cantabrigienses,* I, iii, 291. Records of admission to Lincoln's Inn in 1620 and another to Gray's Inn in 1631 each for a Richard Owen place the origin of the entrant outside of London. "Admissions (1420-1799)," *Lincoln's Inn Admission Register,* I (1896), fol. 49b, p. 186; Foster, *Register: Gray's Inn,* fol. 877, p. 193. Finally, during the 1630's, possibly two men by that name lived in the Inns of Court neighborhood. Children born into the family of Richard Owen are listed in the parish register of St. Dunstan's in the West and of St. Andrews, Holborn. St. Dunstan's in the West Parish Register, April 22, 1638 and Sept. 22, 1639, Guildhall MS. 10,344; "Christenings, 1623-1642," St. Andrews, Holborn, Parish Register, Guildhall MS. 6667/2, entry #3371. But there is no way of definitely connecting any one of these names and events with Shirley's friend.

[78]Costello, *The Curriculum at Cambridge,* pp. 9-17, 32-38, 96-119 and *passim;* Godfrey, *Home Life Under the Stuarts,* pp. 93-94, 96.

[79]Mullinger, *A History of Cambridge,* p. 145.

[80]A valiant effort to illustrate through Shirley's works the playwright's Catholicism is made by Stephen J. Radtke, *James Shirley: His Catholic Philosphy of Life* (Washington, D.C., 1929), pp. 80-98 and *passim.*

[81]The writ of excommunication, dated November 10, 1623, is in Hertford MS. ASA 5/6, no. 108.

[82]The subscription oath is a general one that Charles II in 1662 required of all preachers and teachers. It is in Shirley's own handwriting and reads: "*Jacobus Shirleius* $^{m.a.}$ *olim admissus ad exequendum officium Ludimagistri, im Whitefryers London.*" It is dated August 18, 1662. Guildhall MS. 9539C. Shirley's license to teach appears in the St. Albans Archdeaconry Probate and Administration Act Book (c) 1574-1639. Hertford MS. ASA 26/1, fol. 71.

[83]Shirley's ordination is recorded in the records of the Bishop of London: "Ordinations, 1578-1628," Guildhall MS. 9535/2, fols. 217^V and 218^V.

[84]Dyce gives the information on the verses on the death of Queen Anne; he adds that he received it from Mr. David Laing of Edinburgh, owner of the copy in which the verses appear (Dyce, *Works,* VI, 514, n.6). The present whereabouts of this copy is not known.

[85]Armstrong, *Poems,* pp. 36, 77, 100.

[86]"James Shirley, B.A., Cath. Hall, 1619," written in a copy of Shirley's *Poems* by Dr. Richard Farmer, the principal librarian at Cambridge in the later eighteenth century, is the only direct reference to Shirley for that year, and that not contemporary with the dramatist. The note by Dr. Farmer on Dyce's copy is now in the Victoria and Albert Museum, Dyce Collection, MS. 9132. See the printed notice in Dyce's edition of Shirley, *Works,* I, vi, and n.1. Howarth says that Dyce misread "1617" as "1619"; but the handwriting looks clearly to read "1619." Howarth, "Poems," I, xxxvii.

[87]See Boase and Clark, *Register: Oxford,* II, Pt. I, "Preface," pp. 68-73, on dispensations; and Venn, *Matriculations: Cambridge,* Intro., pp. xv-xxv.

[88]The marriage record appears under the date of June 2, 1618. St. Stephen's Parish Register, 1558-1660, Hertford MS. DP 94/1/1.

[89]See the glossary in W. E. Tate, *The Parish Chest, A Study of the Records of Parochial Administration in England* (1946; rpt. Cambridge, 1960), pp. 303-14; see also pp. 130-32. Alice K. Smith in "The English Country Clergy" gives a definition of a parish clerk (p. 24); see chapter IV

of that work on sources of income, especially pp. 176-225, 243-51 and *passim*.

[90] The marriage license, part of the St. Albans Archdeaconry Records at the Hertford County Record Office, is recorded in two separate sources: "Notes of Admon. Acts, 1557-1669," Hertford MS. ASA 26/1, fol. 67, and "Act Book, 1615-1618," XVIII, Hertford MS. ASA 7/26, fol. 100.

[91] According to a note on the inside back cover of the St. Stephen's Parish Register, Thomas Gilmet—grandfather to James Shirley's Elizabeth—served on the town council through 1604 and died on June 12, 1605. He left buildings and land to his wife Elizabeth. Thomas Gilmet's will is Hertford MS. 46 AW 16. The inventory, among the Archdeaconry Records, is Hertford MS. ASA/25, arranged by year. In his will, Thomas simply calls himself "Yeoman"; at the time, it could mean a wealthy merchant. The rank, a step below that of gentleman, was not necessarily connected with ownership of land, *OED*, s.v. "yeoman." Her will, dated May 19, 1615, elaborates on the pedigree of the family. The will names three sons, Robert, Thomas, and Richard; Elizabeth, daughter of Richard and later Shirley's wife, was given "a bedsted in the best matted chamber." Hertford MS. 58 AW 13. The St. Albans Abbey Parish Register records the baptisms of two Elizabeth Gilmets at the beginning of the seventeenth century: the daughter of Richard Gilmet, on March 7, 1602, and the daughter of Robert Gilmet on July 31, 1603. Shirley married the older girl, and the other Elizabeth presumably married a John Crawley in 1624. Hertford MS. DP 90/1/1; see also "The Parish Registers of St. Albans Abbey, 1558-1689," transcribed by William Brigg and printed as a supplement to *The Herts Genealogist and Antiquary*, I, No. 2 (Oct. 1893), 38-39. The original manuscript papers are in the St. Albans Public Library. A. C. Baugh, "Further Facts About James Shirley," *RES*, 7 (1931), 62-63. Baugh found the marriage license entry in *The Herts Genealogist*, I, 55. The other Elizabeth's marriage is recorded in St. Albans Abbey Parish Register as is her death in 1675 on pp. 146 and 242 respectively.

[92] Mention of the Gilmets as burgesses and mayors appears in the St. Stephen's Parish Register and Draft Minute Books of the Borough Court of St. Albans, no. 297 (1621) and 298 (1619-1620); the *Liber Eleccionum*, a book of the activities of the local burgesses and mayors in the town of St. Albans, fols. 87, 91, 92^V; and the Mayors' Accounts, unnumbered loose folio sheets arranged by year and numbered by yearly groupings, especially Nos. 157 (1617-1618) through 161 (1624-1625). All except the St. Stephen's Parish Register at Hertford County Record Office are at the St. Albans Public Library.

Baugh, the first to discover the St. Albans town records, gave the name *Liber Eleccionum* to that manuscript, No. 312. The Draft Minute Books of the town skip the years 1614 to 1618 and 1622 to 1627; no Gilmets are mentioned in 1628 and 1629. For the surety, see Hertford MS. ASA 26/1, fol. 67. Baugh did not see this second entry of a license to marry on fol. 100 of Hertford MS. ASA 7/26. Richard Gilmet's name appears at least twice more, in notations that he acted as surety for others in securing licenses; see *The Herts Genealogist,* I, 277, 280. On obtaining a license from the bishop (or his representative) in preference to announcing bans, see W. E. Tate, *The Parish Chest,* p. 64.

[93] "Ordinations, 1578-1628," Bishop of London, Guildhall MS. 9355/2, fols. 217^V, 218^V. Shirley is entered twice, under ordinations of *Diaconi* (deacons) and *Presbyteri* (priests). The second entry merely notes his name (spelled "Shelly" in the name headings running alongside the left-hand side of the entries) and *"et supra."* According to Tate, a curate is "properly not the assistant priest of a parish, but any minister having cure of souls, especially a deputy in full charge of a parish, but removable at pleasure by his employer." *The Parish Chest,* p. 305. Tate also explains the curious ecclesiastical and geographical assignments, p. 53.

[94] The Parish Register of St. Nicholas at Harpenden, 1562-1677, is Hertford MS. DP 122A/1/1; that for Wheathampstead, Hertford MS. DP 122/1/1. Bishops' Transcripts of Parish Registers, 1604-1731, include those for Wheathampstead, but the years 1617-1618 and 1619-1620 are missing. Hertford MS. Bundle 179/1-65. Wheathampstead, because it was under the Diocese of Lincoln, was not in the Archdeaconry of St. Albans, but in that of Huntington, Hitchin Division. Probate and Administration Act Books for Huntington Archdeaconry at the Hertford County Record Office skip the years 1617 to 1626, and County Lincoln Record Office has no Huntington records for these years.

[95] Georges Bas, "James Shirley, Pasteur dans le Hertfordshire," *Etudes Anglaises,* 15 (1962), 266-68. The ordination record places Wheathampstead in County Lincoln. Bas points out that the scribe was mistaken; though the town was then under the ecclesiastical rule of the Diocese of Lincoln, it was situated in Country Hertfordshire.

[96] Register Book, St. Alban's Abbey, Hertford MS. DP90/1/1. Shirley's second daughter, Grace, was baptized on May 15, 1622; her death is noted in the register on December 20 the same year. Hertford MS. DP90/1/1. See also "The Parish Registers of St. Albans Abbey," trans. by Brigg, *The Herts Genealogist,* I, 54, 57, 209.

[97] Shirley's promise of the headmastership is in the *Liber Elecconium,* fol. 108^V. See Baugh, "Further Facts," pp. 63-64, and "Some New Facts About Shirley," *MLR,* 17 (1922), 230.

98"The Book of Accounts belonging to the Free Grammar School of the Borough of St. Albans" (1619-1620, 1620-1621), fols. 54-55, in the Headmaster's keeping at St. Albans.

99See in the Mayors' Accounts, St. Albans Public Library, folio sheets under 1619-1620 (no. 158), 1620-1621 (no. 159), and 1621-1622 (no. 160). Each listing refers to the previous year's business; 1619-1620 refers to 1618-1619 and so on.

100*Liber Elecconium,* fols. 118^V, 119.

101Baugh, "Further Facts," p. 65.

102"A Critical Edition of *Love Tricks, or The School of Compliment,*" ed. Nixon Mumper, Diss. Univ. of Pennsylvania 1959, p. 10.

103Baugh, "Further Facts," pp. 63-65.

104The replacement of Shirley's name on the listing with Westerman's is in Administration Acts, XX, Hertford MS. ASA 7/27, fol. 60^V; Westerman's subscription appears on fol. 61^V, and on fol. 82^V of the same volume; the Synodal meeting lists him with no date.

105Robert Peters, in *Oculus Episcopi* (Manchester, 1963), gives detailed information on the administrative affairs of the St. Albans Archdeaconry. Some of my information comes from an earlier version of this book in typescript at the Hertford County Record Office, "The Archdeaconry of St. Albans, 1580-1625; A Study in Ecclesiastical Administration," Bach. Letters Thesis Magdalen College, Oxford, January 1959, pp. 194-208.

106For Shirley's participation in Archdeaconry business, see Administration Acts, XIX (1618-1627), Hertford MS. ASA 7/27, fols. 120, 126; and XX (1622-1627), Hertford MS. ASA 7/28, fols. 20^V, 39^V. Although Shirley began teaching in January, he was not entered in the Act Books until March 26, 1621, for securing a license to teach. Administration Acts, Hertford MS. ASA 26/1, fol. 71.

107See H. R. Wilton Hall, "Records of the Old Archdeaconry of St. Albans, 1575-1637," *St. Albans and Hertfordshire Architectural and Archaeological Society* (St. Albans, 1908), No. 251, p. 153; No. 252, p. 154. The original papers are part of Hall's "Miscellaneous Papers," Nos. 178-262, Hertford MS. ASA 5/4. See also Baugh's discussion of this in "Some New Facts," pp. 233-34, and George Bas's further review in "Two Misrepresented Biographical Documents Concerning James Shirley," *RES,* N.S., 24 (1977), 125-26.

108Baugh, "Further Facts," p. 66.

[109] The writ is part of H. R. Wilton Hall's arranged collection "Miscellaneous Papers," Hertford MS. ASA 5/6, No. 108, fol. 69; other items pertaining to the case are Nos. 102 to 106, 109-110 and *passim* to 128, Hertford MS. ASA 5/6. The Court Papers are a separate series arranged by date in tied bundles, Hertford MS. ASA 9/29 (c. 1580-1635).

[110] The record of Shirley as surrogate is in Hertford MS. ASA 7/28, fols. 24, 42.

[111] The 1655 deposition is Colles v. Lever, Town Depositions, Court of Chancery, PRO MS. C24/787/17.

[112] See the two versions in Armstrong, *Poems,* pp. 13-14, 95. The manuscript is a collection of Shirley's poems, believed to be holograph. Bodl. MS. Rawl. Poet. 88.

[113] Armstrong discusses the manuscript in *Poems,* Intro, p. xxviii; his commentary on the poem is on p. 67. C[harles] H[arding] F[irth], "Calvert, George, lst Lord Baltimore," *DNB* (1886-87).

[114] Hertford MS. ASA 7/27, fols. 71, 74.

II

The Gray's Inn Circle and the Professional Dramatists

Shirley returned from St. Albans to London perhaps as early as April 1624, ready to "set up as a playmaker," according to Anthony à Wood.[1] With his wife and daughter he settled in Cripplegate, an area taking its name from one of the old gates leading into the walled city. Northwest of the city center, it was at once less populous and more rural, like St. Albans, and not even a day's journey from that village. In the early 1620's and the 1630's it became fashionable to spend a season in London and residences of the well-to-do flanked the Cripplegate thoroughfares, St. Giles and Drury Lane. Several of the nobility Shirley would later approach with literary dedications in hopes of patronage had city houses along Drury Lane, including the Earl of Holland, the Earl of Pembroke, and the Tufton daughters of the Earl of Thanet.[2] Shirley's first son, Mathias, was christened in the Church of St. Giles without Cripplegate on February 26, 1625.[3]

Shirley presumably came to London with work in hand, for just ten months elapsed between the last known record of Shirley's presence in St. Albans and proof of the existence of a full-fledged play accepted for the London stage. In the same month that his son was born, Shirley's *Love Tricks, or, The Schoole of Complement* was licensed, on February 11, 1625, for production by the Lady Elizabeth's Men at the Cockpit (Phoenix) Theatre in Drury Lane.[4]

The apparent ease with which Shirley gained acceptance for his first work suggests that he had an associate or patron who served as his intermediary. But with the possible exception of Sir George Calvert, Shirley had no early patron The acceptance of his play and its production in itself reflects the status of the theatres and the acting companies at the time. Anxious for new material and subject to the whims of a varied audience, actors occupied little status in society and risked the possible loss of an evening's receipts should a play fail, a common enough occurrence. To launch a career as playwright meant persuading a company of players to perform one's work; payment to the new author was generally a modest fee, and, should the play do well, the traditional second or third night's profits would become the playwright's recompense. So Shirley's first stage success rested neither on social status nor on patron's influence. His continued success, however, would be increasingly dependent on membership in influential coteries as the production of drama and its content came to be more and more reliant on the court and a select and private audience.

Shirley's first dramatic production was frequently called *The Schoole of Complement*: its popular secondary plot features a school that teaches the proper way to "compliment." Aspiring gentry learn verse making and speeches that are supposed to be the latest manners of the aristocracy. Shirley probably wrote at least a version of the play while he was still in St. Albans. Certainly the "Complement Schoole" section is the one most likely to have been staged by scholar players at the St. Alban's school. Its didactic parade of character types, ranging from Orlando Furioso, a boisterous braggart or "roarer," to Bubulcus, a rich ignorant fool, seems designed to teach young students to make distinctions between the established middle and gentry classes to which membership was bestowed by birth and the would-bes eager to claim rank and achieve status through wealth or marriage.

The poet soon moved from St. Giles, Cripplegate, to Holborn, considerably farther out in the western suburbs. From the hill of High Holborn, open fields led into the country. Most of the new buildings were here, outside of the city, but royal edict regulated even these; as early as 1617 Christopher Beeston ran into difficulty in his efforts to convert an old cockpit into a private theatre. Travel by coach from the Hill in Aldersgate Street to St. Albans was regular, and by 1635 mail was sent through the new post office to places as remote as Ireland and Wales. Along Gray's Inn Lane and Drury Lane, where the Cockpit (Phoenix) Theatre stood, young men connected with the Inns of Court filled many of the houses and inns.[5]

Since the mid-sixteenth century these sons of the gentry and nobility had spent what might be called their finishing school years at the Inns of Court. By the 1630's London was the center of legal business as well as the center of government, culture, and fashion. The influx of people so swelled the plague-ridden city that Charles I eventually denied all those with country seats the freedom to live in the city. Noble and gentrified sons came not only to study law but also to study life at Court and hoped to secure a court appointment through family or friends.[6] Typically, a young man aspiring to financial and social success went from Oxford or Cambridge to study law at one of the Inns of Court. He might live at one of the Inns of Chancery connected with a specific Inn, such as Staple Inn attached to Gray's Inn, and study there before proceeding to formal admission. The Inns of Chancery also served as residences for attorneys and law clerks. As at the universities, many of the sons of gentlemen and nobility never sought formal admission. In his study of the life of John Marston, Philip Finkelpearl reports that about half of those admitted to the Middle Temple at the end of the sixteenth century had been at one of the universities. It was customary to seek acceptance at the same Inn as had relatives or other young men who hailed from the applicant's county. Study at the Inns also attracted non-university and would-be gentry.[7] The mountain of surviving documents in the various courts such as Chancery and Requests testifies that law was a field of opportunity for the aspiring.

The system of education at the Inns was comparable to that of the universities; but study was as much by association as by formal teaching. Only elected barristers called Readers gave formal instruction. They were expected to lecture on particular statutes to the membership of the Inn, but this took place only for approximately three weeks between legal terms, at Easter and again during the summer breaks. Members, according to their rank in the Inn, argued various questions concerning the statute. Somewhat more frequently the new students and the senior members, or Benchers, held moots. No examinations were given. Other pursuits that would prepare young men for service to their King included the study and practice of music and literature. For many who had no intention of being called to the bar the study of law was incidental.[8]

Gentry and aspiring gentry often found that friendships formed at the Inns led to social and economic advancement. Residence there offered as well a solution to the difficulty of securing housing in the crowded city of London. A well known poem published during Shirley's residency near Gray's Inn, *The Young Gallants Whirligigg: or Youths Reakes,* by Francis Lenton, tells of a young man who from grammar school to university to the Inns of Court follows a degrading passage to financial ruin. The dissolute youth wastes his time at the Cockpit and Blackfriars theatres when he should be studying law and squanders his money on fashionable clothes and meals, often paying "an angell for a paltry stoole" to sit on the stage and converse during the play in order to display his attire.[9] Yet not all students at the Inns neglected their legal training. Edward Hyde, the first Earl of Clarendon, a student in the Inns of Court at this time, became "a strict constitutionalist devoted in English law, a committed Anglican both personally and politically, and a man of unusual integrity with the highest moral standards."[10] When the dramatist William Davenant moved into the area in 1628, he lived with Clarendon in his rooms at the Middle Temple Inn. Clarendon's autobiography reveals that he knew a group of young poets and writers whose chief interests were attending plays and visiting gaming houses or socializing with influential people who could advance their careers at Court.[11]

The Inns of Court had a tradition that attracted young writers to their environs; poets and other authors attached to the Inns had produced a considerable part of the important literature of the late sixteenth century. And in the first decades of the seventeenth century, Marston, Ford, May, and Donne had all lived at the Inns. With Shirley in the 1620's were Suckling, Carew, and Davenant, along with Ford and May, to name just a few. Countless others were simply devotees of literature or dilettantes who tried their hand at poetry, translation, or drama. The Inns of Court students made up a substantial portion of the private theatre audiences. Here a struggling young writer might get informed criticism and possibly economic support. People at the Inns who were interested at once in writing and in the law might form groups and write for one another.[12]

The Inns of Court also carried with them a tradition of entertainment amply documented in the records of the individual Inns.[13] Paramount were the Christmas Revels that usually included plays, dancing, feasting, and other amusement. Sometimes Revels were presented at Court. A "Lord of Misrule" was elected to oversee the Revels and to select a "court." Generally the Lord of Misrule presided with mock solemnity over a mixture of events that mimicked the more serious entertainment offered at the banquets given by the Readers at their installation. Accounts of Gray's Inn revels suggest extensive preparation, cost, and duration.[14]

Charles I had replaced with the central apparatus of the royal edict the near autonomy of the city of London. Resistance to royal authority was therefore increasing throughout London. The Inns of Court shared that sentiment; that Parliamentary committees often deliberated in the dining halls of the Inns must have been an influence.[15] At the same time, the character of the city, governed by powerful trade guilds, as a gathering place to shop and meet was giving way before entrepreneurial enterprise and companies whose interests were centered not in London but in countries whose goods could be imported at great profit. Meanwhile grew the liberties of London, those areas outside the city proper and not under the jurisdiction of guilds or municipal government. Among these were the Inns of Court, Blackfriars, Whitefriars, and Southwark. Since these were not under the legal jurisdiction of the sheriffs of London, they attracted a variety of inhabitants. Some were eager to escape the scrutiny of the law: pickpockets, prostitutes, and debtors. Alongside such undesirable types were growing numbers of thrifty Puritan merchants, many of the aristocracy residing in their city estates, and the students and residents living near the Inns of Court.[16]

A merchant class of Puritans eager to participate in business enterprise, the rapid expansion of the city to areas outside of its control, increased legal pressure from the Crown that threatened the city's autonomy: all brought about great social changes. In the Inns of Court the old and the new city mated. Their rich history of celebration and entertainment matched the city's tradition of pageants and feasts, long sponsored by the twelve great guilds. Their masques, mock orations, gaming, and shows were in character with the city's civic shows and fairs.[17] What better environment for a young schoolmaster-priest turned dramatist?

Anthony à Wood's account places Shirley in Gray's Inn.[18] Originally Shirley may have rented a tenement in one of the nearby buildings in Holborn owned by the Inn. He was established there at least by 1627 and probably earlier; his name and address appear on the title page of a textbook published in London that year by Joseph Webbe, a Latin teacher who had devised a new way to teach foreign languages. Entitled *Lessons and Exercises Out of Cicero ad Atticum,* the book was "to be sold by euery Master licensed to teach by that way. As by Mr. Sherley in Rose-alley, at the vpper end of Holborne, towards Grayes-Inne Fields."[19] The address agrees with that given for Shirley in the parish register of St. Andrews, Holborn, for 1628, "of Rose Alley in High Holborn," a tiny street leading north from Holborn near Gray's Inn Lane. The St. Andrews parish register records the birth of three children to Elizabeth and James Shirley between 1628 and 1633. "Thomas Sherley son of James Sherley gent and Elizabeth his wife out of Rose Alley in High Holborne" was baptized on September 11, 1628, and buried on September 22, 1634. John received baptism on May 8, 1631; Mary was baptized on May 26, 1633, and buried on August 1 the same year. That Shirley was comfortably settled during this time is shown by another entry in the parish register noting the burial on October 26, 1630, of "Margarett Goldsberry wife of Thomas Goldsberrey, gent. out of Mr Sherlys house in Rose Ally in high Holborne."[20]

Webbe's reference to Shirley along with the teacher Charles Aleyn's verses to the dramatist on the publication of *The Grateful Servant* in 1630 suggests that the playwright moved from St. Giles without Cripplegate to High Holborn to teach. Aleyn, an usher to Thomas Farnaby, headmaster of a school in the parish of St. Giles, Cripplegate, apparently lived in the parish of St. Andrews, Holborn. He is buried in the churchyard there as a parishoner. Aleyn became Edward Sherburne's private tutor in 1634 when Farnaby left London to establish a school in Kent. That Aleyn's poems treat of classical or historical topics indicates that his friendship with Shirley was a scholarly one; the best known, *The Battailes of Crescey and Poictiers,* was published in 1631.[21] Teaching or tutoring would have given Shirley some income while he was doing his first work for Beeston's company at the Cockpit Theatre. Meanwhile he was making friendships that would later prove valuable to him. He and Aleyn had mutual friends in the Gray's Inn circle: John Hall, Thomas May, and Edward Sherburne.

Teaching or not, Shirley was unusually productive: Beeston licensed two plays in 1625 and another two in 1626, all by Shirley, for his company of players at the Cockpit. Three of the four plays subsequently were printed: *The Wedding* (1629), *Love Tricks, or, The Schoole of Complement* (1631), and *The Maid's Revenge* (1639).[22] This earliest group of plays borrows heavily from older established playwrights, notably Fletcher, Shakespeare, and Jonson. Shirley was experimenting with different types of plays. The romantic comedy *The Wedding* relies strongly on Shakespearean plays; *Love Tricks* is a comedy of gently satiric comment on the manners affected by aspiring country gentry; *The Maid's Revenge* is a tragedy drawing on a well-known collection of Spanish histories. Most evident in these first attempts is the extensive reading and variety of Shirley's sources, ranging from Spanish literature to classical history to the drama and topical events of his time. They illustrate the early influences of his education and teaching. The publications of these early plays all refer to their successful reception on the stage.[23]

During the years between 1625 and 1629, Shirley usually alternated between romantic tragedy and comic realism. During these years the Inns of Court friends would be most influential in helping him to improve his craft. In 1629 and 1630 Shirley apparently arranged for the printing of two of his plays, and the commendatory verses written and published with them give at least some of the membership of the Gray's Inn circle. Of the people who can be connected with Shirley during this time through commendatory poems or other evidence, several had been formally admitted to one of the Inns; the others are directly associated with one another through literary publication. Shirley himself was not officially admitted to Gray's Inn until January 23, 1634, when he was still living in High Holborn. His admission then without a fee was probably the result of his selection to write the masque *The Triumph of Peace,* which the four Inns of Court presented before the Court in February 1634.[24] The Gray's Inn circle formed a literary workshop from the late 1620's to the mid-1630's.

The Wedding was issued in 1629 with verses by five friends. Among them John Ford, Thomas May, and Robert Harvey were formally admitted to the Inns of Court, while William Habington and Edmond Colles were connected to Shirley in other ways, Colles possibly through the St. Albans years.[25] That Shirley met Ford through the Gray's Inn circle seems probable, for although Ford had been a member of the Middle Temple since 1602, in the same year that *The Wedding* appeared he dedicated his own play, *The Lover's Melancholy,* not only to specific members there but to the whole "Noble Society of Gray's Inn." Shirley also shared a future patron with Ford: in 1634 Ford and in 1635 Shirley dedicated plays to William Cavendish, Earl of Newcastle.[26]

Between 1629 and 1632 three of Ford's plays were presented at the Cockpit, where Shirley had presumably become a playwright in residence. Bentley does not include Ford in the category of professional playwright, and his long association with the Middle Temple suggests that he was primarily employed in the legal profession in some capacity; his dedications indicate that he saw himself as an amateur and part-time writer. Ford's tenure with the Inns of Court meant that he knew many of the established residents and could help to introduce younger men like Shirley to other lawyers and writers, even prospective patrons. *The Lover's Melancholy* (1629) names four specific members of Gray's Inn, none of whom can be connected directly with Shirley, but two, Henry Blunt (Blount) and Robert Ellice, along with William Habington, wrote verses in the same year for the publication of William Davenant's *The Tragedy of Albovine, King of the Lombards*.[27]

The example of Ford, older than Shirley by ten years, may have been substantial for the younger man. Both dramatists, perhaps responding to the growing female segment in the audience, portray women similarly, often assigning major roles to them. Shirley's portrayal of women in *The Young Admiral* (1637) is suggestive of Ford's *The Broken Heart* (1633) and *'Tis Pity She's a Whore* (1633), both appearing four years before Shirley's play. Shirley, like Ford, confronts women with choices between love and honor. *The Young Admiral* pleased Sir Henry Herbert, Master of the Revels and representative of court taste: "The comedy . . . being free from oaths, prophaness, or obsceanes, hath given mee much delight and satisfaction in the readinge, and may serve for a patterne to other poetts, not only for the bettring of maners and language, but for the improvement of the quality, which hath received some brushings of late. . . ."[28]

Thomas May, another long-term member of Gray's Inn, held several mutual acquaintances with Shirley. He wrote verses for Philip Massinger, chief playwright for the Blackfriars theatre, knew Ben Jonson as a drinking companion and friend, and commended with verses Charles Aleyn, a fellow alumnus of Sidney Sussex College, Cambridge, on his publication in 1631 of *The Battailes of Crescey and Poictiers*. May was also acquainted with more influential members of the Inns, notably Edward Hyde. From such as May the fledgling dramatist may have learned about the professional and financial practices of young writers. Both astutely dedicated their works to wealthy potential patrons; both gained some access to the Court through patrons. May experienced little success in playwriting and by 1629 had published translations from Roman history and Lucan's *Pharsalia*. He managed to attract the attention of such patrons as Endymion Porter, Kenelm Digby, and Henry Rich, Earl of Holland. Shirley later sought the patronage of these same men by dedicating a play to each, and it may have been through May that he was able to approach them. Despite his anti-Catholicism and his support of Parliament during the Civil Wars, May remained friends with Shirley: witness his commendatory verses to Shirley's *Poems*, published in 1646.[29]

The other Gray's Inn man to contribute verses to *The Wedding* was Robert Harvey. Admitted to the Inn on February 9, 1626, he is listed as the son and heir of John Harvey of London, gent. He may have come from the university, for a Robert Harvey of London matriculated at Magdalen Hall, Oxford as "gen. fil" (son of a gentleman) at age fifteen on November 2, 1621. Harvey wrote commendatory verses for Massinger's publication of *The Roman Actor* in 1630. That he continued to live in the area and presumably practice law as well is evident from a Chancery Court deposition given by Robert Harvey "of Clements Inn in Co. Middlesex, gent aged 34 yeares or thereabouts" dated November 22, 1637.[30]

Kenneth Allot, editor of William Habington's poems, says that Shirley likely was Habington's closest literary friend. When in London, Habington lived in Holborn at his father's house. Noted for his poems to "Castara" (Lucy Herbert), daughter of Lord Powis and later his wife, he wrote one extant play, *The Queene of Arragon, or Cleodora,* performed at Court on April 9, 1640, and on the public stage. It is the ideal courtier play, presented by the Lord Chamberlain to the royal couple with fine scenery and costumes. Habington was a member of a prominent Roman Catholic family and may have strengthened Shirley's sympathies for that faith. Habington joined others to write verses for Shirley's *The Grateful Servant* (1630), and scholars have suggested that the "W.A." who wrote the dedication of Shirley's *Love's Cruelty,* published in 1640 when the playwright was still in Ireland, was in reality Habington, whose name was often written "Abington." The potential patrons whom that dedication names, the Porter brothers, sons of Endymion Porter, were connected with Habington by religious faith and Spanish relatives.[31] Shirley and Habington each wrote a poem about two friends (named EH and WH in Shirley's manuscript version) who made an appointment for a meeting not kept.

Shirley's lines refer to a Catholic association:

> But tis no wounder, for wee do not seeke
> A Christian, where there is noe Catholike.[32]

Habington may have supplied Shirley with the detail of an incident just preceding the composition of *The Wedding* that could have suggested its material. Alfred Harbage has shown that the circumstances in *The Wedding* are curiously similar to those surrounding the marriage of Sir Kenelm Digby and Venetia Stanley. Digby left for a tour abroad in 1620 after securing Venetia's promise of marriage; but when rumors reached her that Digby had died, she encouraged another lover, possibly Sir Edward Sackville. A great deal of gossip ensued on Digby's return, detailed in John Aubrey's *Brief Lives*. Digby did marry Venetia Stanley in 1625, but this fact was not made public until December 1627, when Sir Kenelm left on an adventuring expedition and after two sons had been born to the couple. Digby protests too much Venetia's virtue when he writes his *Private Memoirs* after her death some years later (1633). The characters in Digby's account are all given fictitious names. Many of the events in Shirley's play indicate a familiarity with the Digby affair: a friend tells of the lady's reputation and is challenged by the lover; the lover does not wed his mistress for a time; the lady's character is cleared and the wedding commences.[33]

Habington is a pivotal figure in Shirley's literary career, since his influence and connections were extensive despite his own rather unassertive personality. By 1629 Habington knew both Davenant and Shirley, and although he was never formally connected with the Inns of Court, his steady associations with a number of Gray's Inn residents places him within the circle. Habington by virtue of his family knew well a number of prominent Catholics at Court; his marriage into the Herbert family extended his acquaintances in the Court circle. He may have encouraged Shirley to approach potential patrons in the powerful elite Catholic Court coterie, which included Endymion Porter and Sir Kenelm Digby. In turn, Shirley may have introduced Habington to his own publisher, William Cooke, who published the first edition of Habington's *Castara* in 1634. Possibly Habington worked with friends at Court and at the Inns to help Shirley gain the designation of poet for the masque presented that same year. Habington figures as a connection for Shirley between the early Gray's Inn circle and the later Catholic Court coterie.[34]

In 1630 when Shirley's *The Grateful Servant* was published, it was introduced with ten sets of verses written by eight friends, among them Habington and Aleyn. Others included Thomas Randolph, "Jo." Hall, Robert Stapleton, and Philip Massinger. Although some were not members of the Inns of Court, they were closely connected to the Inns of Court men through their literary verses and publications to several members of the Gray's Inn circle.

One writer who easily became part of the Inns of Court circle was Thomas Randolph. Although a student at Cambridge at the time, Randolph spent several months in London during 1630 while the university was closed by an outbreak of the plague. Although the theatres also were closed from April 17 until November 12, a great deal of theatrical activity was under way, both in composing and publishing. Randolph, Bentley suggests, was writing, perhaps under contract, for the Salisbury Court Theatre during these months. Possibly Randolph brought plays produced at Cambridge to London, where they were acted at Salisbury Court. *The Muses' Looking Glass* was presented by the King's Revels Boys there late in 1630, and *Amyntas* was acted by the Children of the Revels in November 1630. Randolph's *Praeludium* may have been the first play presented by the theatre when it reopened in late November. If Randolph was one of the regular playwrights during this time, he was intimately acquainted with the literary rivalries of the day. It may have been at this period as well that he lost his little finger "in a fray," an incident made famous by his Westminster school friend, William Heminges, in his "Elegy on Randolph's Finger."[35]

John Hall "of Gray's Inn" signs himself to verses written for Philemon Holland's translation of *Xenophon Cyrupa,* published in 1632. Probably the same man wrote verses for Charles Aleyn's *Battailes of Crescey,* published in 1631.[36]

The interrelationships among the people who comprised the Gray's Inn circle are apparent through the verses written for members who published within the group—poetry, drama, essays. Within this larger circle are the friends who also made up part of another group, the Catholic Court coterie. One of the contributors to Shirley's published plays who bridges the two circles was Robert Stapleton, who arrived in London some time after 1625 when he left the Benedictine monastery at Douay, renounced his religion, and returned to England. Much of his known dramatic activity takes place after the Restoration, but he published several translations during the Caroline years, such as *The fourth booke of Virgils Aeneis,* entered for publication by a Shirley publisher, W. Cooke, in November 1634 with commendatory verses not surprisingly by a fellow Catholic, William Habington. Stapleton wrote verses not only for Shirley but also for the Beaumont and Fletcher Folio of 1647.[37]

Like Shirley's *The Grateful Servant* when it was published in 1630, Massinger's *The Roman Actor* on its publication in 1629 contained no less than six sets of commendatory verses, including two written by their mutual friends Ford and May. Some of these supporters were connected with the theatre as actors or playwrights; others, among them Shirley's friend Robert Harvey, were with the Inns of Court. In 1630 Massinger dedicated *The Picture* "To my Honored, and selected friends of the Noble society of the Inner Temple."[38]

By 1630, then, the larger literary group known as the Gray's Inn Circle was taking clear direction, and minor figures allied themselves with established writers and prominent courtiers in that group. What developed during these years was a fairly well knit circle of friends, familiar with each other's literary work and presumably serving as critics and advocates for one another. The Gray's Inn circle worked much like a merchant guild, functioning to protect and support its members, seeking to advance their careers. Certain members, such as Habington, undoubtedly opened the way to the courtier patrons connected with the Court and the Catholic coterie for Shirley and other dramatists, including Davenant. Ford and Massinger gave Shirley access to the established writers and their patrons, becoming the means by which he entered another group, the smaller coterie of professional dramatists. Many of Shirley's acquaintances during this time were simply young men studying at the Inns of Court and developing their interests in drama and playgoing. One such person, for example, probably was Will Atkins "of Gray's Inn" who wrote the only lines commending Shirley's *The Traitor* when it was published in 1635. Atkins had been admitted to the Inn in 1631 and before that had probably lived in the parish of St. Dunstan's in the West, next to Holborn, of which the Scavenger's Rate Assessments list his name along with those of the Catholic courtier Tobie Mathew and the author Izaac Walton for the years 1628-30.[39]

Writers with associations in the Inns of Court addressed a more exclusive audience than earlier authors had known. Expensive private theatres were attracting playgoers of the well-to-do middle class, the gentry, and the nobility, while for most of the year the general London citizenry frequented the public theatres. The Cockpit Theatre, for which Shirley wrote, stood near the town houses of the gentry on Drury Lane and drew much of its audience from the upperclass ladies and gentlemen who lived nearby as well as the Inns of Court students and lawyers.[40] Gerald Eades Bentley classifies the Cockpit as a coterie theatre along with the Salisbury Court Theatre, for which Richard Brome was the principal playwright.[41] The private theatre audience might also include gamesters, military men, city wives, and country gentlemen. All had special seating within the theatre, the exact position being dependent on the ability to pay a fee of sixpence for a seat in the top gallery to half a crown for a private box. A devotee could attend the theatre several times a week and see a different play every night. Most obnoxious to both playwright and players were the courtiers who paid 2/6d. to sit on a stool on stage, doing so simply to distract the audience, call attention to their dress, and make critical comments about the play being performed. Many of the Caroline gentry and aristocracy looked for resemblances between play characters and well known Londoners, whether intended by the playwright or not, and satirical references to specific well-to-do people were frequent.[42] Increasingly, the audience came to shape the subjects and styles of the drama; because it was a self-selected group, the private theatre audience could dictate what sorts of plays were produced and, by extension, who wrote them. Associations and affiliations became ever more important to professional dramatists.

By the early 1630's many playwrights were beginning to concentrate on writing comedies centering on familiar London scenes and situations in an attempt to appeal to the tastes of this audience. In 1632 Shirley's *Hyde Park* and *The Ball* and Brome's *The Weeding of Covent Garden* were staged, to be followed by other comedies set in familiar and popular areas frequented by the wits and gentry in the audience. Trading on the earlier city comedies of Jonson, Middleton, and Marston that illustrated a city changing economically from public market place to private shop, these dramatists continued the commercial theme, using terms having to do with exchange, buying and selling, and accumulation. Some city comedies raise serious questions about new wealth. Criticism most often is expressed in the exploration of relations between sex and money.[43] The theme of the commercialization of social life indicates the dramatists' dependence on London's mixed audiences; and the increased number of prologues and addresses to the reader of published dramas points to the uncertainty playwrights felt about the reception of plays that had to please patrons as well as courtiers, merchants as well as apprentices. Even for the relatively select audience of the private theatres, dramatists wrote plays which reflect the dual character of the city, if only to appeal to the gentry in the audience. Sharp commentary on the nouveaux riches could be taken as expressing the mind of courtiers of old family in the audience. Yet though such people could have their haughty amusement at the recent arrivals, their Court was dependent on new money. The prologue to Shirley's *The Doubtful Heir,* which first was staged in Ireland as *Rosania, or Love's Victory* and later performed in the London public theatre, the Globe,[44] makes it clear that the play was intended for the private Blackfriars stage:

> . . . No shews, no dance,
> . . . here's no target-fighting
> Upon the stage, all work for cutlers barr'd
> No bawdry, nor no ballads; . . .
> But language clean; and, what affects you not,
> Without impossibilities the plot:
> No clown, no squibs, no devil in't. . . .(IV,279)

But there were vacation periods, usually beginning in July and lasting through September, when the Inns of Court men were not around and the gentry and nobility returned to their country estates. At this time, the private theatres depended on the city merchants, tradesmen, clerks, even apprentices—the "cits." And there is evidence that in every audience there was this element. Davenant in his prologue to *The Platonic Lovers* (1635) produced at the private Blackfriars Theatre and Brome in *The Court Beggar* (1639) performed at the private Cockpit Theatre refer to the city audience.[45] References to citizens and the mercantile class in Shirley's plays and those of many of his fellow dramatists restrict their satiric comment generally to Puritan merchants and to newly successful social climbers, separating the old, established guild citizenry from the newer group.

Dramatists liked to write for the private audience, for though it was developing a taste for lavish pageantry, it also was interested in logical plots and clever dialogue more than in the clowning and physical combat that appealed to many of the apprentices and citizens who frequented the public theatres. The witty dialogue in *Hyde Park,* for example, and in Shirley's other London comedies defines the taste of his audience. Dialogue that is more important than action and that depicts character is possible only with a sophisticated clientele, such as might also include playgoers trained in debate and casuistry as the Inns of Court men were.

In the relative ease of his relationship with his audience, Shirley's London comedies anticipate the audience participation in analyzing a play; criticism had become a topic of polite conversation.[46]

But what serious playwrights had to say to this audience was not necessarily what it thought it was hearing. A useful division of the playgoers would be between old nobility and gentry and a composite London class made up of recent social arrivals: prosperous commercial citizens, some of them with purchased titles, along with a number of country gentlefolk trying to adjust to sophisticated urban life. A knowledgeable Carolinian, of course, could break down those categories into fine pieces. The rough dividing line is between people who were socially secure, and therefore tempted to be supercilious toward newcomers, and insecure people eager to take on the manners of the old families—an ancient and modern phenomenon particularly well marked in the elegant Court and theatre world of the seventeenth century. Attending a play critical of the gaucheries and the opportunism of the wealthy merchants or the naiveté of country ladies and gentlemen, both the established set and the new were doubtless confident of being squarely of the same opinion as the playwright and enjoying his favor. Merchants and their wives basking in the friendliness of a Court that needed and sought new money could believe that they had fully arrived and were not at all like their cruder social cousins who merely thought that they had arrived; courtiers of old lineage could believe that they were sharing with the dramatist a private joke on the nouveaux in the audience.

But Shirley can be numbered among playwrights who were in fact commenting on all or much of Carolinian upper class behavior. Most obvious is the scolding of the newcomers for greed and pretension. But such a play as *The Humorous Courtier* or *The Lady of Pleasure* carries another message that should not have pleased the haughtier of the old families: that their claims and manners are not worth copying, that an honest citizen has all the nobility the human race can acquire. Moralist playwrights were also lecturing the monarchy, to which they were staunchly loyal, against its practice of selling titles and its dependence on quick money. The professional dramatists Philip Massinger, Richard

Brome, and Shirley, then, wrote from somewhere just outside the current contented certainties even when their elegance and elevation of language gratified the taste that attended those certainties.[47]

The clearest indication of this ambivalence on the part of the professional playwrights toward their audience and its taste is seen in the prologues written for many plays. The prologue to Shirley's *The Example* (1634) complains about people who set themselves up as arbiters of taste:

> . . . the praise
> Of wit and judgment is not, now a days,
> Owing to them that write; but he that can
> Talk loud, and high, is held the witty man,
> And censures finely, rules the box, and strikes
> With his court nod consent to what he likes.
>
> . . . Nay, he that in the parish never was
> Thought fit to be o' the jury, has a place
> Here, on the Bench, for sixpence; and dares sit,
> And boast himself commissioner of wit:
> Which though he want, he can condemn with oaths . . .
>
> . . . This is a destiny to which we bow,
> For all are innocent but the poets now;
> Who suffer from their guilt of truth and arts, . . .
> If any meet here, as some men i' the age
> Who understand no sense, but from one stage,
> And over partial, will entail, like land,
> Upon heirs-male, all action, and command
> Of voice and gesture, upon whom they love;
> These, though call'd judges, may delinquents prove.
>
> (III,282-83)

Shirley refers to the courtiers who sit on the stage, commenting loudly on the play, but he also seems to be referring to those who prefer only the type of performance that pleased the Court taste and, perhaps, only one particular theatre. Courtiers were becoming interested in developing the accomplishments admired in an elite society—dance, horsemanship, poetry, and drama. Encouraged by the queen, they began to write and produce their own plays. This encroachment on the craft, along with a genuine liking for the audience, moved playwrights to seek an exclusive relationship with discerning patrons. That the relationship was precarious is illustrated by the number of prologues and commendatory verses that complain about the audience and critics or defend them. Some of the complaints no doubt were part of a recognized convention. Dedications to groups of people, such as the dedication by Ford of *The Lover's Melancholy* to the "Noble Society of Gray's Inn," is one illustration of a special relationship with a large segment of an audience.[48] And in a prologue written to *The Imposture* six years later Shirley again comments on the prevailing taste—"A Prologue must have more wit than the play"—but then praises the gentlemen and reassures the ladies:

> . . . You, gentlemen, that sit
> Our judges, great commissioners of wit,
> . . . for the author's sake,
> I' the progress of his play, not to be such
> Who'll understand too little, or too much;
> But choose your way to judge.—To the ladies . .
> In all his poems you have been his care,
> . . . no fright
> Shall strike chaste ears . . .
> No innocence shall bleed in any scene . . .   (V,189)

Shirley's prologue to *The Duke's Mistress,* which was performed before the Court at St. James on February 22, 1636,[49] perhaps describes best the difficulty of pleasing the audience:

> So various are the palates of our age,
> That nothing is presented on the stage,
> Though ne'er so square, and apted to the laws
> Of poesy, that can win full applause.
> This likes a story, that a cunning plot;
> This wit, that lines; here one, he knows not what.
> But after all this looking several ways,
> We do observe the general guests to plays
> Must in opinion of two strains, that please,
> Satire and wantonness; the last of these,

> Though old, if in new dressing it appear,
> Will move a smile from all,—but shall not here.
>
> . . . For satire, they do know best what it means,
> That dare apply; and if a poet's pen,
> Aiming at general errors, note the men,
> 'Tis not his fault: . . .
> But here we quit your fear of satire too, . . . (IV,191)

Though Shirley here indirectly censures current taste for its satire and its "wantonness," he amply employs both in his plays, most notably his London comedies, *Hyde Park* and *The Lady of Pleasure*.

The plays of Shirley, Massinger, and Brome show a striking similarity in the preoccupation with the changing society and the values of various classes within it. These three professional dramatists illustrate the complexity of the larger Inns of Court circle, forming a small coterie within that circle, commenting on the interests, attitudes and manners of the Inns of Court itself, the larger London bourgeoisie, and the elite Court coterie.

Surely the dramatist who influenced Shirley most directly was Philip Massinger. Massinger had a long playwriting career, collaborating notably with Fletcher and, at Fletcher's death in 1625, becoming chief playwright for the Blackfriars Theatre. That Shirley found Massinger's acquaintance important to his own work is evident from the commendatory verses each wrote for the other. Massinger, prior to assuming the position of chief dramatist for Blackfriars, wrote a number of tragicomedies and comedies for Beeston's company at the Cockpit before and after Shirley began his long alliance with that theatre. Sometime between 1621 and 1625 *A New Way to Pay Old Debts,* perhaps Massinger's most scathing indictment of the new middle class, was produced by Beeston's players, and in 1627 they presented his *The Great Duke of Florence.*[50] The influence of the older dramatist on the younger playwright seeking to establish a working relationship with the Cockpit company is suggested by a number of similarities between them in dramatic technique and ideology.

Like Shirley, Massinger was fond of expressing his moral convictions in his plays and often weakened his plot by departing from the narrative to adapt the action to his moral theme. Massinger's moral commentary is more direct than Shirley's; he concentrated his views on politics, religion, and the relationship between the sexes. Despite his criticism of evil rulers in his plays, Massinger holds to a belief in the divine right of kings as in *The Roman Actor* and to the need of rulers to listen to frank advisers such as is depicted in *The Great Duke of Florence.* Frequent allusions to court affairs of his times always make some moral point. Some critics believe that George Villiers, the Duke of Buckingham, is the model for Fulgentio, the king's favorite in *The Maid of Honour,* and again for the admiral of the Carthaginian fleet in *The Bondman.* In *The Emperor of the East,* the playwright suggests through the character of Theodosius the prodigality of Charles I and his lack of grip. *The Picture* takes a sidelong glance at the court of Charles I; a king neglects his duties because he so dotes on his queen, and Massinger makes the point that a wife should not intrude her will or attitude on her husband's business. Massinger was concerned primarily with the changing society of London as a microcosm of the whole country. His criticism of the Court's nepotism, favoritism, and extravagance in such things as expensive masques goes with his concern about the country's unpreparedness for war and the poor treatment of former military men. He came close to equating heredity with virtue, believing the social integrity of the nobility threatened by the financial power of the wealthier tradesmen, and more than one play has this as its centering moral preoccupation.[51]

Massinger's indictment of a changing society is best expressed in *A New Way to Pay Old Debts,* probably written before 1625. The play's main character, Sir Giles Overreach, is generally agreed to be modeled on the character and career of Sir Giles Mompesson. Having received a patent from King James for the sole manufacture of gold and silver thread, Mompesson used copper instead, which resulted in laming, blindness, and death. Massinger's Overreach is struck down for betraying his obligations in a trust given him by the King and for trying to rise above his social position; he becomes the projection of the evil that will later be identified with capitalism. The character of Welborne embodies ancient right and rank; Timothy Tapwell represents the new accession of prestige without tradition.[52] The play argues that efforts to cross class barriers are dangerous and destructive of society as a whole.[53]

Lady Frugal and her daughters in *The City Madam* (1632) are additions to the argument. These women are made to look ridiculous in their attempts to act in dress and manner as the nobility; at the same time, Mr. Plenty as a representative of the nouveau riche remarks that he pays his tailor for his clothes when they are delivered, unlike men of title. But in the end title is all to Massinger; people are worthy only if they keep to their social place. In the same play he gently satirizes the activities of fashionable ladies who want to be affiliated with the Court. Massinger contends that city women should move in their own spheres.[54]

Massinger undoubtedly influenced Shirley's more delicate treatment of the shift in social power. *The Lady of Pleasure* (1635), centering on London customs and places, illustrates Shirley's ambivalence toward country and city gentry and nobility. A wealthy couple representing the landed gentry comes to London to acquire the affectations and culture the city offers. Lord Bornwell speaks for the simple virtues of the landed gentry. It was more fashionable to cast slurs on the pastoral life as does Lady Bornwell, who represents a new monied class in its attempts to merge into the nobility of birth and breeding. Yet Shirley also comments on the sophistication of the aristocracy, superficial but hard and impenetrable to an outsider such as Lord Bornwell. He fares best in the outcome because he knows his place. Lady Bornwell, unfaithful to her marriage, is Shirley's gravest examination of the newly monied class in its quest for status and title. Shirley exhorts his audience to look not to social position but to the true nobility that comes from within. In *The Lady of Pleasure* as in other work that is most typical of him, Shirley's didacticism and correctional satire address more than one social class.[55] In *The Ball* (1632) Shirley takes a look at the pastimes of rising courtiers and their affectations. There are references to Sir Marmaduke's "patent for making vinegar" and his involvement in various citizens' projects—draining fens, operating iron mills, making buttons. The character of Bostock in the play serves as Shirley's critical and strongly partisan comment on those who claim honor through noble relatives or connections: "...for we inherit nothing truly/ But what our actions make us worthy of" (III,63).

At times Massinger's plays, like Shirley's, were censored by Sir Henry Herbert, Master of the Revels, for making obvious dramatic allusions to Court figures and for incorporating current events into their plots. At a time when England and Spain were at peace, Massinger's *Believe as You List* (1631) was denied licensing because its plot referred to the deposing of the King of Portugal by the King of Spain. The play had to be rewritten, the setting changed to ancient Rome. King Charles read Massinger's now lost play, *The King and the Subject,* and in 1638 Herbert censored it at the King's direction since certain lines referred to the various methods the King used to raise taxes.[56]

Shirley had similar trouble. The Master of the Revels required him to revise *The Ball* and remove certain parts because "there were divers personated so naturally, both of lords and others of the Court...."[57] What people at court the characters represent is mere conjecture, but Barker and Bostock perhaps were modeled on real people; so possibly was Lord Rainbow, the "May Lord" and "bubble of Nobility" whose actions with the ladies are inconsistent with his words to Bostock on honor (III,63). Although Jack Freshwater is a stereotype, it may be that Monsieur le Frisk, the French dancing master, derives from one of Henrietta Maria's servants. Scholars have generally agreed that, although the printing of *The Ball* designates Chapman as coauthor, the play is largely Shirley's creation, Chapman having been called in for revision of those offensive parts to which the Master of the Revels objected, and set to diffusing the identities of characters who were clearly parodies of court figures. If Chapman did revise and change names (Lord Loveall becomes Rainbow, Sir Lionel is changed to Marmaduke), he may have inserted the brief masque that defends the chaste activities of the balls. The revision is careful to use very few "noble" people in the altered cast but it is clear that all are of the upper class.[58]

Massinger and Shirley wished to instruct as well as entertain. But the courtly audience of the late 1620's and the 1630's, when it did not turn to mere show, was interested in the wit and humor afforded by the social pretensions of the changing middle class rather than in the effects of a strong merchant class on the economic and social future of the nation. Shirley took a middle course, commenting on the manners and morals of the various classes that made up the world of London, and perhaps more successfully than Massinger or Brome managing to establish with his theatre audience a spirit of cooperation in poking fun at those outside of its circle and coterie, allowing the audience to believe itself above and separate from the targets of the wit and humor, yet implicitly remarking on social climbing in a serious way.

Brome's plays, like Shirley's London comedies, are occupied with court abuses, political and social. They provided their fastidious and sophisticated but somewhat shallow audience with domineering women, intricate plots culminating in one big, sensational scene, and the use of names and places well known to their fashionable audiences. Brome is more critical of the Court and its indulgences than are Massinger and Shirley and has a more narrow and perhaps less philosophic view of London society.[59] More than Massinger and Shirley, he places his comedies in London, using an almost reportorial colloquial dialogue, and his plays capitalize on current events and places. Shirley's *Hyde Park* (1635), for example, offers without much critical comment an intimate glimpse of the interests and pleasures of a monied, leisure class. The debate between Fairfield and Carol is a piece of showmanship, designed to display wittily the typical pastimes of a young woman in that stratum: playing "gleek" (cards), attending plays, going to the foot races and horse races, being seen at Springgarden and the "Sparagus" (II,490). The independence that is desirable to a woman, a topic that would be of great interest to Restoration audiences,[60] Carol defines when she advises the widow Bonavent to keep her freedom: her pets, jewels, private tailor and doctor might be taken away if she remarries, and now she can talk as she likes at the table, dance, and go to bed when she pleases

(II,475). The dominating woman in *A Mad Couple Well Matched* (1636), which has been described as Brome's closest anticipation of the Restoration comedy, is a subtle satire on the puritanic, strait-laced wife who is a conniving hypocrite; the friendship plot in the play can be viewed as a satire on the court's fad of the precieuse. Brome criticizes pretense, social climbing, and coterie affectation, the last in his "roaring boy" clubs, a lower-class parallel to a court coterie.[61] Both elements appear as well in Shirley. *The Humorous Courtier* (1631) is Shirley's most consistent attack on courtiers. Shirley's ridiculous courtier is a comment on the singleminded greed for power or status. Hypocrisy is played by the villain Orseolo, who affects misogyny. Greed appears in four variations through Volterre, Contarini, Comachio, and Depazzi. The theme smacks of Jonson's *Volpone*.

In 1629 Shirley's *The Wedding* was issued with a list of the cast naming parts for fourteen actors. In that same year, Massinger's *The Roman Actor* and Lodowick Carlell's *The Deserving Favourite* also published cast lists, and Ford's *Lover's Melancholy* included an actor list. Three of the four plays were presented by the King's Men at the Blackfriars Theatre; Shirley's play was acted by the Queen's Men at the Cockpit. Actor lists appeared in two more of Massinger's plays printed in 1630: *The Picture,* produced by the King's Men, and *The Renegado,* written for the Queen's Men. As Bentley points out, printing the actors' names and their roles with a play edition was a noteworthy departure from custom. He suggests that the inclusion of cast lists may have resulted from cooperation among the playwrights. That each was deeply interested in the works of his colleagues is evident from the verses that Ford, Massinger, and Shirley wrote for one another in the years 1629 and 1630.[62] The cooperation indicates a need to establish solidarity against attack. Another possibility is that the inclusion of actors' lists was a requirement imposed by the companies, who became the owners of the playwright's work.[63] In either case, professional playwrights were entering a defensive league with one another and with actors, for both were now under assault.

On the one side, the Puritans were denouncing them. The protection acting companies earned when King James I placed them under royal patronage in 1603 had raised their status. But Parliament in 1625 had been presented with *A Shorte Treatise against Stage-Playes;* Massinger's *The Roman Actor,* played in late 1626, is generally thought to be the profession's reply to this attack. Publishing cast lists was one way of legitimating the professions of dramatist and actor. Meanwhile the professional authors, in their solicitation of audiences of wealth and rank, were facing competition from amateur courtier dramatists writing at the urging of the queen. A theatre war between the two sets of authors put under siege the reputations of playwrights, theatre houses, and actors. Shirley's friends who wrote commendatory poems for the publication of *The Grateful Servant* all refer to literary attacks on the playwright. The number of verses is unusual, particularly for Shirley, whose publications seldom include any commendatory pieces.[64]

The differences between the two factions, both of which had members within the larger Gray's Inn circle, represent a growing division among playwrights and writers and their attitudes toward their craft, brought about in part by the changing tastes and interests of a Cavalier court. The private audience connected with the Court viewed attendance at plays as an opportunity to display the cultural refinement it cultivated as well as a diversion from the growing political unrest around it. While upper-class taste could find gratification in sophisticated plot and dialogue, and did so to Shirley's advantage, masque and pageantry were becoming the fashion. Courtiers began to write somewhat vapid but visually spectacular dramas that appealed to Queen Henrietta Maria. Davenant was most attuned to this taste, and his appointments of servant to the Queen and later of poet laureate confirm his ability to please.[65] Massinger's biographer T. A. Dunn writes of courtly authors, followers of Ben Jonson, who called themselves the Tribe of Ben.[66] Not all of the Tribe joined the courtier faction: Randolph was part of that group, and he allied himself with Shirley against his critics. After he suffered a stroke in 1628, Jonson was no longer the assertive influence on the drama he had been, but his followers, such as Davenant, Carew, and Suckling, carried on his critical tradition albeit with less experience and knowledge. Through their own works and their attacks on the established professional dramatists' plays produced at the leading private theatres, they attempted to make the drama conform to the fashionable masque-like presentations admired by the Court.[67] The uneasy relations between Ben Jonson and the architect and masque designer Inigo Jones as they collaborated in a series of court masques bespeak the clash in sensibility between serious writers—for both Jonson and Jones were serious—and the courtly audience for whom they wrote, responsive to the graceful word or movement rather than to genuine feeling or ideas.[68] The professionals disdained, even when they had to accommodate, the prettiness of Court and Cavalier taste, the contrived elevation of language, the expensive masques, the Platonic love fashion. And while partisans in both camps could look with hostility or with humorous condescension on the social climbing of new wealth, it was the professionals—more inclined to moral statement in any event—who were the more explicit in their condemnation, for the Court was drawing on new money for the dramatic presentations that offended the professional playwrights. In remarking about the professional dramatists' reaction to their audience, Clifford Leech refers to the "emotional refinement of Ford and Shirley, the compromises of Davenant, the sense of unease in Massinger, the constant impatience of Brome."[69] The rivalry among acting companies expressed these clashes in social attitudes and in concepts of craft. In the end the King's Men at Blackfriars was supreme after a brief period from 1628 to 1630 when the Cockpit and Red Bull enjoyed considerable popularity. Until 1636 when the theatres were closed once again by outbreaks of the plague and Shirley left for Ireland, the Cockpit stood second only to the Blackfriars in reputation, in part because of Shirley's productivity.[70]

Verses written by Thomas Carew for William Davenant's publication of *The Just Italian* contributed to the dispute. Carew wrote to praise Davenant's play, presented at Blackfriars in November of 1629 and printed very quickly in January 1630. It had not been well received on the stage. Shirley's *Grateful Servant,* presented in December of 1629 and printed in February of 1630, had been a resounding success. Carew's poem alludes to the Cockpit and

Red Bull theatres, "where not a tong/Of th'untun'd Kennell, can a line repeat/Of serious sense: but like lips, meet like meat; Whilst the true brood of Actors, that alone/Keepe naturall vnstrayn'd Action in her throne..." at Blackfriars play to empty audiences.[71] It was a broadside attack on the actors, implicating playwrights and theatres as well and blaming audiences for poor judgment.

Georges Bas, in his study of Carew's verses and those written for Shirley, has noted that Thomas Craford's verses to Shirley for *The Grateful Servant* were a direct rebuttal to Carew's poem:[72]

> I doe not praise thy straines, in hope to see
> My verses read before thy Comedy;
> But for it selfe—that cunning I remit
> To the new tribe, and Mountebanks of wit
> That martyre ingenuity...
> And had that stage no other play, it might
> Have made the critticke blush at cock-pit flight,
> Who not discouering what pitch it flies
> His wit came down in pitty to his eyes
> And lent him a discourse of cocke and bull
> To make his other commendations full:
> But let such Momi pause, and give applause
> Among the brood of actors, in whose cause,
> As Champion he hath sweat...
> Let 'em vnkennell malice, yet thy praise
> Shall mount secure, hell cannot blast thy bayes.   (I,lxxx)

John Fox begins, "Present thy work unto the wiser few,/That can discern and judge;...be therefore boldly wise,/And scorn malicious censurers;...Because thou dost not swell with mighty rhymes,/Audacious metaphors; like verse, like times./Let others bark; keep thou poetic laws,..." "Jo. Hall" remarks, "Who would write well for the abused stage,/When only swelling words do please the age,/And malice is thought wit? To make't appear/They judge, they mis-interpret what they hear... Thee and thy strains I vindicate, whose pen/Wisely disdains to injure lines, or men:...Let purblind critics still endure this curse,/To see good plays, and ever like the worse." Referring perhaps to the

Blackfriars' predominance, Charles Aleyn opens his verses, "Tush, I will not believe that judgment's light/Is fix'd but in one sphere, and that dull night/Muffles the rest;..." Thomas Randolph's poem begins with a stanza of grandiose verbiage, mocking the style of the critics of Shirley: "I cannot fulminate or tonitruate words,/To puzzle intellects..." and goes on: "...others with disturbed channels go,/And headlong, like Nile-cataracts, do fall/With a huge noise, and yet not heard at all...." Robert Stapleton refers to flowery language and obfuscation: "...thy Muse... doth not use/To wear a mask or veil, which now a days/Is grown a fashion,..." Shirley's friend Habington hints that the playwright's adversaries lean on influential and prestigious supporters: "My name is free, and my rich clothes commend/No deform'd bounty of a looser friend,/Nor am I warm i' th'sunshine of great men,/By gilding their dark sins;..." Along with Randolph, Habington refers to the Cockpit specifically: "... thou'st given a name/To the English Phoenix, which by thy great flame/Will live in spite of malice to delight/Our nation, doing art and nature right...." Massinger joins in the attack on the style of the opposing camp: "...I dare not raise/Giant hyperboles unto thy praise,/Or hope it can find credit in this age,... Here are no forc'd expressions, no rack'd phrase,/No Babel compositions, to amaze/The tortur'd reader, no believ'd defense/To strengthen the bold atheist's insolence,/No obscene syllable, that may compel/A blush from a chaste maid;..."[73]

Such a crowd of indignant defenses of Shirley undoubtedly had more to occasion it than Carew's remarks, which refer to the theatres and actors at the Cockpit and the Red Bull and their audiences' lack of taste rather than to a specific play or playwright. Bas suggests that the conflict was primarily over the contention that the King's Men were superior to the actors at the Cockpit and Red Bull.[74] Shirley's preface to *The Grateful Servant* defends the actors:

> I dare not owne their character of my selfe,
> or play, but I must ioyne with them that have
> written, to doe the Comedians iustice, among whom,

> some are held comparable with the best that are, and
> have beene in the world, and the most of them
> deseruing a name in the file of those that are eminent
> for gracefull and vnaffected action. Thus much Reader
> I thought meet to declare in this place, and if
> thou beest ingenuous, thou wilt accuse with me,
> their bold seuerity, who for the offence of being modest
> and not iustling others for the wall haue most
> iniuriously thrust so many actors into the
> Kennell—now—
> *Panduntur portae, I uvat ire*—(II,5)

But Bas believes that the virtues of the playwrights were at issue as well. Davenant had his champions, Carew and Suckling, working as an advance guard to prepare the way for his success, while he aspired perhaps to replace Massinger at the Blackfriars. Yet his own play performed there was not liked and his earlier work, *Albovine* (1628), which he had printed in 1629, had never been performed.[75] Commendatory verses printed with *The Emperor of the East* in 1632 offer evidence that Massinger was receiving unfavorable commentary from the Blackfriars critics. Massinger's friends John Clavell, William Singleton, and Henry Parker defend him against "the gallants" in the audience who disliked the play.[76]

Shirley never developed a literary association with Davenant so far as is known. Perhaps each questioned the other's originality; Shirley was older than Davenant by about ten years, and might naturally resent rather than be complimented by a younger man eager to supplant him. The elevated verbiage that Shirley's friends attributed to his opponents is characteristic of Davenant's work.[77] His dialogue shifts from everyday conversational speech to stately and ornate hyperbole, particularly when he is attempting to depict the Platonic love cult popularized by Queen Henrietta Maria. More than most authors, Davenant aimed to please and to entertain. His *News from Plymouth* (1635) includes a conventional quarrel between masculine liberty and the female search for equality and freedom in marriage; a brief threat of tragic possibilities is soon dispelled in a lively and cheerful picture of seventeenth-century life. Whether he sincerely embraced the ideals of Platonic love (his malady, which ended in embarrassing disfigurement to his nose, announces that he did not practice them), Davenant became the leader of the fad, writing some six plays about it between 1634 and 1642.[78]

Both of Davenant's biographers describe him as a consummate opportunist. In a chapter entitled "The Search for Patrons," Arthur H. Nethercot writes: "His whole method of campaign, in fact, lay in this plan: to publicize himself; to become known to all the great people who could help him upward; to fight, to write, to carouse and discourse, to flatter and compliment, until he was accepted and welcomed in that bright world above him, which was so unlike that in which he had been reared."[79] What eventually paid off for Davenant was the support of two powerful patrons in the Court, Endymion Porter and Henry Jermyn. Alfred Harbage pictures Davenant as a young man "strongly attracted by the glamour of fashionable circles, sincerely devoted to poetry, but alert to find achievement whether as a poet, a soldier, or a courtier. Affable and vivacious, he was finding popularity in a widening circle of friends. Most of these friends were young men of his own age, better connected than he, but as yet of no more importance in the world. Unfortunately for him, they were inclined to set up as *bon vivants* as well as wits, and he shared their pleasures."[80]

Prominent among these new friends was John Suckling, who had been admitted to Gray's Inn in 1627.[81] Suckling was the supreme courtier; Harbage refers to him as "almost a symbol of the Cavalier legend."[82] He combined wealth (an inheritance he spent extravagantly), wit, a love of gambling and socializing, and a tendency toward ostentatious display tantamount to pageantry, particularly in demonstrating loyalty to his king. Best known of his exploits was his contribution to King Charles' cause in the Bishops' Wars of a troop of one hundred men, attired in white silk and mounted on splendid horses. Yet many of his contemporaries saw him as a coxcomb with little valor or virtue. And Suckling had produced slight literary work by 1630, although he was to have an elaborate production of his play, *Aglaura,* presented at Blackfriars in 1638. For the fifth act the company could choose between a tragic and a happy ending. Suckling spent several hundred pounds on costumes for the players and then gave them to the actors, a highly unusual and an extravagant gesture. This display occurred long after the appearance of the verses in *The Grateful Servant* that chronicle the controversy between cavalier critics and professional playwrights. Suckling's reputation had preceded his production by many years.[83]

Although he was not the gallant Suckling was, Davenant rode the coattails of the Sucklings and Carews and thus continued to be associated with the Court coterie. Such an association yielded him the poet laureateship in 1637. The following year, Brome in his prologue to *The Antipodes* announced:

> Opinion, which our Author cannot court,
>   . . . has, of late,
> From the old way of Playes possest a Sort
> Only to run to those, that carry state
> In Scene magnificent and language high;
> And Cloathes worth all the rest, except the Action,
> And such are only good those Leaders cry;
> And into that beleefs draw on a Faction,
> That must despise all sportive, merry Wit,
> Because some such great Play had none in it.[84]

It is clear that Davenant was angling for the control of a theatre and had for some time been interested in writing for one of the major acting companies. He wrote plays for the Blackfriars while Massinger was still principal playwright there in 1633 and 1634; Brome's last play for that company can be dated 1632 or 1633. Davenant also was writing for the Cockpit in 1640 and 1641 when Brome returned to the Salisbury Court Theatre, although in May 1641 the Cockpit produced Brome's *Jovial Crew*.[85] The ever ambitious Davenant had adeptly used his position of poet laureate to secure permission to build a theatre, posing a direct threat to all of the established acting companies and the professional playwrights under contract with those companies. By October of 1639 Davenant had agreed to forego the privileges of his patent, probably because he saw a way to become manager of one of the established playhouses with the help of his powerful court friends. His failure to establish a new theatre could also be explained in part by probable opposition from the Lord Chamberlain, who held financial interests in the Salisbury Theatre, and from Sir Henry Herbert, Master of the Revels, who owned a share in the same theatre and presumably appealed to his kin, Philip Herbert, Lord Chamberlain to the King.[86]

In May 1640, Davenant seized upon his advantage. William Beeston, who had become manager of the Cockpit in 1638 after his father Christopher Beeston died, was in prison for having presented an unlicensed play which referred to political activities of the King regarding a journey he had made to the north. The management of the company was turned over to Davenant.[87] Now that he was in charge of a theatre, he could emphasize courtly interests and fashions on the stage, including the courtly love fad. And he could effectively control the jockeying for positions of principal playwright for one of the three major acting companies.

These events placed Brome in a difficult situation. He had been under contract as principal dramatist to the Salisbury Court Theatre but also furnished plays to the Cockpit company. Indeed, the offending play was likely Brome's *The Court Beggar,* acted at the Cockpit. It refers not only to the King's trip north but also to courtiers who contrive to secure patents or acquire monopolies or estates to be dissolved.[88] Brome was particularly antagonistic to Davenant's and Suckling's tendency to incorporate the interests of Platonic court ladies and Cavalier mannerisms into the theatre, and the play offers a sweeping blow at the courtier Davenant aspired to represent. It features a character named Court-Wit, who writes a masque for a lady of the Court and attempts as well to secure a patent to be instructor to all actors. A reference to building a theatre on barges on the Thames presumably refers to Davenant and his royal patent of March 1639, allowing him to build a theatre in Fleet Street. The location of that proposed theatre would have been painfully near both the Salisbury and the Cockpit theatres. All this, along with references to his diseased nose, confirms that Court-Wit is modeled on Davenant.

Finally, a character named Sir Ferdinando appears to be a caricature of Suckling; he is depicted as a ladies' man, coward, gambler, and would-be soldier who gains unearned success at court.[89] Ten years after the first war of the theatres, Brome had scored his final coup in the intermittent and prolonged dispute between the courtiers and the professional dramatists. By 1640, when he finished *The Court Beggar,* the skirmishes had been joined by a more prevalent anti-Cavalier sentiment, a precursor to the coming Civil Wars.

Though Shirley's plays have their similarities with Brome's and with Massinger's, and all wrote primarily for private and select audiences in closed theatres, they differ in their attitudes toward the mercantile class and the aristocracy. Massinger had little tolerance for social newcomers. Brome, the pragmatist, is something of a muckraker of noble folk and merchants and dealt with political practices such as the abusive monopolies. Shirley is a critical commentator on both classes, concerned with universal values of honor and friendship, love and loyalty. He never fully dissociated himself from the mercantile class, yet he moved among the ruling classes. He satirized the merchants through his comments on city government increasingly dominated by wealthy Puritan merchants, and he ridiculed the social pretension of the wives and daughters of the merchants. His was the bias of the old established merchant guilds as they confronted the new individual tradesmen.

Shirley was able, unlike Massinger and Brome, to establish a form of drama that involved cooperation between author and audience, and the product of this cooperation anticipates the later comedy of manners. In a successful comedy of manners, there must be one group representing fashionable life and another composed of pretenders; the difficulty for Caroline playwrights, according to one critic, is that they could not count on a fixed status and makeup of either group or situation, for the society was continually changing.[90] Shirley's formal schooling and his intimate knowledge of the court gave him an advantage over both Brome and Massinger; manners and place were well established and formal at court, and pretenders could be clearly distinguished and could play their intrigues within conventions easily recognizable to them and to an audience. But this son of a draper, this curate and schoolteacher who twice married daughters of merchants and had two barber-surgeon sons, was gentler on commercial society than were his playwright colleagues. And he could be sharp with the upper classes. His comedies of manners are distinctive for the initial detachment he shows towards his characters. The impartiality of his observations makes his work in a way more pessimistic than that of either Massinger or Brome. And it is inseparable from his harshest characteristic: an appearance almost of disdainful aloofness from the concerns and interests of those who patronized him.

Notes

[1] Wood, *Athenae,* III, 737.

[2] John Parton, *Some Account of the Hospital and Parish of St. Giles in the Fields, Middlesex* (London, 1822), pp. 107, 347-49, 372.

[3] St. Giles Without Cripplegate Parish Register, Guildhall Library MS. 6419/2.

[4] Herbert, *Dramatic Records,* p. 31; Arber, *Stationers,* IV, 472. See also Bentley, *JCS,* V, 1144-47.

[5] This description of the Holborn area is indebted to P. W. William Ryan, *Stuart Life and Manners* (London, 1912), pp. 144-47; Jeaffreson: *Middlesex Records,* II, 125-26; Joseph Quincy Adams, *Shakespearean Playhouses* (New York, 1917), pp. 351-53; John Stow, *A Survey of London* (1603), ed. Charles L. Kingsford (Oxford, 1908), I, 87; and Norman G. Brett-James, *The Growth of Stuart London* (1935; rpt. London, 1973), pp. 59-62.

[6] Lawrence Stone, *The Crisis of the Aristocracy* (Oxford, 1965), pp. 385-88, 394-98, 400-02, 690-92.

[7] Philip J. Finkelpearl, *John Marston of the Middle Temple* (Cambridge, MA, 1969), pp. 4-7.

[8] Finkelpearl, pp. 6-10. Finkelpearl remarks that only fifteen per cent of those admitted to one of the Inns actually were called to the bar during the years 1570 to 1600.

[9] Finkelpearl, pp. 12-15.

[10] Martine Watson Brownley, "Why Clarendon Served the Stuarts," *Biography,* 4, No. 2 (Spring 1981), 119.

[11] Alfred Harbage, *Sir William Davenant: Poet Venturer* (1935; rpt. New York, 1971), pp. 35-36.

[12] Finkelpearl, *Marston,* pp. 19-27, 30-31.

[13] See D. S. Bland, "A Checklist of Drama at the Inns of Court," *Research Opportunities in Renaissance Drama,* 9 (1966), 46-51.

[14] Finkelpearl, *Marston,* pp. 34, 38-44. The "Lord of Misrule" may have given Jonson the idea for the antimasque he introduced within the court masques.

[15] Finkelpearl, pp. 64-66.

[16] Susan Wells, "Jacobean City Comedy and the Ideology of the City," *ELH,* 48, No. 2 (Spring 1981), 38-39, 42.

[17] Wells, pp. 46-47.

[18] Wood, *Athenae*, III, 738.

[19] Vivian Salmon, "James Shirley and Some Problems of 17th Century Grammar," *Archiv,* 197 (1961), 288.

[20] "Christenings, 1623-1642," St. Andrews, Holborn, Parish Register, Guildhall MS. 6667/2, Entries #1077, 2152, 2995; "Burials, 1632-1642," St. Andrews, Holborn, Parish Register, Guildhall MS. 6673/2, Entries #5130, 5607. If Shirley's mother was the "Katheryne Chetwyn" who was buried in the parish of St. James, Clerkenwell, Shirley also may have been settling the affairs of her haberdashery business. The entry reads, "Katheryne Chetwyn, widow, in South Ile" under date of May 26. "Burials, 1551-1663," *St. James, Clerkenwell, Parish Register,* Harleian Society, 17 (London, 1887), 189. See also Bentley, *JCS,* I, 227, and Chapter I, n.11 in this study.

[21] See the commendatory verses written to Shirley in Dyce, *Works,* I, lxix-cv; see also Armstrong, *Poems,* pp. 40-41. Correspondence from Sherburne dated October 26, 1686, to Anthony a Wood notes that Aleyn "was of Cambridge of Sydney College . . . one of the ushers to my Master Farnaby and afterwards private instructor to me for some time in my father's house. dyed before the Rebellious Times and lyes buried in St. Andrews Holborne, under the North Church Wall. . . ." BM MS. Wood F44, fol. 268. *The Calendar of State Papers* for 1631-33 states that he was an usher to Farnaby and teaching in 1632. *Cal. SP Dom.,* 1631-33 (1862), Ser. 2, V, 467. See also Venn, *Alumni Cantabrigienses,* I, 16; *Poems and Translations of Sir Edward Sherburne,* ed. F.J. Van Beeck (Assen, 1961), xxi-xxii; "Burials, 1632-1642," St. Andrews, Holborn, Parish Register, Guildhall MS. 6673/2, Entry #250.

[22] Bentley, *JCS,* V, 1132, 1144, 1163; Herbert, *Dramatic Records,* p. 31.

[23] Robert S. Forsythe, *The Relations of Shirley's Plays to the Elizabethan Drama* (New York, 1914), pp. 48-63, 117-36, 137-49, 322-31.

[24] Foster, *Register: Gray's Inn,* fol. 906, p. 202. The entry reads: "Jas Shirley of High Hol Mdx gent one of the Valets of the Chamber of Q H M *absque fine.*" Herbert, *Dramatic Records,* p. 54. The masque itself will be discussed more extensively in Chapter III of this work.

[25] Commendatory verses written to Shirley for *The Wedding* are in Sister Martin Flavin, *A Critical, Modern-Spelling Edition of the 1620 Quarto of 'The Wedding' by James Shirley* (New York, 1980), pp. 309-13. On the Colles family, see Chapter I of this work.

[26] William Allan Neilson, "Ford and Shirley," *Cambridge History of English Literature,* ed. A. W. Ward and A. R. Waller (1907-16; rpt. New

York, 1933), VI, 223-35; M. Joan Sargeaunt, "John Ford at the Middle Temple," *RES,* 8 (1932), 69-71; Sir Henry F. Macgeagh and H. A. C. Sturges, comp. *The Register of Admissions to the Honorable Society of the Middle Temple, 1501-1781* (London, 1949), I, 123; Ronald Huebert, *John Ford: Baroque English Dramatist* (Montreal, 1977), pp. 11-12; Bentley, *JCS,* III, 449-50; Herbert, *Dramatic Records,* p. 32; Gerald Eades Bentley, *The Profession of Dramatist in Shakespeare's Time* (Princeton, 1971), pp. 34, 287; A[rthur] H[enry] B[ullen], "Ford, John," *DNB* (1885-86).

[27]Arthur H. Nethercot, *Sir William Davenant: Poet Laureate and Playwright-Manager* (New York, 1938), p. 82; Bentley, *JCS,* III, 197-98, 434-39; Andrew Gurr, *The Shakespearean Stage, 1574-1642* (Cambridge, 1970), p. 163; Bentley, *The Profession of Dramatist,* pp. 33-34; Alfred Harbarge, *Cavalier Drama* (1936; rpt. New York, 1964), p. 162.

[28]Herbert, *Dramatic Records,* pp. 19-20, 35.

[29]Allan Griffith Chester, *Thomas May: Man of Letters, 1595-1650* (Philadelphia, 1932), pp. 6-7, 32, 36-8, 40, 42-44, 49, 51; Dyce, *Works,* I, xciii. Cf. Chapter I of this work.

[30]The case referred to debts incurred by John Verney and involved his widow, Katherine, along with William Barkley, Esquire, and Giles Clotterbooke, noted as three of the defendants asked to respond to a Bill of Complaint of Samuel Cramner, citizen and alderman of London. Harvey was the witness to a bill of sale for goods and chattels in payment of Verney's debt in January 1635. Clements Inn was attached to the Inner Temple, but no record of a Robert Harvey admitted to that Inn is to be found. See Town Depositions, Court of Chancery, PRO MS. C24/623, Pt. I. Boase and Clark, *Register: Oxford,* II, Pt. 2 (1571-1622), Matriculations, ii, 397; Foster, *Register: Gray's Inn,* fol. 829, p. 177.

[31]Herbert, *Dramatic Records,* p. 58; Kenneth Allot, ed. *The Poems of William Habington* (London, 1948), pp. xxvii-xxix; Dyce, *Works,* I, lxxxi; A[rthur] H[enry] B[ullen], "Habington, William," *DNB* (1890).

[32]Allot, *Poems of Habington,* p. xxxviii; Bentley, *JCS,* IV, 520-25. See also Chapter III of this work.

[33]Alfred Harbage, "Shirley's *The Wedding* and the Marriage of Sir Kenelm Digby," *Philological Quarterly,* 16 (1937), 35-40; Sir Kenelm Digby, *Private Memoirs of Sir Kenelm Digby, Gentleman of the Bedchamber to King Charles I* (London, 1827). Also see Aubrey, *Brief Lives,* I, 224-26, and BM MS. Aubr. 6, fol. 99, p. 101^V.

[34]Allot, *Poems of Habington,* pp. xviii, xxi, xxvii-xxviii; Arber, *Stationers,* IV, 288.

[35] W. J. Lawrence, "New Facts from Sir Henry Herbert's Office Book," *TLS,* 29 Nov. 1923, p. 820; Bentley, *JCS,* IV, 540-41; V, 967, 969-71, 989-90.

[36] Williams, *Dedications,* p. 85. A John Hall was admitted to Gray's Inn in 1619, the son of Robert Hall of Gray's Inn, gent. Foster, *Register: Gray's Inn,* fol. 760, p. 155. He may be the John Hall who became a successful lawyer by the mid-1630's. In August 1633, King Charles requested that "John Hall an attorney" be sent for to assign the position of foreign postmaster to Matthew de Quester. *Cal. SP Dom.,* 245, #41, p. 197. There was also Dr. John Hall, who had married Shakespeare's daughter Susanna and with her was made executor of the playwright's will. This Hall died in 1635, leaving his wife his house in London and his study of books. He notes of the manuscripts, "burn them or do with them as you wish." George Chalmers, *An Apology for the Believers in the Shakespeare Papers* (London, 1797), pp. 6, 247. In his will Hall notes that he would have given the manuscripts in his possession "to Mr. Boles." Prerogative Court of Canterbury (PCC), Wills, 114 Pile, PRO. Yet another John Hall is identified as a schoolmaster in the St. Andrews, Holborn, parish register: "Joseph Hall, son of John Hall schoolmaster and of Mary his wife was born in his father's house in Plough Yard in Fetter Lane and baptized March 29, 1641." This John Hall died in his house in Fetter Lane on August 2, 1646. "Christenings, 1623-1642," St. Andrew's, Holborn, Parish Register, Guildhall MS. 6667/2, Entry #6399; "Burials, 1642-1653," St. Andrews, Holborn, Parish Register, Guildhall MS. 6673/3, Entry #14174.

John Fox, another contributor, may be the musician who received a grant of denization in 1635 and 1636 as one of His Majesty's musicians. *Cal. SP Dom.,* 313, Feb. 10, 1636, p. 220; 290, June 12, 1635, p. 122. Yet he is not among the musicians listed in the detailed manuscript account of Bulstrode Whitelocke, which gives the royal musicians and those of the private theatres along with numerous other musicians hired to perform in the Inns of Court masque, *The Triumph of Peace.* See the article by Murray Lefkowitz, "The Longleat Papers of Bulstrode Whitelocke; New Light on Shirley's *Triumph of Peace," Journal of the American Musicological Society,* 18, No. 1 (1965), 42-60.

[37] "Dido and Aeneas," *Virgilius Maro Publius.* Film 8018, Reel 1044, BM; Arber, *Stationers,* IV, 304; Williams, *Dedications,* p. 177; Bentley, *JCS,* V, 1186-87; Hugh Aveling, *Northern Catholics: The Catholic Recusants of the North Riding of Yorkshire, 1558-1700* (London, 1966), p. 251.

[38] *The Plays and Poems of Philip Massinger,* ed. Philip Edwards and Colin Gibson (Oxford, 1976), I, xxi. Neither play was entered in the Stationer's

Register, but *The Roman Actor* was licensed for the stage by Herbert in October 1626 and *The Picture* was licensed in June 1627. Herbert, *Dramatic Records,* pp. 31, 32. See also Bentley, *JCS,* IV, 815-16; T. A. Dunn, *Philip Massinger: The Man and the Playwright* (London, 1957), pp. 219-21.

[39] Dyce, *Works,* I, lxxxii; "Scavenger's Rate Asessments 1628-1630," Parish Rate Assessments, St. Dunstan's West, Guildhall MS. 3783. According to Wood's *Fasti,* Will Atkins was created doctor of civil law in November 1642. Part II (1820), IV, col. 43; fol. 872, p. 192.

[40] William A. Armstrong, "The Audience of the Elizabethan Private Theatres," *RES,* NS 10, No. 39 (1959), 234-38.

[41] Bentley, *JCS,* III, 52-4; IV, 47-49, 61-62; VI, 192-93.

[42] Armstrong, "The Audience of the Elizabethan Private Theatres," pp. 238-43, 245-47.

[43] Herbert, *Dramatic Records,* p. 34; Wells, "Jacobean City Comedy and the Ideology of the City," pp. 37-38, 48-50; Kathleen McLuskie, "Caroline Professionals: Brome and Shirley" in *The Revels History of Drama in English,* ed. Philip Edwards *et al.* (New York, 1981), IV (1613-1660), pp. 241-46, 252-55.

[44] Bentley, *JCS,* V, 105-06; Dyce, *Works,* IV, 278-79. Quotations from Shirley's works in the text are generally from Dyce and are followed by a reference to volume and page. When later preferred editions of individual plays are used, footnotes contain the proper citations.

[45] Kenneth Richards, "Theatre Audiences in Caroline and Early Restoration London: Continuity and Change," *Das Theater und Sein Publikum* (Vienna, 1977), pp. 167-70, 173, 175; see also Gurr, *The Shakespearean Stage,* p. 148.

[46] Michael Neill, " 'Wits most accomplished Senate': The Audience of the Caroline Private Theaters," *SEL,* 18 (1978), 342, 346, 351, 354.

[47] Clifford Leech, "The Caroline Audience," *Shakespeare's Tragedies and Other Studies in Seventeenth Century Drama* (1950; rpt. London, 1961), pp. 161, 163-64, 170-73.

[48] Neill, " 'Wits most accomplished Senate'. . . ," pp. 342-47; Armstrong, "The Audience of the Elizabethan Private Theatres," pp. 242-43.

[49] Herbert: *Dramatic Records,* pp. 37, 56.

[50] Bentley argues that both dates are too late for Massinger to be writing for the Cockpit theatre. See *JCS,* IV, 781-88, 801-02. Earlier productions of these plays would place them during Shirley's years in St. Albans.

Because Shirley makes no mention of Massinger in his introduction to the Beaumont and Fletcher folio, Massinger's biographer, T. A. Dunn, assumes they were not very close friends. *Massinger,* pp. 27-29.

[51]Dunn, *Massinger,* pp. 147, 166-76. On Massinger's portrayal of women in his plays and his own religious beliefs, see Dunn, pp. 114-31, 176-91. See also Edwards, *Plays and Poems of Massinger,* I, xvi-xvii.

[52]Edwards, *Plays and Poems of Massinger,* III, 517, n. 2; Michael Neill, "Massinger's Patriarchy: The Social Vision of *A New Way to Pay Old Debts,*" *Renaissance Drama,* 10 (1979), 187-89, 197.

[53]S. Gorley Putt, "The Complacency of Philip Massinger, Gent," *English,* 30 (Summer 1981), 107.

[54]Edwards, *Plays and Poems of Massinger,* IV, cf. Acts I, ii, iv; IV, iv; V, iii.

[55]Richard Morton, "Deception and Social Dislocation: An Aspect of James Shirley's Drama," *Renaissance Drama,* 9 (1966), 242-44; *A Critical Edition of James Shirley's 'The Lady of Pleasure,'* ed. Marilyn J. Thorssen, Garland Series (New York, 1980), pp. 40-41, 45-47, 57-59, 63; Edgar L. Chapman, "The Comic Art of James Shirley: A Modern Evaluation of His Comedies," Diss. Brown University 1964, pp. 139-44, 148, 155-59, 162-63; Thomas Marc Parrott and Robert H. Ball, *A Short View of Elizabethan Drama* (New York, 1943), pp. 274-75; Kathleen M. Lynch, *The Social Mode of Restoration Comedy* (New York, 1926), pp. 36-40; Joe Lee Davis, *The Sons of Ben: Jonsonian Comedy in Caroline England* (Detroit, 1967), 87-90 and *passim.*

[56]Herbert, *Dramatic Records,* pp. 19, 22, 33; Dunn, *Massinger,* pp. 43-44; Bentley, *The Profession of Dramatist,* pp. 155, 167-68, 172-73.

[57]Herbert, *Dramatic Records,* p. 19.

[58]Forsythe in *The Relation of Shirley's Plays to the Elizabethan Drama* (pp. 407-09) discusses the various critics and their theories. See also *The Ball,* ed. Thomas Marc Parrott in *The Plays and Poems of George Chapman: The Comedies* (London, 1914), pp. 869-87; F. G. Fleay, *A Biographical Chronicle of the English Drama, 1559-1642* (London, 1891), II, 238-39; Bentley, *JCS,* V, 1077-79; Dyce, *Works,* III, 3; Hunter, *Chorus Vatum,* V, 62; Dana McKinnon, "*The Ball* by George Chapman and James Shirley: A Critical Edition," Diss. Univ. of Illinois at Urbana 1965, Introduction, pp. ix-xl.

Shirley presumably did not know, for instance, the Earl of Newcastle at this time (the dedication of *The Traitor* in 1635 to him states that Shirley is ambitious to be known to Newcastle), but the character of Lord Bonvile in *Hyde Park* is suggestive: "Next to a woman,/He loves a running horse.—" See later references to Newcastle's interest in women and horses in *Mercurius Britannicus,* No. 13, 16 Nov.—23 Nov. 1643, p. 103, Thomason Tracts, BM E 75; *Cal. SP Ven.,* 23 (1632-36), No. 129, March 25, 1633, p. 87. See also F. S. Boas, *An Introduction to Stuart Drama* (London, 1946), pp. 356-57; Hanson T. Parlin, *A Study in Shirley's Comedies of London Life, Bulletin of the University of Texas,* No. 371 (Nov. 15, 1914), pp. 59, 62, 64.

[59]R. J. Kaufman, *Richard Brome: Caroline Playwright* (New York, 1961), pp. 10-11, 13-15. See also C. E. Andrews, "Richard Brome," *Yale Studies in English,* 56 (1913), 55-64.

[60]Dyce, *Works,* II, 457-541; Dale Underwood, *Etherege and the Seventeenth-Century Comedy of Manners* (New Haven, 1957), pp. 152-53; Theodore Miles, "Place Realism in a Group of Caroline Plays," *RES,* 18 (1942), 431-38.

[61]Richard Jefferson, "Some Aspects of Richard Brome's Comedies of Manners: A Re-Interpretation," Diss. University of Wisconsin 1955, p. 164; Kaufman, *Richard Brome,* pp. 13-16. Kaufman asserts that Brome argues that one should not attempt to rise above his place in society (p. 15, n.20). See also Catherine Shaw, *Richard Brome,* (Boston, 1980), pp. 17, 31.

[62]Bentley, *JCS,* I, 223-25, 246; III, 116, 449-50; IV, 809-10, 813-14, 816-17; V, 1165.

[63]Stephen Orgel, "The Royal Theatre and the Role of King," *Patronage in the Renaissance,* ed. Guy F. Lytle and Stephen Orgel (Princeton, 1981), pp. 267, 270; Bentley, *The Profession of Dramatist,* pp. 82, 143, 264, 269-71; Gurr, *The Shakespearean Stage,* pp. 140-41.

[64]Dyce, *Works,* I, lxxiii-lxxxi; Bentley, *JCS,* IV, 816; V, 115-18. Jack R. Ramsey gives the fullest and most convincing argument concerning the competition among professional playwrights. His detailed discussion shows that Shirley and Davenant carried on a ten-year rivalry, each seeking the favor of the prestigious private theatregoers and of the influential members of the Court coterie. That Davenant "won" is demonstrated by his appointment as poet laureate and his considerable success after the Restoration. See "A Critical Edition of James Shirley's *The Grateful Servant,*" Diss. University of Michigan 1971, pp. 102-30.

[65]Harbage, *Davenant,* pp. 49-50, 64-65; Neill, " 'Wits most accomplished Senate,'" pp. 344-47 and *passim;* Nethercot, *Davenant,* pp. 149-50, 166; Bentley, *JCS,* III, 194-95, 211-12, 216-18.

[66]Dunn, *Massinger,* pp. 37-40; see also Davis, *The Sons of Ben,* pp. 8, 29-30.

⁶⁷Harbage, *Cavalier Drama,* pp. 156-57.

⁶⁸Roy Strong, "A Royalist Arcadia: Charles I," *Splendor at Court: Renaissance Spectacle and the Theater of Power* (Boston, 1973), pp. 213-18; D. J. Gordon, "Poet and Architect: the Intellectual Setting of the Quarrel between Ben Jonson and Inigo Jones," *Journal of the Warburg and Courtauld Institutes,* 12 (1949), 152-55, 157-58, 160-63, 165-67, 170-71, 175-76.

⁶⁹Clifford Leech, "The Caroline Audience," *Shakespeare's Tragedies,* p. 161; see also pp. 163, 172-74.

⁷⁰Bentley, *JCS,* I, 223-26.

⁷¹Herbert, *Dramatic Records,* p. 33; Arber, *Stationers,* IV, 190; Greg, *Bibliography,* I, #429, pp. 579-80; Nethercot, *Davenant,* pp. 80-81, 84-85; Bentley, *JCS,* I, 224-25; III, 204-05; V, 1115-18.

⁷²Georges Bas, "James Shirley et 'Th' Untun'd Kennell' une petite guerre des theatres vers 1630," *EA,* 16 (1963), 11-14.

⁷³Dyce, *Works,* I, lxxxiii-lxxxi.

⁷⁴Bas, "James Shirley . . . guerre des theatres vers 1630," pp. 20-22.

⁷⁵Bas, "James Shirley . . . guerre des theatres vers 1630," pp. 15-21.

⁷⁶Edwards, *Plays and Poems of Massinger,* I, Introduction, pp. xl-xli; Dunn, *Massinger,* pp. 31-33.

⁷⁷Yet these works show similarities. The role of Fredeline in Davenant's *The Temple of Love* (1635) is close to that of Lord A in Shirley's *Lady of Pleasure* (1635), and her questionable ethics compare to those of Confident Rapture in *The Example* (1634). Lady Ample in *The Wits* (1634) by Davenant brings to mind Shirley's witty women in his realistic London comedies, such as *The Witty Fair One* (1628) and *Hyde Park* (1632). And Alteza in *The Just Italian* (1629) commits an indiscretion similar to that of Lady Bornwell in *The Lady of Pleasure.* See also Charles Squier, "The Comic Spirit of Sir William Davenant: A Critical Study of His Caroline Comedies," Diss. University of Michigan 1963, pp. 26, 49-50, 65, 87-90, 111, 123n.

⁷⁸Nethercot, *Davenant,* pp. 127-29.

⁷⁹Nethercot, *Davenant,* pp. 75-76.

⁸⁰Harbage, *Davenant,* p. 43; Ramsey, "A Critical Edition of James Shirley's *The Grateful Servant,*" pp. 121-22.

⁸¹Foster, *Register: Gray's Inn,* p. 180.

⁸²Harbage, *Cavalier Drama,* p. 109.

[83]Harbage, pp. 109-10; Bentley, *JCS,* I, 58; V, 1198.

[84]*The Dramatic Works of Richard Brome: Containing Fifteen Comedies Now First Collected in Three Volumes,* ed. John Pearson (1873; rpt. New York, 1966), III; Kaufman, *Richard Brome,* p. 151; Edmund K. Broadus, *The Laureateship* (Oxford, 1921), p. 225.

[85]John Freehafer, "Brome, Suckling, and Davenant's Theater Project of 1639," *Texas Studies in Literature and Language,* 10 (Fall, 1968), 370, 380-81; Bentley, *JCS,* III, 52, 71-72.

[86]Kaufman, *Richard Brome,* pp. 151-52; Bentley, *JCS,* II, 421; Freehafer, "Brome, Suckling, and Davenant's Theater Project of 1639," p. 377.

[87]Kaufman, *Richard Brome,* pp. 152-53.

[88]Freehafer, "Brome, Suckling, and Davenant's Theater Project of 1639," pp. 367, 370, 374.

[89]Kaufman, "Suckling and Davenant Satirized by Brome," *MLR,* 55 (1960), 335-44; Bentley, *JCS,* III, 61-65. See also Act IV. i, ii of Brome's *The Court Beggar* in *The Dramatic Works of Richard Brome,* I, ed. Pearson.

[90]William H. Hickerson, "The Significance of Shirley's Realistic Plays in the History of English Comedy," Diss. University of Michigan 1932, p. 22; see also Kaufman, *Richard Brome,* pp. 10-15; Underwood, *Etherege,* pp. 152-53.

III

The Court Coteries and Court Patronage

The Court, writes David M. Bergeron, was the "single most significant institution for the support of drama" in the seventeenth century.[1] After James I placed the theatrical companies under royal patronage, actors could call themselves gentlemen and were expected to provide entertainment at Court through performing plays or in specific roles in masques.[2] With the accession of Charles I, the patronage of the arts, including painting, music, and drama, much extended. Charles and his French queen were raised in a period of great European artistic achievement, particularly in Italy and Flanders. Both were Catholic cultures, developing a baroque style which emphasized a sensuous but didactic theatricalism in art, music and drama, specifically in the masque. Charles himself collected paintings and along with Queen Henrietta Maria participated in performances of masques at court.[3]

"The custom of publication by patronage," notes Margaret B. Pickel in a study of Charles I as patron of the arts, "was as much part of the social and business organization of the seventeenth century in England as our system of competitive and commercial publication is an accepted part of modern civilized life."[4] Yet

Charles practiced no method of patronage; he simply hired and supported individuals according to his taste and desire. The office that came closest to a regular dispensation of governmental patronage was that of "Surveyor of the King's Works," a title given to Inigo Jones. Specifically it required the supervision of building in the king's interests. Jones licensed all new construction but in fact achieved far-reaching changes in architecture, painting, and drama, all though an *ad hoc* series of functions assigned to him by means of royal "commissions." Poets and painters were likewise on retainer, including Mytens, Van Dyck, and Hollar. Occasionally a poet held an office in the royal household, generally one in name only with few if any specific duties. The poet Thomas Carew became a member of the King's Privy Chamber and Shirley was made valet to the Queen. Just as Charles personally hired his painters, the dramatic presentations he allowed were private shows for the Court, not the large public shows such as Queen Elizabeth had condoned.[5]

Noblemen were similarly employing painters or serving as patrons to poets and musicians. Thus the poet and dramatist Ben Jonson could secure a pension from the King, enjoy the patronage of the Earl of Newcastle, and receive the "author's night" play receipts for new plays presented at the private and public theatres.

Poets, playwrights, scholars, and artists were all dependent on wealthy patrons, both for financial gifts and for the more durable appointments that opened at Court, university, and church. Securing a noble patron was the means to honors or privileges if not an office. Honors included knighthood or other title; privileges could bring pensions, annuities, monopolies.[6] Literary patronage, then, was inseparable from social and political patronage.[7] Printing presses made it possible for many people to become authors, and the number of eligible petitioners went out of all proportion to the number of available patrons. "The period from 1560 to 1640," writes Lawrence Stone, "is thus one of exceptionally intensive intellectual and artistic training, squeezed between centuries of ignorance on the one hand and centuries of dilettantism on the other."[8] Poets learned to seek a number of patrons rather than to rely on one; patrons often served many authors at once.

Just how important a patron was to a professional writer Philip Massinger reveals in his appeal to Philip Herbert, Earl of Montgomery and fourth Earl of Pembroke, the first of many solicitations, which his editors date at some time between 1615 and 1620. Massinger implies that gaining a literary reputation is impossible without "A noble Fauorer." With a patron, "I might write and doe/Like others of more name."[9]

In pursuit of patrons, an author might publish a piece in a large and expensive folio and affix a dedication to one or more members of the aristocracy. Thomas May dedicated his translations of Lucan's *Pharsalia* in 1627 to the Earl of Devonshire, but he also dedicated separately eight of the ten books of the work to other noblemen.[10] Play publication also helped to raise the reputation of the playwright as author. The cost of purchasing these quartos and folios reflected the audience of the theatre, mostly the educated and well-to-do private theatre-goers.[11] It was an exclusive audience dictating its interests and tastes, which the royal couple had a major part in shaping.

What seventeenth-century drama presented to this audience was not richness of language but graceful gesture, along with an attention to outward appearance that was apparent at first in the masque and subsequently dominated the play. Themes dealt with the interests, pastimes, gestures, speech of the Court, rather than with the development of character. Professional dramatists, including Massinger, Brome, and Shirley, were powerless to stay the tide of royal preference. A dilettante coterie of noble dramatists and a considerably more select and homogeneous audience of courtiers combined to sway English drama towards a theatre of style and mannerism.

In June 1634, James Howell wrote from Westminster to Philip Warwick at Paris: "The Court affords little news at present, but that there is a love called Platonic Love, which much sways there of late; it is a love abstracted from all corporeal gross impressions and sensual appetite, but consists in the contemplations and ideas of the mind, not in any carnal fruition. This love sets the wits of the town to work; and they say there will be a masque shortly on it, whereof Her Majesty and her Maids of Honour will be part."[12] The masque was probably William Davenant's *Temple of Love*, performed on Shrove Tuesday, 1635, by the queen and her attendants. Henrietta Maria had introduced the Platonic idea through a pastoral turned masque, *The Shepherd's Paradise,* presented first at Whitehall on January 9, 1633, and featuring a series of debates on the topic with nine different settings, and lasting nearly eight hours. On March 5, Shrove Tuesday, the pastoral had been transformed into a masque, with similar adaptations to the staging of it at Somerset House. Its author was Walter Montague, a member of the queen's Court coterie who converted to Catholicism in 1635. That year Davenant presented *The Platonic Lovers,* the fullest exposition of the theme, which also appears to satirize it.[13]

Drama in the Platonic mode puts the hero and heroine to striving for the satisfaction of love and friendship amidst the contrary pull of parents, previous obligations to country, and so forth. Larger issues of crown and state are merely background for the private concerns of love and friendship. The Platonic vogue also expressed itself in poetry, which typically emphasized constancy, humility, service, beauty, and virtue. Several of Shirley's friends wrote verses about Platonic love: William Habington carried the idea to an earnest intensity in his *Castara*. Some of the nobility, especially women, became benefactors to a coterie of servants who wrote verses dedicated to them. These included Elizabeth, Countess of Rutland, and Lucy (Percy), Countess of Carlisle, whose Platonic name was Aminta. Other courtiers merely wooed through poetic compliment made publicly, or in private through intimate verse. Platonism became an art of talking about love or a disputation on love in verse. All varieties were imitated at court—from warm relationships to the humble, self-effacing contemplation of a man for a beautiful chaste woman to the love between a man and a woman that transcends all physical considerations and concerns itself with the soul.[14] None of this was new. What was new consisted in the emphasis on the manner of revealing this love, a self-consciousness that entirely robbed the work of the ability to express genuine sentiment, arouse passion, and effect change. All of the external elements were there but little of the internal emotion capable of stimulating thought or catharsis.

Puritans were antagonistic to a love cult promulgated by a Catholic queen and articulated in a stylized and ceremonious manner that smacked of rites. Other critics had more mundane quarrels with the fashion. Dramatists suggested that some practitioners abused the cult as a means to sexual adventure; many dramas refer to citizens cuckolded by wives who were aping "the court way." Playwrights parodied the fawning language and extravagant compliment. Among these was Shirley, especially in *The Ball*, for which the Master of the Revels roundly scolded him. Shirley's skepticism about the mode may have cost him the queen's favor. Although his poem, "Love for Enjoying," is clearly an anti-Platonic poem, another entitled "To His Mistris Confined" could serve as an expression of Platonic love, and "Epithalamium," which Shirley wrote for the marriage of his patron Thomas Stanley some years later, makes the reference to union of soul and body that is common in Platonic poetry. Many were ambivalent towards the vogue. Alfred Harbage sums it up in this way: "Throughout the century we can in fact discern both a more old-fashioned tendency, concerned with morals, continuing the love and honour tradition of the court of Queen Henrietta Maria, and a new one, libertinistic, realistic, interested in man as a social animal."[15] Shirley's strength and weakness is that he tried to depict both modes, as indeed he saw the Court representing both tendencies. The fashion introduced by the queen in all its purity was not always kept pristine by her court followers. Shirley succeeded admirably in illustrating the fashion and its abuse.

When Sir Henry Herbert, Master of the Revels, entered Shirley's *The Gamester* in his note book, he remarked that it came from a story suggested to Shirley by Charles I. Although licensed in November 1633, it was not performed before the King and Queen until the following February. Presumably Shirley was amply rewarded. Herbert reports that the King said it was the best play he had seen in seven years. We have in this play, then, the sort of entertainment Charles preferred.[16] The story is similar to the comedies of Fletcher; it includes tricks, disguisings, a touch of possible disaster averted at the last minute, some wit mixed with farce—all combined to make a play setting lust against chastity, love against loyalty. Yet Shirley's play, unlike the typical work of Fletcher, is grounded in London and takes in a great deal of local color on the "gaming life."

Shirley's emphasis in this and other plays on the proper conduct of love and honor corresponds to the Cavalier taste for form and social manner as opposed to impassioned commitment. His restrained, elegant expression fits perfectly with the Caroline liking for decorum and culture, often called "wit." It is a self-consciousness that seems to suit Shirley's temperament better than that of either Brome or Massinger, an awareness of the artifice even in participating in it.[17] Yet *The Gamester,* like much of Shirley's other work, has a frankness that is among his virtues and a counter to the stylization his century imposed on his work. His Wilding as the "gamester" undergoes a well motivated conversion and his agony over his supposed cuckolding is genuine. His frank proposal that his wife act as his pander comes in the first scene of the play and contains all the information an audience needs to know about the main plot, which, unlike Fletcher's plots, is not especially intricate.[18] The Barnacles are the satirical stereotypes of the middle class, monied and stupid. But Shirley through Old Barnacle shrewdly comments on the antagonism between citizen and courtier:

> . . . we that had
> Our breeding from a trade, cits, as you call us,
> Though we hate gentlemen ourselves, yet are
> Ambitious to make all our children gentlemen:
> In three generations they return again. . . .
> the courtiers make
> Us cuckolds; mark! we wriggle into their
> Estates; poverty makes their children citizens;
> Our sons cuckold them: a circular justice!   (III,201)

Hazard, another gamester, makes observations on several characters who simply cross the stage; all are of the gentry class or higher—a lord, a knight, and a country gentleman. In keeping with the suggestion that money can buy justice, Shirley suggests the attitude towards marriage when Hazard as the ideal gamester proposes and in the same breath talks to the young woman of her dowry.

Roy Strong in his study of the Court and art comments on the contributions that made England the art center of European civilization in the 1630's. The culmination of the spoken and visual arts of the period was the masque. The two men most responsible for the development of this unique composite of art, music, and drama were Ben Jonson and Inigo Jones. Until 1631 Jonson was the preeminent masque writer, working with Jones to produce a series of spectacular shows combining verse and prose, music and dance, scenery and staging with elaborate machinery. From the reign of James I with the presentation of the *Masque of Blackness* in 1605 to the last Court presentation in 1640, this special art form had central place at Court. Original presentations were given each Twelfth Night and Shrovetide with numerous other masques written and presented as occasional pieces by various noblemen, often in honor of the king and queen. In time the masques were used as propaganda for the Court. Davenant's *Britannia Triumphans,* for example, was presented in 1637, during the ship-money trial. It asserts the correctness of the naval policy of the king.[19]

Ben Jonson and Inigo Jones sought through the masque to honor their sovereigns James I and his son who thoroughly embraced the concept of the divine right of kings; and so successful was Jonson in complimenting James's pedantry (meanwhile displaying his own erudition) that in 1616 he was granted a pension of 100 marks for regularly providing the Twelfth Night masque.[20] Strong demonstrates that the masque was designed to depict the Court itself in mythic and allegorical form.[21] Stephen Orgel's study of the Jonsonian masque suggests that Jonson's purpose in making the audience an essential part of the masque was to celebrate the royal spectators: the playgoers in effect were performing in a display of deference to the royal couple.[22] Such devices as perspective stage scenery make the Crown the center of the presentation, able to bring harmony from disorder in scenes pitting chaos against order, and nature against art, usually architecture.[23] All the elements of the masque are directed towards a statement of the just, wise, and peaceful rule of the king represented by figures of classical myth or personified by the ideal virtues such as love and fame. Gardens, perfectly balanced villas, rainbows, seas, gods and goddesses, abstractions personified as Fame, Justice, Truth—all make a recurring statement of the divine purpose of kings. Jonson's use of the antimasque, antic presentations which alternated with the more serious dramatic material, accorded with James I's taste and was intended primarily to depict the opposite of these virtues and emblems.[24] Power is equated with love, and opposition and rebellion are dismissed by a king who represents order and peace. Though masques were enjoying a new popularity, and had supplanted the more splendidly and reflectively verbal drama of Shakespeare's stage, they are traditional in one way. They celebrate the "ceremonial ordering of human life" that is increasingly scrutinized during the Jacobean era.[25]

Then Jonson and Jones quarreled. In part it was the egotism of a well established and pensioned writer clashing with that of a traveled and increasingly popular architect-engineer-painter. But the interests and personality of King Charles worked against Jonson. Charles was impressed by ritual and form; he disliked debate or criticism. Jonson's strength was in his realistic representation of London life on the one hand and on the other his classical learning, which required thought and intellect. The playwright's tendency to lecture or teach the Court was not destined to please Charles or his queen.[26] Also Jonson's interests were in the urban life of his times: his classical knowledge was not easily adapted to the concerns of Platonic love. Nor was he particularly interested in marriage and the rising female element in the Caroline audience. His plays such as *Bartholomew Fair* show the changing social order as one of upheaval and disorder rather than a reaffirmation of unity and divinely ordained kingship.[27] When Jonson composed his first masque for King Charles in 1631, the emphasis was on design and show rather than content; Jones's influence prevailed to make the poet's part simply description of a work conceived in visual terms.[28] By the time Shirley was called upon to compose the poetry for the Inns of Court masque in 1634, Jones had supplanted Jonson. Nowhere is this more evident than in the several contemporary accounts given at the time about Shirley's *Triumph of Peace;* all stress the visual elements—dress, properties, scenery: pageantry at its height.[29]

The Jonsonian masque had nevertheless been clearly established as an art form by 1631 when Jonson last worked with Inigo Jones. This was not to be the end of Jonson as masque writer. Jonson's patron, William Cavendish, Earl of Newcastle, commissioned the poet to write two masques for presentation to their majesties, one on the occasion of their visitation to the Earl's estate at Welbeck in 1633, the other for their visit to Bolsover in 1634. In *Love's Welcome at Bolsover* Jonson included a comic dance by rough workmen which is introduced by a surveyor named Iniquo Vitruvius, an obvious satire directed at Jones.[30]

In the years 1633 and 1634 Shirley was at the height of his popularity. The dedication of *The Bird in a Cage* in 1633 had made evident his royalist and anti-Puritan sympathies, and his acceptance in the Court coterie dominated by the queen had further assurance when he was selected by the Inns of Court to write a masque that would demonstrate their loyalty and support of the queen's artistic endeavors.[31] William Prynne's *Histriomastix* had lamented the performance of plays and likened to whores women who took part in any such presentations. The lawyers were in a sensitive position, for Prynne had been a member of Lincoln's Inn.[32] Shirley's long association with the members of Gray's Inn and others in the Inns of Court made his selection likely. Yet while Herbert's records designate Shirley as the author, as do the title pages on the several editions that appeared in the same year, the playwright's name appears in few of the many private accounts of the masque, several of them describing the events in great detail, especially the procession of the Inns of Court before the actual presentation of the masque.[33] The thorough account in the *Memorials of Bulstrode Whitelocke,* a member of the Inns of Court committee which oversaw the production, tells how much the musicians Simon Ives and William Lawes were paid and lists the total expense of the masque— £20,000—but nowhere mentions Shirley's name or fee.[34] The extensive records that Whitelocke kept concerning the masque's musical component, including specific diagrams depicting the positions to be taken by the musicians, are described in detail in Murray Lefkowitz's article on the Longleat Papers.[35] We now know the names of the cast and of the musicians at the Blackfriars and Cockpit theatres as well as many English and foreign musicians employed at Court. Uncatalogued Middle Temple manuscripts give details of the organization, administration, and cast of the masque. These show a total cost of £15,000 with Shirley paid £120. Inigo Jones received £200, but probably part of that fee was to pay workmen.[36] Similarly extant are drawings of the elaborate settings designed by Inigo Jones for the masque.[37] In the masque the organization and lyric poetry were of lesser interest than the music and scenery. This masque, indeed, created a sensation for its cost and its sumptuous trappings.[38]

That Shirley was called upon to write the most famous masque historically of the entire period is somewhat ironic. Shirley, in fact, was not a masque writer; few masques are used in his plays and his comments on the form are not favorable. Yet he excelled in lyric poetry that was largely descriptive, and his moral didacticism, the matter of a masque, is much in his plays. And while the words of a masque did not command the major attention, the text of *The Triumph of Peace,* which critics now dismiss as the most disjointed of all masque scripts, had three editions within a year.[39] The selection of Shirley as author for the splendid display illustrates the workings of literary patronage with its religious and political implications and the central importance of coterie membership.

In *The Triumph of Peace* Shirley manages to lecture, expose, and correct all of the social classes in England, and he brings in not only the typical allegorical figures such as Fancy, Opinion, and Confidence, but also merchants and tradesmen, such as a tailor, a feather maker (frequently the trade of Puritans), and a carpenter. What is significant is that Shirley's *Triumph of Peace* questions in part the wisdom of the absolute power of kingship. In a series of antimasques Shirley depicts some Court abuses, including monopolies granted by the Crown. The figures that pass by, a jockey, a country fellow, a philosopher, and so forth, are all intended to remind the king of grievances against monopolies. The final statement of Shirley's masque cautions that the king cannot rule without law.[40] The poet's thesis is that for its survival Peace needs Law and Justice, which the reigning King and Queen bring to England. These three allegorical figures allow Inigo Jones large scope for spectacular entry. Here is Shirley's description of the entrance of Peace:

> ... there appears in the highest and foremost
> part of the heaven, by little and little to
> break forth, a whitish cloud, bearing a chariot
> feigned of goldsmith's work; and in it sate
> Irene, or Peace, in a flowery vesture like the
> spring, a garland of olives on her head, a
> branch of palm in her hand, buskins of green
> taffeta, great puffs about her neck and
> shoulders. (295-96)

Several antimasques take up the entire first act of the masque. Here we have Opinion, Novelty, and Admiration—all prevalent in the Court—but Fancy, who insists on an antimasque, is the genius of the scenes and conjures up all the various spectacles. The antimasque was an element of the production that catered to the tastes of the middle classes, and Shirley was able to play this fact into the antimasques themselves. In one segment, local tradesmen enter roughly and rudely, demanding a view of the proceedings and concurrently and humorously showing the manners and aggressiveness of lower class Londoners. A scene featuring a tavern and its customers serves as background for Shirley's main critical claim in the piece, an attack on projectors and the common practice at Court of selling monopolies. Shirley also comments on highwaymen, local justices, hunters, gamesters—all in dumb show and dance.[41] All of these short scenes present elements of peace, law, and justice operating ideally and being abused. The antimasques, which in their inclusion of tradesmen and servants aim to show the all-embracing rule of King and Queen in peace, with justice and law, allow Shirley to introduce some realistic humor and commentary into a production given to personification and grand show.

In the main masque appear some of Shirley's loveliest lyrics, which are sung. The final cloud-like apparition portrays Morning, who gloriously descends to end the night and the masque:

> Come away, away, away
> See the dawning of the day,
> Risen from the murmuring streams;
> Some star shew with sickly beams,
> What stock of flame they are allow'd,
> Each retiring to a cloud;
> Bid your active sports adieu,
> The morning else will blush for you.
> Ye feather-footed Hours run
> To dress the chariot of the Sun;
> Harness the steeds, it quickly will
> Be time to mount to eastern hill.
> The lights grow pale with modest fears,
> Lest you offend their sacred ears,
> And eyes, that lent you all this grace;
> Retire, retire, to your own place.
> And as you move from that blest pair,
> Let each heart kneel, and think a prayer,
> That all, that can make up the glory
> Of good and great may fill their story. (303-04)

As was customary, all of the lyrics end with praise and honor to King Charles and Queen Henrietta Maria.

Shirley's masque was itself parodied in a brief work entitled *The Tragedy of the Cruelle Warre* (1643). Written by a member of the Parliamentary faction, it attacks the false image of national unity presented in *The Triumph of Peace*. Because Shirley wrote for the Inns of Court, the author chose to personify Law and Justice. That *The Tragedy of the Cruell Warre* frequently makes little distinction between the masque and the antimasque illustrates that the Court masque was not well known outside the milieu.[42] It depicts the expense and tragedy of war rather than the triumph of peace. The antimasques are used to picture the discord the Cavaliers effected in the name of the King. The characters Opinion and Fancy represent the spirit of the Cavaliers—presumptuous and rebellious against counsels of reason. The cause of the Cavaliers is labeled papist for giving arms to the Roman Catholics in contravention of the practice in the times of Elizabeth and James. In general the pamphlet gives the views of those Protestants wishing to compromise with the King on condition that he recognize the prerogatives of Parliament and disavow the religious politics of Archbishop Laud and Catholicism.[43]

The famous masque assured Shirley's reputation and his circle of friends and patrons spread rapidly; he was able to address himself to some of the most influential men in England. Having already gained formal entry into the Court coterie in 1633 with his appointment to the office of Valet to the Chamber of Queen Henrietta Maria,[44] he was even more conspicuous within it, and in time he would enter the circle headed by the Earl of Newcastle. Shirley was in a position to observe through his own experience and through his associates at Court and the Inns the tastes and manners of the most influential coterie in Caroline England, centered around Queen Henrietta Maria. Patronage connections, along with dedications, trace his gradual alliance with the Court coterie and his brief membership in that select group before he left for Ireland in the spring of 1636.

A number of figures associated with Roman Catholicism were among those Shirley in the 1630's chose as friends or potential patrons. Most of the people to whom Shirley addressed his work during this time were of noble families that had been Catholic for generations: the Earl of Rutland, William Tresham, Esq., Sir Edward Bushell, Lady Jane Pawlet, and Sir Edward Golding, among others. Shirley's poetry also includes several elegies on the deaths of members of noble Catholic families.[45] At this time a fresh Catholic revival was in progress at the Court under the influence of French-born Queen Henrietta Maria: conversion became the vogue, and attendance at the Queen's Chapel at Somerset House a fashion.[46] Patron and poet converts, along with some Catholics by family tradition, made up a Court coterie.

The appointment to office in the queen's household may have been through the influence of Shirley's close friend William Habington, one of the Court's poet Catholics like Sir John Suckling and William Davenant. Habington is a figure in a network of connections. In 1636 he was considered for the post of the queen's agent to Rome. The position went to another who presumably had more influence with two powerful young courtiers close to the Queen, Henry Jermyn and Tobie Mathew. These two were patrons to William Davenant, whose talents served more directly the Platonic vogue.[47] Tobie Mathew was supplicant to Lady Carlisle, so much so her devotee that he was referred to as "Lady Carlisle's dog."[48] His position nevertheless was powerful enough to win the poet laureateship for Davenant. Joined with [H]Abington's name in the 1637 Middlesex Sessions Rolls for not going to church is that of Robert Stapleton. Both are said to be "late of St. Giles in-the-Fields" parish and are noted "gentlemen." An entry in that parish register for the year 1636 records the death of a stillborn child of Robert Stapleton.[49] His association with Shirley and Habington was literary. Stapleton achieved a measure of prominence at Court and presumably began his writing during the 1630's, though his extant plays date from the Restoration.[50]

Francis Manners, the sixth Earl of Rutland, was among the upper-class Englishmen, most of them Catholic, to whom Shirley turned for patronage, perhaps prodded by his courtier Catholic friends and his own analysis of the balance of power at Court. The Earl was the subject of Shirley's dedication of *The Grateful Servant* in 1630.[51] It was a good choice, for the Earl was one of the wealthiest and most influential men in England, in part through his daughter's marriage to George Villiers, Duke of Buckingham, favorite of James I. A member of the Inner Temple, Chief Justice of Eyre, Lord Lieutenant of Lincolnshire until 1627, seated on the Privy Council, the Earl of Rutland possessed nearly every honor despite his Romanism.[52] Shirley's address to him reflects not only generous patronage from the Earl but also personal acquaintance: he speaks of "gratitude to your Lordship, whose clear testimony to me was above a theatre" and calls him the "volume of our English honour," perhaps in reference to *The Booke of Honour: or Five Decades of Epistles of Honour*, dedicated to the Earl in 1625 by Francis Markham.[53] Shirley may have been introduced to the Earl through the Tufton girls, daughters of the Earl of Thanet, for Rutland's second wife was the daughter of Sir John Tufton.[54] A manuscript poem written by Shirley to Diana Tufton, married to Sir Robert Curson, and Mary Tufton, the wife of Sir Edward Bishop, who had come to the Inner Temple in November 1620, addresses the sisters as married but still childless. On the basis of the poem, R. G. Howarth in his study of Shirley's poetry proposes that the two had entertained the poet in their London town houses before the birth of Sir Edward's heir in December 1627.[55] Possibly Shirley was looking to one or both husbands as possible patrons. A revision of the poem was published in the 1646 collection, but it addresses only Lady Diana Curson while her marriage was yet young enough for the poet to encourage her to beget heirs. The printed version is headed "at his Departure," and suggests that Shirley may have stayed with Lady Curson at another time as well, perhaps before he left for Ireland in 1636.[56] Although her husband was seated at Waterperry in Oxfordshire, it is more likely that Shirley visited her at her home in London. There is no indication that the Cursons or Bishops were well known patrons, but they were Roman Catholics and related to other, more powerful aristocrats.[57]

William Tresham, to whom Shirley dedicated *Love Tricks* in 1631, unlike the Earl of Rutland was a young man with little wealth or influence. William was probably a member of Gray's Inn, newly admitted: there are two entries of that name, one for March 1633 and another for August 1633, the second identifying the member as the son of Sir Lewis Tresham.[58] A possible relative is Sir William Tresham, a Catholic, who owned a town house in Clerkenwell by 1619.[59] The dedication, pleasantly frank, admits that Shirley was taking the opportunity of addressing the play to Tresham on the knowledge that he had enjoyed it on stage; no other means of knowing the young man, Shirley says, presents itself. The playwright makes the pointed remark "the flowings of your blood will instruct you how to merit."[60]

Perhaps the most interesting dedication, that of *Changes, or Love in a Maze* in 1632, is to Lady Dorothy Shirley, the wife of Sir Henry Shirley. The playwright refers to "your name/To whose clear virtue truth is bound, and we,/That there is so much left for history."⁶¹ The arms shown in the portrait of the playwright are of the Shirley branch of Eatington, and those of Lady Dorothy's husband, who was still living at the time. It seems unlikely that the poet would be audacious enough to claim a blood relationship on the basis of coincidence in name only, and it is an indication that Shirley did not formally apply for a coat of arms.⁶² Perhaps Shirley meant to honor the lady's family; she was a Devereux, the second daughter of Robert Devereux, second Earl of Essex. Lady Dorothy became a widow in 1634 and remarried in the Queen's Chapel at Somerset in 1635, which indicates she was a practicing Catholic. She presumably lived in London from time to time; her name appears in the 1634 Calendar of the Westminster Sessions Rolls for not attending church in her parish of St. Martin's-in-the-Fields.⁶³

The following year Shirley presented *The Witty Fair One* in published form to another Catholic, Sir Edward Bushell, making an unusual reference to Bushell's "candid censure of some unworthy poems which I have presented to the world."⁶⁴ The reference could be to poems or plays circulated in manuscript, a common practice, although it is fairly certain that his poem *Echo and Narcissus* was issued from the press in 1618 and published several years later again with the *Poems* in 1646.⁶⁵ Presenting poems to the "world" usually meant publication, and by 1633 Shirley had printed a number of his plays, some of which Sir Edward may have criticized.

The piece that best indicates Shirley's leaning and personal interests during this time is a little allegory called *A Contention for Honour and Riches,* presented in 1633 to Edward Golding, Esq., of Colston Bassett in the County of Nottinghamshire. Though Shirley remarks that is was "meant for innocent mirth," it reads much like a moral treatise written by a young schoolmaster for his scholars.⁶⁶ He may have intended the masque as a lesson to his pupils at the St. Albans Grammar School or, if he did teach in London in 1625 to 1627, to his young charges there. It is honor rather than riches that the scholar first receives, Shirley says, perhaps thinking of his own experience; riches come easily not to the study but to the city man and the merchant. That the allegory had been written earlier is quite possible, but the reference " . . . the memory of your own act and virtue to pay ourself" particularly suited the time and the patron. Golding's name appears in an entry of December 3, 1633 in the Middlesex Sessions Rolls, "Edward Gouldinge late of Colston Bassett Co. Nottingham Gentleman" indicted for recusancy. There he is described as "late of St. Margaret's Westminster," and it is likely that Shirley had met him first in London.[67] The reference to Golding's act and virtue would apply exactly to a recusant's refusal to compromise his religion, and would indicate that Shirley's Catholicism put a stress on the moral component of religion. Shirley's hostile "dedication" in the same year to the Puritan William Prynne of *The Bird in a Cage* is narrowly moralistic.[68]

That Shirley was moving among people whom we know or conjecture to be Catholic is not sufficient grounds for thinking him a convert. After all, it simply made sense to cultivate people of influence at Court, and those closest to the Queen in religion and dramatic interests had a great deal of power. But there are some elusive references that, along with his associates, make the assumption plausible. One "Jacobus Shirley, gent" of the parish of St. Giles-in-the-Fields appears in an entry for July 15, 1646, in a Recusant Roll that records convictions of the General Session of the Gaol-Delivery for the City of Westminster, one of three courts that convicted for recusancy.[69] The list appears to be a summary of convictions for the years 1643 to 1646. The Shirley in question evidently had not attended church for the past 30 weeks: he was fined 30s. and the fee was a shilling for each absence. That the man was not a merchant is clear from other entries in the list that note the profession of the recusant.[70] Then we have such allusions as that in the issue for January 4-11, 1644 of a civil war newssheet, *Mercurius Britannicus,* which calls the Court a debauched child unable to be revived ". . . by his Grandfather *Ben Jonson,* and his uncle *Shakespeare,* and his couzen-Germains *Fletcher,* and *Beaumont,* and nose-lesse *Davenant,* and Frier *Sherley* the Poets." "Frier" suggests that the playwright's Catholicism was common knowledge, though it should be noted that the author, Captain Thomas Audley, was a Puritan who would be eager to malign all poets.[71]

Whole the tone of many of Shirley's plays was moral and to that extent reflective of a religious temperament, references to religion are few. Even as a matter of deliberate policy, this would be understandable. It was a dangerous business, this of practicing any other than the Anglican faith, and Shirley was neither a wealthy man, able to afford the high fines imposed on papists, nor a secure favorite or nobleman confident of protection from the queen. Any representations of formal Roman worship would not have passed the censor of plays, Sir Henry Herbert.[72] The Court circle did not demand religion in its drama, but Henrietta Maria's liking for pageantry and formal presentation may have come in part from the splendor of Catholic worship. The taste of this select and narrow group demanded wit, ingenious plotting, and even the satiric treatment of its own exaggerated manners and fashions, especially as these could be represented in caricatures of the aspiring merchant class.

And the Queen's preference for the masque ultimately demanded that playwrights endeavor to use the form. Shirley was no exception. That he was not a successful masque writer and had little liking for the masque is evident in his works. Despite this, he managed to secure the designation of the Inns of Court as "maker" of their splendid show of support for the crown. This illustrates the importance that connections and membership in coteries came to play in forwarding the career of the dramatist. Shirley's active assocation with the Inns of Court circle paid off. And his dedications to members of the Catholic nobility during the late 1620's and early 1630's, prior to the Inns of Court masque, no doubt put him in favor among the Court coterie. Although the plays dedicated to possible Catholic Court patrons range from the early comic *Love Tricks* to the more somber *The Traitor,* they are significant in the judgment he used in selecting, for instance, the theme that would appeal most to the potential benefactor. Young Treshman enjoyed *Love Tricks* on the stage; *Changes* would appeal to Lady Dorothy Shirley; *The Grateful Servant* fits the dedicatee, the Earl of Rutland, almost with unintended irony.

Shirley was attentive to persons at Court likely in the inner circle of the Catholic group, and his reputation and connections with persons affiliated with the coterie eventually led also to his being made valet to the Queen. He was to make liberal use of the inner workings of that group in his plays, generally appealing to the prevalent taste for wit, love and honor themes, and local color. Others, notably Davenant, followed his example with even greater success. Shirley hardly was calculating enough to convert to Catholicism in hopes of attracting attention and patrons even though others presumably did so. What ultimately led to his failure to gain the coveted poet laureateship was his penchant for preaching even while catering to current taste. Another decision on his part also removed him from the popular mind: the move to Ireland.

Notes

[1] David M. Bergeron, "Women as Patrons of English Drama," *Patronage in the Renaissance,* eds. Guy F. Lytle and Stephen Orgel (Princeton, 1981), pp. 277-79, 282.

[2] Stephen Orgel, "The Royal Theatre and the Role of King," *Patronage in the Renaissance,* pp. 267, 270.

[3] Malcolm Smuts, "The Political Failure of Stuart Cultural Patronage," *Patronage in the Renaissance,* p. 167.

[4] Margaret B. Pickel, *Charles I as Patron of Poetry and Drama* (London, 1936), p. 159.

[5] Smuts, "The Political Failure of Stuart Cultural Patronage," pp. 169-73, 175-77.

[6] Linda Levy Peck, "Court Patronage and Government Policy: The Jacobean Dilemma," *Patronage in the Renaissance,* pp. 29-30; see also Peck, *Northampton: Patronage and Policy at the Court of James I* (London, 1982), pp. 24-26.

[7] Arthur F. Marotti, "John Donne and the Rewards of Patronage," *Patronage in the Renaissance,* p. 207. The intertwining of literary, social, and political patronage is particularly well illustrated by the powerful court patron the Earl of Northampton, in the reign of James I. See Peck, *Northampton,* pp. 51-52, 54-55.

[8] Lawrence Stone, *The Crisis of the Aristocracy* (Oxford, 1965), pp. 703-04, 722.

[9] *The Plays and Poems of Philip Massinger,* ed. Philip Edwards and Colin Gibson (Oxford, 1976), I, Intro. pp. xviii, xxiii-xxiv, xxix. See also Massinger's dedication of *The Duke of Milan* (1623) to Lady Katherine Stanhope and *The Renegado* (1630) to George Hading, Lord Berkeley, who was related to Lady Stanhope.

[10] Patricia Thomson, "The Patronage of Letters Under Elizabeth and James I," *English,* 7 (1949), 280.

[11] Stephen Orgel, "The Royal Theatre and the Role of King," pp. 270, 272-73.

[12] Howell, *Letters* (London, 1754), I, 255, quoted in Pickel, *Charles I as Patron,* pp. 29, 33, 35-36.

[13] "Comedies, festivities, and balls are the order of the day here, and are indulged in every day at Court for the prince's sake, while all the greatest lords vie with each other in entertaining him at noble and sumptuous

banquets." *Cal. SP Ven.,* 23 (1632-1636), no. 581, Dec. 21, 1635, p. 491. Specific contemporary references to the masques are in Knowler, *Strafford's Letters,* I, 177 (*The Faithful Shepherdess*), 207, 525; II, 130, 140, 148, 150; *Cal. SP Ven.,* 23 (1632-36), no. 100, p. 63; no. 240, p. 184; no. 127, p. 86, no. 249, p. 190; no. 352, p. 275; no. 427, p. 334, no. 534, p. 445; no. 588, p. 499. Confusion about the pastoral, later produced as a masque, is explained in John Orrell, "Productions at the Paved Court Theatre, Somerset House, 1632/3," *N & Q,* 23 (May-June 1976), 223-24. See also Stephen Orgel, *The Illusion of Power, Political Theatre in the English Renaissance* (Berkeley, 1975), pp. 19-24, and John Peacock, "The French Element in Inigo Jones's Masque Designs," in *The Court Masque,* ed. David Lindley (Manchester, 1984), pp. 156, 161.

[14]Gunnar Sorelius, *The Giant Race Before the Flood: Pre-Restoration Drama on the Stage and in the Criticism of the Restoration* (Nairobi, 1964), p. 119; J. B. Fletcher, *The Religion of Beauty in Women* (New York, 1911), pp. 181-82, 184-86, 193-94, 197; G. F. Sensabaugh, "Love Ethics in Platonic Court Drama, 1625-1642," *Huntington Library Quarterly,* I (1937), 279-80; C. A. Ackerman, "Fashionable Platonism in Caroline Poetry," Diss. University of Michigan 1955, p. 37; Raymond A. Anselment, "The Countess of Carlisle and Caroline Praise: Convention and Reality," *SP,* 82, No. 2 (Spring 1985), 214-15, 218-24, 226-31.

[15]Alfred Harbage, *Cavalier Drama* (1936; rpt. New York, 1964), p. 164. See F. S. Boas, *An Introduction to Stuart Drama* (London, 1946), pp. 356-57; Hanson T. Parlin, *A Study of Shirley's Comedies of London Life, Bulletin of the University of Texas,* No. 371 (Nov. 15, 1914), pp. 59, 62, 64. Parlin does not believe Shirley was satirizing the new love convention; the masque clearly shows the fashion of balls in a pure light, but of course the play had been revised and possibly portions cut. See also Sorelius, *The Giant Race,* p. 110; G. F. Sensabaugh, "Platonic Love and the Puritan Rebellion," *SP,* 37 (1940), 458-62, 480-81; Ackerman, "Fashionable Platonism," pp. 112, 116-17, 132, 178-79; Armstrong, *Poems,* pp. 2, 7, 37-8.

[16]Herbert licensed the play on November 11, 1633, and records a performance of it at court (with the plot idea attributed to King Charles I) on February 6, 1634. Herbert, *Dramatic Records,* pp. 35, 54-55. The French *Heptameron* by Marguerite of Navarre was also a source; see Robert S. Forsythe, *The Relations of Shirley's Plays to the Elizabethan Drama* (New York, 1914), p. 367. Dyce, *Works,* III, 183-277.

[17]Michael Neill, " 'Wits most accomplished Senate': The Audience of the Caroline Private Theaters," *SEL,* 18 (1978), 355-57, 359.

[18]Wilding's characterization anticipates the libertine of Restoration drama, and this explains why Shirley's *The Gamester* became a popular revival

play. Three different adaptations were presented on the English stage between 1711 and 1827, in the later years because it was taken for an attack on gambling. Gebhard J. Scherrer, "James Shirley's Reputation, 1624-1833," Master's thesis Brown University 1948, pp. 50, 52-62; Forsythe, *The Relations of Shirley's Plays to the Elizabethan Drama,* pp. 31-41. See also Stephen Ronay, "*The Gamester,* A Critical Edition of the 1637 Quarto with Introduction and Notes," Diss. University of Chicago 1948.

[19]Strong, *Splendor at Court: Renaissance Spectacle and the Theater of Power* (Boston, 1973), pp. 213, 241.

[20]Stephen Orgel, *The Jonsonian Masque* (Cambridge, MA, 1965), p. 69.

[21]Strong, *Splendor at Court,* p. 216.

[22]Orgel, *The Jonsonian Masque,* pp. 64-65.

[23]Strong, *Splendor at Court,* pp. 216, 218-19.

[24]Orgel, *The Jonsonian Masque,* pp. 72-76.

[25]Cyrus Hoy, "Masques and the Artifice of Tragedy," *Elizabethan Theatre,* 7 (1980), 121.

[26]Peter W. Thomas, "Charles I of England: The Tragedy of Absolutism," in *The Courts of Europe: Politics, Patronage and Royalty, 1400-1800,* ed. A. G. Dickens (London, 1977), pp. 195, 204; see also Thomas, "Two Cultures? Court and Country Under Charles I" in *Seventeenth-Century England, A Changing Culture,* ed. W. R. Owens (Totowa, NJ, 1981), p. 271.

[27]Anne Barton, "Harking Back to Elizabeth: Ben Jonson and Caroline Nostalgia," *ELH,* 48, No. 4 (Winter 1981), 720.

[28]Orgel, *The Jonsonian Masque,* pp. 80, 195.

[29]Some of these contemporary references are cited in footnote 13 of this chapter, but see in particular G. Garrard to the Earl of Strafford, Dec. 6, 1633; Jan. 9, 1634; Feb. 27, 1634, in Knowler, *Strafford's Letters,* I, 167, 177, 207; *Cal. SP Ven.,* 23 (1632-36), no. 235 (Jan. 4, 1634), 180; no. 258 (Feb. 17, 1634), 195; Scudamore Papers, #8168 (Jan. 11, 1634), PRO MS c115/M31; Cal. SP Dom. 240, no. 14 (Feb. 3, 1634), no. 65 (Feb. 14, 1634), PRO MS SP 16.

[30]W. Todd Furniss, "Ben Jonson's Masques," *Three Studies in the Renaissance: Sidney, Jonson, Milton* (New Haven, 1958), pp. 164-67.

[31]See Shirley's dedication to William Prynne and the play in *James Shirley's 'The Bird in a Cage': A Critical Edition,* ed. Frances Frazier

Senescu (New York, 1980). *The Bewties* was licensed for presentation on January 21, 1633 and published as *The Bird in a Cage* the same year. Herbert, *Dramatic Records,* p. 34; Greg, *Bibliography,* I, #480, p. 627. The title page reads: "*The Bird in a Cage.*/A Comedie,/As it hath been presented at the Phoenix in Drury Lane./The Author James Shirley, Servant to her Majesty."

[32]*STC,* #20464. F. G. Fleay believes the pastoral in which the Queen and ladies acted on Christmas 1633 was Shirley's *Arcadia.* It was not licensed by Herbert and presumably privately performed. "Annals of the Careers of James and Henry Shirley," *Anglia,* 8 (1885), 407. He suggests that the work which raised the ire of Prynne was Montague's *Shepherd's Paradise.* See Fleay, *A Biographical Chronicle of the English Drama, 1559-1642* (London, 1891), II, 118.

[33]Herbert, *Dramatic Records,* p. 54; Greg, *Bibliography,* II, #488, pp. 632-34. It is interesting that William Cooke was able to register the masque for printing on Jan. 24 before it was to be presented on Feb. 3, 1634. See Arber, *Stationers,* IV, 287. See also Bentley, *JCS,* V, 1154-63. Descriptions of the masque occur in Whiteway's Diary, 1618-1634, pp. 194-95, BM MS. Egerton 784; George W. Johnson, *Memoirs of John Selden* (London, 1835), pp. 202-05 and in the records of the various Inns of Court: George Godwin, *The Middle Temple; The Society and Fellowship* (London, 1954), pp. 82-83; Frederick A. Inderwick, *A Calendar of the Inner Temple Records* (London, 1895-1901), II, xlvii-xlviii, 210, 212-14, 217-20, 226; *The Pension Book of Gray's Inn, 1569-1669,* ed. Reginald J. Fletcher (London, 1901-1910), I, 316-20.

[34]Bulstrode Whitelocke, *Memorials of the English Affairs from the Beginning of the Reign of K Charles I to the Happy Restoration of K Charles II* (Oxford, 1853), IV, 280.

[35]Lefkowitz, "The Longleat Papers of Bulstrode Whitelocke; New Light on Shirley's *Triumph of Peace,*" *Journal of the American Musicological Society,* 18, No. 1 (1965), 42-60.

[36]*The Middle Temple Documents Relating to Shirley's 'The Triumph of Peace,'* ed. Tucker Orbison, Malone Society Collections, XII (1983), 33-84.

[37]Percy Simpson and C. F. Bell, *Designs by Inigo Jones for Masques and Plays at Court* (1924; rpt. New York, 1966), pp. 79-82 and Stephen Orgel and Ray Strong, *Inigo Jones: The Theatre of the Stuart Court,* 2 vols. (Berkeley, 1973), I, 46-7, 63-6; II, 538-45, 554-55.

[38]See the discussions of the staging of the masque in Orgel and Strong, *Inigo Jones: The Theatre of the Stuart Court,* I, 63-66; II, 538-45;

Andrew J. Sobol, "New Documents on *The Triumph of Peace,*" *Music and Letters,* 47 (Jan. 1966), 10-26; Allardyce Nicoll, *Stuart Masques and the Renaissance Stage* (New York, 1938), pp. 49, 97-99, 101 and *passim.*

[39]*Triumph of Peace,* ed. Clifford Leech in *A Book of Masques: In Honour of Allardyce Nicoll* (Cambridge, 1967), pp. 275-313. Quotations in the text refer to this edition. The title page on the British Museum copy (C12/f15) reads after the title: "Invented and Written" with the author's name followed by "of Grayes Inne,/Gent." At the Victoria and Albert Museum, the last page of one copy (#9113) gives Inigo Jones as scene painter and Lawes and Ives as the musicians who composed the music. Another copy (#9114) notes that it is the third impression and at the end a notation begins "A/Speech to the King/and Queenes Maiesties." For critical comments on the masque itself, see David Lindley's Introduction to *The Court Masque* and David Norbrook, "The Reformation of the Masque," in *The Court Masque,* ed. Lindley, pp. 94-95, 104; Robert Withington, *English Pageantry: An Historical Outline* (Cambridge, 1918-1920), I, 117-19; Pickel, *Charles I as Patron,* pp. 144, 148, 157; Nicoll, *Stuart Masques and the Renaissance Stage,* pp. 36, 38, 47, 49, 97, 99; Enid Welsford, *The Court Masque* (Cambridge, 1927), pp. 225-28; A. Wigfall Green, *The Inns of Court* (New Haven, 1931), pp. 128-29, 132; F. S. Boas, *An Introduction to Stuart Drama* (London, 1946), p. 393. Paul Reyher remarks, however, that Shirley was the best of the masque writers; he became known by abandoning the principles of Jonson and conforming to public taste. *Les Masques Anglais* (Paris, 1909), pp. 202-03.

[40]Strong, *Splendor at Court,* pp. 224-31 *passim,* 232.

[41]Leech, *Triumph of Peace,* pp. 290-93.

[42]Lois Potter, "*The Triumph of Peace* and *The Cruel War:* Masque and Parody," *N & Q,* 27 (Aug. 1980), 345-48.

[43]Jean Jacquot, "Une Parodie du *Triumph of Peace,* masque de James Shirley: Note sur l'edition, par Jean Fuzier, de *The Tragedy of the Cruell Warre,*" *Cahiers élisabethains: Etudes sur la Pré-Renaissance et la Renaissance Anglaises,* 15 (April 1979), 77-80; Georges Bas, "More About the Anonymous *Tragedy of the Cruell Warre* and James Shirley's *The Triumph of Peace,*" *Cahiers élisabethains,* 17 (1980), pp. 49-53. Bas suggests that the author is Bulstrode Whitelocke, well known as a moderate Puritan and member of the "peace party," and a staunch advocate of negotiation and compromise. Also see Jean Fuzier, "English Political Dialogues 1641-1651: A Suggestion for Research with a Critical Edition of *The Tragedy of the Cruell Warre* (1643)," *Cahiers élisabethains,* 14 (October 1978), 49-68.

⁴⁴Marvin Morillo, "Shirley's 'Preferment' and the Court of Charles I," *SEL,* I (1961), 101-06, 110, 112-14; Pickel, *Charles I as Patron,* pp. 114-15.

⁴⁵Catholic nobility and Roman converts are discussed in Gordon Albion, *Charles I and the Court of Rome; A Study in 17th-Century Diplomacy* (Louvain, 1935), pp. 157, 195-97, 204, 208-09, 212, 215; Max Beloff, "Humphrey Shalcrosse and The Great Civil War," *EHR,* 54 (Oct. 1939), 692; John H. Jesse, *Memoirs of the Court of England During the Reign of the Stuarts, Including the Protectorate* (Philadelphia, 1840), II, 292-97; Brian Magee, *The English Recusants; A Study of the Post-Reformation Catholic Survival and the Operation of the Recusancy Laws* (London, 1938), pp. 140, 146, 148; David Mathew, *Catholicism in England,* 2nd ed. (London, 1948), pp. 69, 75, 85, 89; *Calendar of the MSS of His Grace the Duke of Portland Preserved at Welbeck Abbey,* HMC 13R (London, 1893), I, p. 2; "A" Series Archives, Westminster Cathedral MS. XXX (1641-54), 173-74; Armstrong, *Poems,* pp. 15, 34, 35.

⁴⁶In his letter dated May 19, 1635, Garrard wrote to the Earl of Strafford in Ireland that a great number of people were worshiping at the Queen's Chapel at Somerset House and at the French ambassador's house in London, so many that the Archbishop of Canterbury protested. Knowler, *Strafford's Letters.* I, 426.

⁴⁷*The Poems of William Habington,* ed. Kenneth Allot (London, 1948), p. xxix.

⁴⁸Malcolm Smuts, "The Political Failure of Stuart Cultural Patronage," p. 171.

⁴⁹Jeaffreson, *Middlesex Records,* Sessions Rolls, III, 61; St. Giles in the Fields Parish Register, p. 4^V (in the keeping of the Rector).

⁵⁰Bentley, *JCS,* V, 1186-87.

⁵¹Dyce, *Works,* II, 3-4; Jack R. Ramsey, "A Critical Edition of James Shirley's *The Grateful Servant,*" Diss University of Michigan 1971, p. 153; Greg, *Bibliography,* II, #429, p. 579.

⁵²Mathew, *Catholicism in England,* p. 75; *MSS of His Grace the Duke of Rutland Preserved at Belvoir Castle,* HMC 12th R, App. IV (London, 1905), I, xvii, 468, 471-73, 480-81 and *passim;* "A" Series Archives, Westminster Cathedral MS. XXII (1628), 486; XXIII (1628-29), 73; XXIV (1630-31), 291-92; XXVII (1635-36), 31-32.

⁵³Whitelocke, *Memorials of the English Affairs,* II, 88, 248; *STC,* #17331.

⁵⁴W[illiam] A[rthur] J[obson] A[rchbold], "Manners, Francis, VI Earl of Rutland," *DNB* (1893).

[55] Howarth, "Poems" I, xi-xii.

[56] Armstrong, *Poems,* pp. 10, 63, 94.

[57] Fleay, *Biographical Chronicle,* II, 235.

[58] Foster, *Register: Gray's Inn,* fols. 896, 900, pp. 199, 200.

[59] John W. Stoye, *English Travellers Abroad, 1604-1667* (London, 1952), p. 354; Norman G. Brett-James, *The Growth of Stuart London* (London, 1935), p. 215.

[60] Since Shirley urges the young man to "grow you up" and observes that the youth had seen the play when it was first presented on the stage six years before, we might assume the playwright was addressing a boy of 15 or 16 years who would have been 9 or 10 years old when he first saw the performance.

[61] Armstrong, *Poems,* p. 10. Knowler, *Strafford's Letters,* I, 373; Evelyn P. Shirley, "Who Was Henry Shirley, The Author of 'The Martyr'd Soldier'?" *N & Q,* 1st Series, 12 (July 14, 1885), 26-27. See also Chapter I of this work.

[62] Evelyn P. Shirley, *Stemmata Shirleiana; or The Annals of the Shirley Family,* 2nd ed. (Westminster, 1873), pp. 119, 106-20.

[63] See Chapter I, n.34; E[dward] I[rving] C[arlyle], "Shirley, Sir Robert," *DNB* (1897-98); Westminster Sessions Rolls Calendar, VIII, Part 2 (April 1633-September 1634), Westminster Public Library MS. West. Sess. Roll 39/175, p. 204.

[64] Dyce, *Works,* I, 275; see also *James Shirley's 'The Wittie Faire One,' A Critical Edition of the 1633 Quarto with Introduction and Notes,* ed. Esther Melvina Power (Chicago, 1945).

[65] Dyce, *Works,* I, xlv-xlvi; Armstrong, *Poems,* pp. 70-71. In a letter dated June 24, 1635, to the Earl of Strafford, Garrard mentions, "Also Sir Edward Bushell, a Querry to the Queen, died this last week." Knowler, *Strafford's Letters,* I, 434. See also Leslie Hotson, *I, William Shakespear* (New York, 1938), p. 145. In some copies of the play "Edmund" is given for "Edward" Bushell.

[66] Dyce, *Works,* VI, 289. Colston Bassett is a village in southeast Nottinghamshire, only fifteen miles south of Newark where Shirley would spend time during the Civil Wars.

[67] Jeaffreson, *Middlesex Records,* Sessions Rolls, III, 138. Many references to the Golding family appear in the parish register of Colston Bassett; see pp. 59, 61, 62. This register is bound with an old Indenture and is at the Nottingham County Record Office, MS PR 6971. Quarter Ses-

sions Minute (QSM) books for the county include, however, a listing of those not attending the parish church and names recusants: "Edward Goulding of Colston Bassett armig (+ Ellinora his wife)," vol. 12 (typed summary transcripts), Jan. 11, 1641—Oct. 7, 1642, QSM, Nottingham County Record Office TS, p. 5. See also *Memoirs of the Life of Colonel Hutchinson written by his Widow Lucy [Aspley]* (London, n.d.), p. 93; Peter Young, *Newark and the Civil Wars* (HMSO, 1964), Appendix I, p. 90.

[68]Dyce notes that Shirley used the piece as the basis for *Honoria and Mammon. Works,* VI, 2-3. On Shirley's dedication of *The Bird in a Cage* to Prynne, see Senescu, *The Bird in a Cage,* pp. ivff. and 3-4.

[69]Pipe Series, 17th Charles I (1642), PRO MS E377/49.

[70]On fees for recusancy, the best source is Hugh Bowler, "Some Notes on the Recusant Rolls of the Exchequer," *Recusant History,* IV, No. 5 (April 1958), 182-90; see also Martin J. Havran, *The Catholics in Caroline England* (Stanford, 1962), pp. 92-101.

[71]Marvin Morillo, " 'Frier Sherley': James Shirley and *Mercurius Britanicus,*" *N & Q,* 7 (1960), 338-39.

[72]Frank Fowell and Frank Palmer, *Censorship in England* (London, 1913), pp. 50-51, 72, 75, 78.

IV

Shirley in Ireland, 1636-1640

Sir William Brereton, who later became a Parliamentary commander during the civil wars, kept a diary of his travels in 1634 and 1635 and wrote of Dublin on July 9, 1635, that it was the "fairest, richest, best built city I have met with in this journey (except Yorke and Newcastle)." He mentions, however, the poor harbor and notes that "the king's ship which lies here to scour the coasts (which is said to be the *Ninth Whelp,* and the *Bonaventure,* a tall stout ship) is constrained to remove for harbour...."[1]

On June 12, 1636, less than a year after this entry, the Lord Deputy of Ireland, Thomas Wentworth, later Earl of Strafford, arrived at Hampton Court for consultation with King Charles. Five months later, on November 23, 1636, he returned to Ireland with a large entourage in the King's guardship, the *Ninth Whelp.*[2] According to Allan H. Stevenson, who conducted a thorough study of Shirley's years in Ireland, the playwright almost certainly was on that ship. But it is unknown whether he went at the specific invitation of the Lord Deputy or to join his old friend John Ogilby who had accompanied Wentworth on an earlier trip to Ireland as dancing tutor to the Lord Deputy's children. Ogilby had planned to build a theatre in Dublin, for which he would need a playwright "in residence." As early as 1631 Ogilby lived in Gray's Inn Lane in London; by 1633 he kept a dancing school at Black-Spread Eagle Inn.[3] When a severe outbreak of plague led to the closing of the London theatres on May 12, 1636, Shirley may have decided to take advantage of an opportunity to continue writing plays and thereby support his family. Shirley's remove to Ireland provides no certain indication that the playwright was on intimate terms with the Lord Deputy. None of Shirley's published plays, and only two brief poems, are dedicated to Wentworth.[4]

Wentworth believed that a representative of the King in Ireland should have a proper court. This included a playwright and an acting troupe. During his stay there from 1633 to 1641, the Lord Deputy acquired a good deal of money and land, built hunting boxes, gave fine entertainments at Dublin Castle (which he greatly enlarged), and built a magnificent house near Nass at a cost of £22,000.[5] As early as 1633, Richard Boyle, the first Earl of Cork, mentions in his diary that he saw a play acted by the Lord Deputy's gentlemen, perhaps under the direction of Ogilby.[6] In the summer of 1637, Wentworth made a progress into the southern provinces of Ireland, where he was entertained quite splendidly, especially at Limerick, with a tableau of "seven planets in a very special and heavenly motion."[7]

From what we know of his character, the Lord Deputy took his official duties seriously. As a Protestant Royalist, he had the job of attempting to enforce English religious rule and yet not antagonizing the established Irish Catholic families who controlled the wealth of the country. From an English viewpoint, Wentworth in his early years succeeded as a financial administrator, in that no large expenditures had to be drawn from the English exchequer to support the English presence in Ireland.[8] Yet Wentworth, nicknamed "Black Tom," was not popular. The self-righteous Lord Deputy, convinced of his ability to weaken the Catholic position in Ireland by a new plantation of English Protestants, often simplified situations and, once having made a decision, ruthlessly adhered to it.[9] He refused to admit Catholics to the Irish Parliament: in an argument about this he imprisoned and fined the

Sheriff of Dublin.[10] In 1634, as the result of a military court-martial, Wentworth ordered the shooting of Francis Annesly, Lord Mountnorris, Vice Treasurer and an officer in the army. Both Irish and English nobility unsuccessfully protested the severe directive.[11] And in July of 1637, Wentworth imprisoned the young Earl of Kildare, fining him £ 3,000 for refusal to deliver some documents in a suit over lands between the Earl and Sir Robert Digby.[12] In one of many letters to his close friend, William Laud, Archbishop of Canterbury, Wentworth asserts: "Again, I am not afraid of any Man's complaint, being well assured in myself, that whoever questions me shall work towards my greater Justification, and manifest the more my Integrity and Faith to his Majesty."[13]

One poem written to the Lord Deputy by Shirley is in the form of an epilogue to *The Royal Master,* composed presumably for a command performance at the Castle on New Year's Day 1638, which undoubtedly was a gesture to honor the Lord Deputy's presence. In the poem, the playwright refers to the Lord Deputy's recent marriage in 1633 to his third wife, Elizabeth Rhodes, and to the "fair top branch" of the family, William, about twelve years old at the time and Wentworth's son by a former marriage. The other poem, written just before Shirley left Ireland in the spring of 1640, is entitled "To the E[arl] of S[trafford] upon his recovery."[14] Wentworth's illness was perhaps gallstone attacks, one of which he refers to in a letter to the Earl of Nithisdale in May of 1636, noting that his delay in coming to England at first had been bad weather but now "so violent a Fit of the Stone" would keep him confined for ten days.[15] On his last return to Ireland in 1640, Strafford was seriously ill with gout and dysentery and was confined at Chester for some days enroute.[16]

What is interesting here is the circumstance in which Shirley found himself, a Catholic in a country controlled by Protestants, with a Lord Deputy who saw it as his duty to uphold the principles of kingship and the Church of England. On the whole, Strafford's policy was to impose conformity when it was related to official situations, such as not allowing Catholics in the Parliament. The gentry in Ireland at this time comprised Catholic old English and the new English aristocracy created by a monarch anxious to raise funds by giving grants of Irish land to ambitious courtiers. Londonderry Plantation in northern Ireland, for example, was leased by the King to raise ready money. Strafford, however, influenced Charles to stop such practices and succeeded in transferring Londonderry to royal management, away from its corrupt management by the City of London.[17] The Lord Deputy threatened to enforce recusancy fines on the Catholic gentry in an attempt to get contributions for the royal treasury. Naturally they resented this; but he also had not the cooperation of Protestant gentry, headed by the Earl of Cork. Aubrey notes that Strafford forced the Earl of Cork to pay a £1,500 yearly fee, which the Lord Deputy restored to the English church.[18]

Shirley's poem to the wife of perhaps the most powerful nobleman in Ireland, James Butler, the Earl of Ormonde, entitled "To the excellent pattern of Beauty and Virtue, L[ady] El[izabeth], Co[untess] of Or[mond]" gives evidence of past patronage. Shirley refers to "my gift . . . A servant's wish . . . which with the year thus enters." The poem also refers to the Countess' sons, the second of whom had been born in June 1639, and alludes to a coming child: "And may that unborn blessing timely bud. . . ." So Shirley almost certainly composed the poem for the New Year 1640. R. G. Howarth believes that Shirley himself was timely and wrote the poem in 1642 when the Earl became a Marquis; but the poet had been away from Ireland for two years then and apparently had returned to the patronage of the Earl of Newcastle. And Shirley never directed any poem or play to the Earl of Ormonde himself, asserting in his poem to the Countess, " . . . I never learn'd that trick of court to wear/Silk at the cost of flattery. . . ."[19]

Ormonde, though he had Catholic brothers and sisters and was friend or relative to most of the Catholic gentry in Ireland, resembled the Earl of Strafford in being a dedicated Protestant amidst a largely Catholic-Irish nobility. Like most wealthy and titled heirs left in childhood with massive holdings, Butler (until he came of age) had been under the guardianship of the Court of Wards, which aimed at protecting the youngster's inheritance. Because the laws prohibited Catholics from inheriting money or lands, Catholic children received Protestant guardians. Ormonde, as a Catholic by birth, was brought up in England at Lambeth Palace under the wardship of Archbishop Abbot of Canterbury and became a Protestant. The Irish hoped that his religion would give them a means of conciliation with the King and Royalists. Butler remained a Protestant and Royalist and later became Lord Lieutenant of Ireland and in the Civil Wars commanded the Irish Royalist army.[20]

Another probable patron of Shirley during these years, George Fitzgerald, 16th Earl of Kildare and an extensive property holder, also had grown up under the supervision of the Court of Wards. The Earl of Cork had purchased the wardship for £ 6,600, later sealing the bargain by marrying his fourth daughter to the young Earl in 1630.[21] Fitzgerald befriended Shirley soon after the poet came to Ireland; as Shirley says in his dedication of *The Royal Master* to the Earl in 1638: "It was my happiness, being a stranger in this kingdom, to kiss your lordship's hands. . . ."[22] We may presume that Fitzgerald generously encouraged Shirley. The Earl had need of entertainment, certainly after the Lord Deputy ordered him incarcerated in connection with Fitzgerald's suit against Sir Robert Digby over lands. This does not mean that the young Earl languished in jail; wealthy noblemen could live very comfortably in prison, and Fitzgerald at least once asked for a sort of "parole" so that he might go to his estate to take the air. When he gave up the disputed lands, he was released in March 1638. Shirley's dedication was written just before his spring 1637 trip to England: " . . . my Affaires in England hasten my departure, and prevent my personall attendance." The association presumably endured throughout the playwright's stay in Ireland, but during the Civil Wars the Earl supported the English Parliamentary side, subsequently serving it in various positions.[23]

Attached to the court of the Earl of Strafford, Shirley did not approach many of the Irish aristocracy. During his years in Ireland, three other noblemen—all of them English—received dedications, Richard, Lord Lovelace, George, Lord Berkeley, and the powerful courtier, Henry Rich, Earl of Holland.

To Richard Lovelace, created Lord Lovelace of Hurley (Berkshire) in 1627, Shirley dedicated in 1637 what is perhaps his best play, *The Lady of Pleasure*. Several other works were dedicated to the nobleman in 1637 and 1638, indicating his generosity as a patron.[24] George, Lord Berkeley, held a fine reputation for being patron to aspiring and established writers and poets. These included Massinger, Webster, and Robert Burton, the last dedicating to him *The Anatomy of Melancholy*.[25] The remarks Shirley makes in his dedication of *The Young Admiral* to Lord Berkeley candidly refer to this; the playwright had "long since prepared my particular ambition to be known to you, that I among other, ...by some timely application, derive upon me your lordship' influence...."[26] As if to set forth his qualifications, Shirley adds that the play had been presented at Court before the king and queen. Henry Rich, Earl of Holland, was Shirley's judicious choice to receive the dedication of *Hyde Park,* also in 1637. Shirley notes that the play took its title from "your lordship's command...when it was presented...upon first opening of the Park."[27] The statement suggests earlier patronage. In particular the dedication reveals that despite his remarks to the contrary, Shirley knew "the ways of flattery" and could be both calculating and shrewd. The Earl held numerous influential positions, including the chancellorship of the University of Cambridge and, since the previous year, appointment as first lord of the bedchamber. Most important, he was a member of the inner "council of courtiers" to the King and doubtless able to advance the career of a petitioner simply because of his associations at Court.[28]

It is likely that these dedications to English noblemen were written during Shirley's brief visit to England in the spring of 1637. All three plays were entered in the Stationers Register on the same day, April 13, 1637, by Andrew Crooke and William Cooke, with whom the playwright apparently had a publishing agreement during these years.[29]

But Shirley's trip to England that spring was primarily to enlist actors for a permanent acting troupe in Ireland.[30] John Ogilby had been a member of Wentworth's personal household for more than three years, and in February 1637, a few months after Shirley's arrival, he was named Master of the Revels for Ireland.[31]

Ogilby proceeded with building his theatre in Werburgh Street, directly across from the Castle in Dublin. Intended for the dominant Irish-English aristocracy, and therefore presumably a "private" playhouse, the theatre opened about Michaelmas 1637. From the many commendatory verses heralding the publication of Shirley's *The Royal Master* the following year, this was probably the opening play at the Werburgh Street Theatre.[32] That Shirley's trip was successful is demonstrated by the number of references to former London actors in Ireland. Parochial assessments, for instance, list Thomas Cooke and William Cooke, who also appear as actors at the Red Bull.[33] On December 28, 1637, the infant son of a Thomas Jordan was christened at St. John's Church, Dublin; an actor by that name had performed at the Salisbury Court playhouse in London.[34] A William Perry was housekeeper for the Dublin playhouse in 1641; he paid its parish assessment of 5s. for the poor. Similarly an actor of that name was associated with the old Fortune theatre.[35] From Shirley's old Queen's Company, William Allen, Michael Bowyer, Hugh Clark, and William Robbins may have traveled to Ireland, for nothing is known of these men from May 1636 until 1641, when they became members of the King's Men in London. Another scholar would add Edward Armiger and Richard Weekes to the Irish group, both of whom had been at the Fortune theatre in London.[36]

With an experienced group of actors, Shirley would have little difficulty producing well-known English plays and some new ones of his own. In his *Poems* (1646), the playwright includes a number of prologues and epilogues he wrote for plays performed in Ireland. These include *No Wit to a Woman's* (probably Middleton's *No Wit, No Help Like a Woman's*), Jonson's *Alchemist,* and three of uncertain authorship, *The General, The Toy,* and *Irish Gentleman.*[37]

Of most interest, however, are Shirley's own new plays presented on the Irish stage: *Rosania, Or Love's Victory* (published as *The Doubtful Heir*), *The Gentleman of Venice, The Constant Maid, The Politician, St. Patrick for Ireland, The Royal Master,* and possibly two plays no longer extant, *The Tragedy of St.*

Albans and *Look to the Lady*.[38] The plays tell us something of the dramatist's experiences and attitudes in these four years, as well as the tastes and interests of the preponderantly English "Irish" court, not the least those of the Lord Deputy. Shirley limited his sphere of acquaintances and his sources for play materials to the narrow range of court life. He was well suited for the job: since the early 1630's his talents had been channeled more and more towards the tastes and interests of the London courtly elite who patronized the private theatres.

Rosania, Or Love's Victory, licensed under that name in 1640 and published in 1652 under the title *The Doubtful Heir,* is obviously rewritten from an earlier play of Shirley, *The Coronation.* Robert Forsythe demonstrates that the two works are congruent in both cast and plot. This repetition of situation and stock types from *The Opportunity* to *The Coronation* to *Rosania,* all most likely having Spanish sources and all written within a few years' time, argues persuasively for the playwright's extensive and direct use of Spanish drama and story for many of his plays.[39] The realistic subplot is aligned with the main story from the beginning. It involves a blunt Captain, fallen into debt, who demonstrates a clever wit in his treatment of his creditors, the citizen merchants. He tricks them into enlisting in the military while he mulcts them of their money. This subplot gives a sense of the patronizing attitude that apparently the soldiery, as well as the nobility, held toward the merchant class. It is one of few of Shirley's plays in which citizens and merchants take a substantial part. Shirley may have enlarged the blunt soldier role from that of *The Coronation* because of the actors with whom he was working in Ireland.[40]

Two prologues were written for *Rosania.* In the one for the Dublin performance, Shirley explains why he chose "Rosania" for the title, claiming that it was in deference to the current popularity in England of naming plays after ladies' names—such as *Aglaura* and *Claricilla.* Here is an obvious reference to the rivalry professional playwrights felt toward the courtier dramatists, Suckling and Thomas Killigrew, the respective authors of the plays to which Shirley refers.[41]

Another Dublin play, *The Gentleman of Venice,* uses a familiar subject of Shirley's dramas—the problems of inheritance. Throughout the play Shirley comments on the contrast between social position and personal worth. In payment for his success at war, Giovanni asks the hand of the noble lady, Bellaura. Because of his inferior social position, she quickly rejects his request. Yet earlier Bellaura tried to enlighten Giovanni by telling him of the perils and sins of court life; her own refusal ironically demonstrates the artificiality of the court's values. Of course, once his true heredity is established, her "heart hath wings to meet him." There is still the element of correction and criticism in the playwright directed at the gentry. Yet in another way Shirley caters to his audience. He uses an entire scene in this play to give an intimate view of a seventeenth-century whorehouse.[42] In particular, Shirley reflects a growing tendency to use the double entendre in suggestive dialogue, as between the prostitute Rosabella and the spendthrift Malipiero. Even *The Gamester's* tavern scenes seem mild in comparison.

In *St. Patrick for Ireland* Shirley attempted something different from his earlier dramatic style, combining history, romance, tragedy, and miracle. In writing this interpretation of Ireland's history, Shirley may have been responding to the Court at Dublin's interest in more serious fare. What we know of Lord Deputy Wentworth suggests this, and Shirley's prologues written for plays produced in Ireland imply to some extent that he had failed at trying to please his audience, which he accuses of being hypercritical and "sick" in taste.[43] If a reconciliation with his public was Shirley's aim, then we may have an explanation for his presenting the pre-Christian natives of Ireland as pagans, which has led some critics to consider the play insulting to the Irish. The real point of Shirley's depiction of heathen Ireland may be to dignify further the triumph of Irish Christianity. Well in keeping with his own Catholic sentiments, this was a gracious nod towards the Irish Catholic gentry in his audience. At the same time, the play could offer a political allegory of Ireland's progress in his own day, an elaborate compliment to the Lord Deputy's role in Irish history. Shirley held a peculiar position, one that expected him to praise both the Irish religious tradition and the Irish Protestant hierarchy. Shirley perhaps merely voiced his hope for the future of Ireland.[44]

The play is staged almost as a pageant, and Shirley ambitiously applies the techniques of an elaborate masque, including spectacles, chanting, and processions. Many scenes take place before an altar—usually pagan; shocking even for a heathen culture is Corybreus's device of posing as a god so that he can rape Emeria.[45] The play contains much violence balanced in part by comedy and song. Several stories which have been interwoven come together in the third act, but perhaps the most spectacular scene occurs in the fourth act as the evil Milcho leaps into the flames he has lighted in an attempt to kill St. Patrick and the Queen.[46] There is a fine exotic touch in the serpent scene, trading full on Irish tradition, with serpents creeping in to stroke the sleeping Saint who, awakening, commands them:

> Hence, you frightful monsters!
> Go hide, and bury your deformed heads
> For ever in the sea! from this time be
> This island free from beasts of venemous natures.[47]

It must have taxed the strength and ingenuity of the little band of actors to perform such a broad and showy spectacle.

The Royal Master, the best of the romantic comedies produced in Ireland and a montage of Shirley's earlier work, centers on a topic he never tired of, court affectations and affairs. The theme is a common one, the play contrasting two types of ambition. Shirley meant to see *The Royal Master* staged in England as well, for he says as much in his dedication of the play in spring 1637 to the Earl of Kildare. He notes that the play has never been performed and that he expects it to be when the English theatres open again.[48] We may suppose that Shirley had written the play during the time the London theatres were closed, probably between May 1636 and before March 1637. It presumably was performed in Ireland, however, in the fall of 1637 and again before the Lord Deputy in 1638. Most likely Shirley took the play with him to England in the spring of 1637, hoping that the London theatres would open, but they remained closed until October. That Shirley left a copy in England is apparent, for Andrew Crooke, a London publisher who had issued other plays by Shirley, licensed it for publication with John Cooke and Richard Serger on March 13, 1638, over a month before its approval for presentation on the London stage.[49]

During his lifetime, over twenty-five publishers and booksellers were to take part in the publication and sale of Shirley's works. Most of Shirley's published plays had been set in type by Thomas Cotes for Andrew Crooke and William Cooke, booksellers in St. Paul's Churchyard. Since between 1637 and 1640 Crooke and Cooke entered many of Shirley's plays in the Stationers Register, Allan Stevenson suggests that before Shirley left for Ireland he had agreed to publish several of his plays with the two. Stevenson plausibly argues that the plays issued in print during these years, when London theatres were closed much of the time because of the plague, represent a large part of the repertoire at Dublin.[50] Andrew Crooke entered *The Royal Master* and *The Opportunity,* two Shirley plays written for Dublin audiences and subsequently published in Ireland. The title page of *The Royal Master*, dated 1638, notes that it was to be "sold at Castle Gate in Dublin" by Edmund Crooke and Thomas Allot. Thomas Allot, Richard Serger, and John Crooke, whom the will of Edmund Crooke, a brother of Andrew, mentions as being partners to him, all were stationers associated with the publication of Shirley's works. The four men possibly took turns working in the Dublin shop, Stevenson suggests. The play was also published in London by John Crooke and Richard Serger the same year. Shirley switched to Richard Whitaker with John Raworth as printer when he published two other Dublin plays, *St. Patrick for Ireland* and *The Constant Maid,* both issued in 1640. Yet four other plays brought out in 1640 appeared under the stationers Andrew Crooke and William Cooke separately or together: *The Coronation, Love's Crueltie, The Opportunity,* and *The Humourous Courtier.* And John Crooke continued to publish Shirley's masques during the 1650's. Shirley's association with Crooke and Cooke apparently was a profitable one, and he surely had stationers of repute. Andrew Crooke served as Master of the Stationers Company in 1665-

1666.[51] Shirley seldom used the same publishers for his plays as he later employed for his grammar books, but most of his publishers had shops in or near that great booksellers' market, St. Paul's Churchyard.

What is interesting biographically about the printing is the commendatory verses. Nine people composed ten pieces on *The Royal Master*.[52] They give us a good listing of the playwright's Dublin acquaintances, and the coterie of writers and aesthetes centered on the Court of the Lord Deputy.

John Ogilby's long friendship with Shirley is well documented. By the mid-1620's Ogilby may have been acquainted with a large number of courtiers, law students, and noblemen. After establishing a name for himself as a dancer, he had been able to attract as pupils some of the children of the elite whose summer houses stood along Gray's Inn Lane near his dancing school. So expert was he, the story goes, that he was invited to dance in one of the grand masques staged by the Duke of Buckingham; Ogilby injured and lamed himself on that occasion and presumably afterward devoted himself to instruction. When Thomas Wentworth was appointed Lord Deputy of Ireland, Ogilby received an appointment in the Deputy's household as teacher, later becoming one of Wentworth's guard troop and subsequently deputy master of the revels. His acquaintance with Shirley likely began in the London years.[53] And their friendship would extend beyond the Irish years as well, possibly during the Civil Wars. On the 6th of May in 1650, Ogilby gave testimony in a suit involving Sir Rowland Egerton's infant son and Sir John Egerton. Ogilby's deposition notes that he lives in the parish of Blackfriars, London, and is "aged 50 years or thereabouts."[54] In 1651 Shirley, along with Davenant, wrote verses to Ogilby on his paraphrase of Aesop's *Fables*.[55]

Of the group of nine, three others could be called writers of some note. It is possible that Richard Bellings had known Shirley in London, for Bellings was a member of Lincoln's Inn.[56] While there he had written a sixth book to Sidney's *Arcadia,* first published in 1629. He returned to Ireland and by 1641 was a member of the Irish Commons; thereafter he was active politically, particularly in the Irish Catholic Confederacy, serving as a secretary in the Supreme Council of the Confederacy in 1642. He later wrote a history of Irish affairs from 1641 to 1643. Bellings, a Roman Catholic, remained a Royalist on the Anglo-Irish side; a friend to the Earl of Ormonde, he sailed with the Earl for France in 1650.[57]

W. Smith's lines to Shirley indicate that he was a close acquaintance: "Dear Friend, I joy my love hath found the means/To wait upon, and vindicate thy scenes/From some few scruples of the weaker sex,/Whose nicer thoughts their female minds perplex: . . ." He is probably the William Smith who wrote "To Ireland—" which begins, "Hayle, sacred island! whom no threat, no art/Could tempt to falter in the passive part . . ." and ends with a rousing "On, sprightly hearts, you, whom the French, the Dutch,/The Pole, the Spaniard court and love so much. . . He's thoroughly arm'd, who to the field can bring/Th' interests of his fayth, countrie and king." Years later this Royalist wrote a poem "On the unnatural murder of my King."[58] It may be that Shirley's friend is also the William Smith to whom Allibone's *Dictionary* assigns two dramas: *Freeman's Honour,* and *St. George for England.* And most likely he is the same Wm. Smith who composed verses for Henry Burkhead's publication of *Lirenda's Miserie.*[59]

A little poem by "T.I." in the commendatory collection remarks, "Thy Muse I honour'd, ere I knew by sight/Thy person, . . ." The identity of T.I. is open to speculation. Allan Stevenson has made a plausible guess: Thomas Jordan, the actor, who was probably in the troupe and became the city poet of London after the Restoration. Jordan often signed his name "T.I." In 1637 Jordan dedicated *Poetical Varieties* to "Mr. John Ford of Gray's Inn" (not the playwright). He also wrote commendatory verses to many playwrights, including Richard Brome, and verses to Thomas Stanley, later Shirley's patron, on Stanley's marriage to Dorothy Enyon.[60] Jordan had been an actor not with the Queen's Men but in the rival Red Bull theatre in London earlier in the 1630's. That Jordan, if he were in the acting troupe in Dublin, would be on intimate terms with Shirley is likely. They pursued common interests in the Interregnum of the 1650's; Jordan was busy writing private masques and this too occupied Shirley.[61]

John Jackson appears to be a gentleman who pursued the arts as a dilettante, and in this to exemplify the commendatory group as a whole. Jackson tells us he had studied poetry: "I'll tell him I have read/The laws of Flaccus with a serious head, . . ."[62] The only other poem assigned to a man who might be Shirley's friend is verses contributed to Sir Rowland Cotton's collection, *Perantetia spectatissimo* . . . , published in 1635.[63] A notation in the Irish House of Lords calendar for 1625 records a warrant to pay John Jackson £15/6/8d. for the press of fifty footmen and their conduct from Cumberland to Liverpool for service in Ireland.[64] Similarly, a John Jackson, esquire, was in the Irish Parliament in 1634 representing Carrick-on-Shannon, County Leitrim.[65] A letter of 1641 from the King to the Lord Lieutentant of Ireland requests that a John Jackson be given a captain's place in the standing army of Ireland when his turn comes.[66]

There is little that can be said definitely about "W. Markham," who in his commendatory verses insists that Shirley should become the next poet laureate.[67] An extant register of petitions to Lord Deputy Wentworth, dated 1638, records Wm. Markham for money owed him by three other men.[68] It is tempting to place W. Markham with the Markham family of Ollerton, Nottinghamshire, famous Roman Catholic Royalists during the Civil Wars and presumably friends of Shirley while he was in Nottingham with the Earl of Newcastle in the early 1640's. Yet no known W. Markham appears in the pedigree of the Markhams of Ollerton.[69]

Another friend, Drury Cooper, probably was an Englishman from Nottinghamshire. The Coopers in that county were a well-known Roman Catholic family who fought for the King in the Civil Wars.[70] But Shirley's friendship with Drury Cooper possibly started as early as his years at Cambridge. Drury Cooper, son of William of Thurgarton, Notts., was matriculated pensioner at Trinity College, Cambridge in 1619, made B.A. in 1621 and M.A. in 1624. If Shirley were at Cambridge studying for his M.A. during 1619-21, he more likely met Drury Cooper there.[71] Cooper may have met Shirley in London; this same young Drury Cooper was admitted to Gray's Inn on November 1, 1620 and perhaps was part of the large Gray's Inn group during the 1620's.[72] But at the writing of his poem, Drury Cooper was in Ireland: "And when my Shirley from the Albion shore/Comes laden wth the Muses, all their store/Transfers to Dublin, . . . Shall we not welcome him with our just votes?"[73] A "Capt. Cooper" is named in charge of the Lion's *Fifth Whelp* in a note dated May 25, 1633 to the Lord Deputy from the Lords of Admiralty. That this is probably Shirley's friend Drury Cooper is suggested by an earlier petition dated July 3, 1632, of "Capt. Dawtry Cooper" to the King, requesting employment at sea for Ireland. He says in his petition that he had two years earlier been given charge of the *Ninth Whelp* but had been recalled.[74] The friendship may have continued if Cooper returned to Nottinghamshire during 1642-44.

The Francis Butler who contributed another commendatory poem is probably the Francis Butler whose name appears many times during the period of the Civil Wars in the papers of James Butler, the Earl of Ormonde. That Francis Butler was an active Royalist, serving under the Earl first as ensign to Captain Samuel Loftus and later as Sgt. Major in Sir Henry Tichbourne's regiment.[75] Shirley's friend may have been knighted as well; in 1643 the King granted one Sir Francis Butler the estates of several Irishmen outlawed on charges of high treason.[76]

The least recognizable member of the group, James Mervyn, wrote two poems to Shirley, one in English and one in Latin. Almost nothing can be found of him other than what he says of himself in his verses: he would be placed in a Limbo of poets, or on the border of being a poet if there were such a place—as, he adds, there is a Limbo for Patriarchs.[77]

This small group, with the exception of Richard Bellings, appear to be young men connected more directly with England and the Lord Deputy's unit than with Ireland and the old Irish aristocracy. Shirley clearly viewed his stay in Ireland as temporary; his commendatory verses betray a desire to return to England, and the separation from London, his home base, must have been painful to him and only undertaken out of financial necessity.

Nonetheless, he kept his currency on the London scene through his publishers and sought to cultivate through dedications London patrons.

In the summer of 1639 Shirley dedicated to Henry Osborne, Esquire, a play written years before, *The Maide's Revenge*. Osborne visited the Dublin Court of the Lord Deputy during that summer, apparently to gain secretarial experience. According to Stevenson, he probably came with his cousin, Sir Edward Osborne, whom Strafford had invited to visit. If Henry was the older brother of Dorothy Osborne, he would have been only twenty.[78] Shirley's reference to the "English stage," as though that stage were distant from him, implies that he wrote the dedication in Ireland. More details of Shirley's plays can be gleaned from this dedication. He remarks that *The Maide's Revenge* is his second tragedy to be presented on stage, and that it has been "many years" since he looked at the play. Shirley had probably taken to Ireland several of his old plays, intending to use them on the stage there; perhaps *The Maide's Revenge* was one he decided not to use but to profit from through publication, even though "it come late to the impression." He honors Osborne, Shirley says in the dedication, "nor is it upon guess, but the taste and knowledge of your ability and merit; . . ." As in his poem to the Countess of Ormond, Shirley makes reference to flattery: "I never affected the ways of flattery: some say I have lost my preferement, by not practicing that Court sin; . . ."[79] In any event, Shirley thought of Osborne as a young man of possible generosity.

That would be reason for the dedication of *Love's Crueltie* to George and Charles Porter, sons of Endymion Porter and heirs to wealth and title. The play and dedication were published in England in 1640. We do not know that Shirley had "manifold obligations . . . to . . . captain Endymion Porter," although it is possible.[80] Porter was one of the central figures in the Catholic Court coterie and a favorite of Queen Henrietta Maria. Undoubtedly Shirley had met him, and Porter, while championing the preferment of William Davenant, also may have been generous to Shirley. But the dedication is signed "W.A." Probably Shirley entrusted his friend, William Habington (Abington) to publish the play and write the dedication in the playwright's absence, and Habington may have been indebted to Porter more directly. Certainly, Habington was a friend of Endymion Porter; he includes a poem "To my honoured Friend, Mr. E. P." in his published poems entitled *Castara,* in 1634.[81]

From Shirley's dedication of *The Opportunity* in 1640 to Captain Richard Owen, which speaks of "my return with you, from another Kingdom" and expresses gratitude for a safe journey home, we know quite precisely when the playwright returned to England. Stevenson notes a letter in the Earl of Strafford's correspondence reporting that Captain Owen, commander of the *Ninth Whelp,* had been ordered to patrol Scottish waters on April 8, 1640 and then to travel from Dublin to Chester on April 11th. Another dispatch in Strafford's letters, dated the 12th of April, says that the *Whelp* would come to Dublin in two to three days. So probably Shirley returned from Dublin to Chester with Owen about April 16, 1640.[82] The dedication indicates that Shirley and Richard Owen had traveled together before—perhaps that was during the first voyage to Ireland. Warm and sincere, it praises Owen's "clear judgment and excellent abilities" in poetry and speaks of their conversations together on the voyage. Their friendship possibly began at Merchant Taylors' School, grew at Oxford, and continued during the Gray's Inn years. The sentiments expressed indicate that the author expected no reward, a dedication in the present-day sense of the word.[83]

That Shirley was dedicating plays to likely English patrons and publishing some plays in England indicates that he considered his stay in Ireland temporary. Only of necessity in a time of plague had he ventured to Ireland; perhaps he had even left his family in England, though his gratitude to Richard Owen for a safe journey back to London suggests that his family may have been with him.

The four years in Ireland proved disappointing for Shirley in more than personal ways. He apparently regarded his years there as exile from his beloved London. Shirley must have been enticed by the offer of a lucrative contract such as that enjoyed by Brome; his financial needs could not be met by publishing and possible gifts from dedicatees alone. His choice may have been made based on the thought of a few months' visit until the plague abated rather than several years; otherwise, he might once again have returned to teaching.

Shirley's plays written for the Irish stage, his choice of friends and patrons, all suggest a man whose preference clearly lay in England with the London stage. Indeed, the plays themselves frequently repeat his earlier characters, situations, and themes. In prologues and epilogues Shirley wrote for plays, his own and those of other playwrights, Shirley complains about the size of the audience. Prefacing a play no longer extant called *The Toy,* he claims that nothing good seems to please the Irish playgoers.[84] For one of Fletcher's plays he begins: "Are there no more?" and remarks: "Were there a pageant now on foot, or some/Strange monster from Peru or Afric come, . . . any drum will bring. . . Spectators hither; nay, the bears invite/Audience."[85] And when he writes for a Middleton play he comments: "I'll tell you what a poet says; two year/He has liv'd in Dublin, yet he knows not where/To find the city."[86] In still another prologue to the *Irish Gentleman* he laments that "art and wit are not honored nor fruitful in Ireland."[87] Shirley's Dublin audience was select and courtly; perhaps the English Deputy General had alienated too many Irish and the average playgoer chose not to attend the theatre patronized by the Earl of Strafford. *St. Patrick for Ireland* illustrates that Shirley neither understood nor cared to appreciate Irish culture. Professionally Shirley sensed that he was not keeping his name current and endeavored to publish several of his plays, dedicating them to English-Irish or simply English nobility and gentry. His association with the Earl of Strafford's group in Ireland must have hurt him politically as well, for the Earl's unpopularity and subsequent downfall and execution could not have helped the dramatist. And so his dedication of a play to the sea captain who finally returned him to England from Ireland for the last time is fitting.

Notes

¹Brereton, *Travels in Holland, the United Provinces, England, Scotland, and Ireland, 1634-1635,* ed. Edward Hawkins, The Chetham Society (London, 1844), I, 37.

²George, Lord Goring, wrote to Edward, Viscount Conway, on June 12, 1636, that the "Lord Deputy kissed their Majesties hands at Hampton Court this day." *Cal. SP Dom.,* 1635-36, 326, p. 554; Knowler, *Strafford's Letters,* II, 6-8, 38-39; Lady Burghclere, *Strafford* (London, 1931), II, 37, 59.

³Stevenson, "Shirley's Years in Ireland," *RES,* 20 (1944), 20-22; Aubrey, *Brief Lives,* II, 101; Theophilus Cibber, *The Lives of the Poets of Great Britain and Ireland to the Time of Dean Swift* (London, 1753), II, 265-66.

⁴On Shirley's poems to Strafford, see Armstrong, *Poems,* pp. 8-11 and Howarth, "Poems," II, 233-34, 242-43.

⁵C. V. Wedgwood, *The King's Peace 1637-1641, The Great Rebellion* (New York, 1955), pp. 164; Hugh F. Kearney, *Strafford in Ireland, 1633-41, A Study in Absolutism* (Manchester, 1959), pp. 164, 172. Kearney gives a useful annotated bibliography of Strafford scholarship by both Irish and English historians, pp. viii-xi.

⁶T[homas] F[inlayson] H[enderson], "Boyle, Richard, lst Earl of Cork," *DNB* (1885-86); see also Boyle's *Diary, The Lismore Papers,* ed. A. B. Grosart (London, 1886-88), p. 6.

⁷Wedgwood, *The King's Peace,* p. 181.

⁸Kearney, *Strafford in Ireland,* pp. 32, 38, 169, 217; Aidan Clark, *The Old English in Ireland, 1625-42* (Ithaca, 1966), pp. 118, 121.

⁹Thomas L. Coonan, *The Irish Catholic Confederacy and the Puritan Revolution* (Dublin and New York, 1954), pp. 45-47; David A. Chart, *The Story of Dublin* (London, 1907), p. 76; David Mathew, *The Age of Charles I* (London, 1951), pp. 83, 92.

¹⁰*Cal. SP Ven.,* 1632-36, #302, 255-256.

¹¹*Cal. SP Ven.,* 1632-36, #603, 515 and n.

¹²*The Journal of Sir Simon D'Ewes from the Beginning of the Long Parliament to the Opening of the Trial of The Earl of Strafford,* ed. Wallace Notestein (London and New Haven, 1923), pp. 226, 404; *Cal. SP Ire.,* Conway Papers. 1633-1647, 256, #42, p. 165. See also J[ohn] T[homas] G[ilbert], "Fitzgerald, George, 16th Earl of Kildare," *DNB* (1889-90).

¹³Knowler, *Strafford's Letters,* I, 28.

¹⁴Howarth, "Poems," II, 242-43; Armstrong, *Poems,* p. 64; Bentley, *JCS,* V, 1139-42; Dyce, *Works,* VI, 428-29.

¹⁵Knowler, *Strafford's Letters,* I, 6.

¹⁶Howarth, "Poems," II, 233.

¹⁷Wedgwood, *The King's Peace,* pp. 164-65.

¹⁸Kearney, *Strafford in Ireland,* pp. 38-41; Aubrey, *Brief Lives,* I, 115.

¹⁹Armstrong, *Poems,* pp. 9-10, 63; Howarth, "Poems," II, 238-39.

²⁰The Court, in turn, appointed a guardian. A nobleman who gained such a wardship over large properties held a lucrative position, reaping the income from the child's estate while managing it. And for profitable wardships the guardians would pay handsomely. The King himself frequently received money for assigning wards. Coonan, *The Irish Catholic Confederacy,* pp. 55-56; Wedgwood, *The King's Peace,* p. 403; Clark, *The Old English in Ireland,* p. 16.

²¹Clark, *The Old English in Ireland,* pp. 86, 116.

²²Dyce, *Works,* IV, 103; *The Royal Master* was entered in the Stationers Register in London by Andrew and John Crooke and Richard Serger. Arber, *Stationers,* IV, 472.

²³*Cal. SP Ire.,* 256, 1633-1645, 165; *Cal. SP Dom.,* Sig. Off. III, #108, 140-41, 173, 184; Register of Petitions to the Earl of Strafford, 1637-38, BM MS. Harl. 430, fol. 210, p. 402.

²⁴Williams, *Dedications,* #22448, 25436, 10667; Dyce, *Works,* IV, 3.

²⁵Williams, *Dedications,* #4159, 17641, 22463, 23124, 24987, 24176, among others. Lord Berkeley was admitted to Gray's Inn on February 2, 1623. Foster, *Register: Gray's Inn,* fol. 802, p. 169; J[ames] M]cMullen] R[igg], "Berkeley, George, 8th Baron Berkeley," *DNB* (1885-86).

²⁶Kenneth J. Ericksen, *A Critical Old-Spelling Edition of 'The Young Admiral' by James Shirley* (New York, 1979) pp. 3-4.

²⁷Dyce, *Works,* II, 459.

²⁸C.V. Wedgwood, *The King's Peace,* pp. 147-48. The Earl received numerous dedications, including the poet George Wither's *Emblems* in 1635 and two others in 1637 alone. Williams, *Dedications,* #25900, 7365, 13265. See also *Cal. SP Ven.,* 1632-36, #422, Feb. 3, 1635, 329; #429, March 2, 1635, 337; #460, April 13, 1635, 367; #558, Oct. 19, 1635, 466; #653, May 9, 1636, 558 and n.

²⁹Arber, *Stationers,* IV, 381; see also pp. 123-24 of this Chapter.

³⁰Stevenson, "James Shirley and the Actors at the First Irish Theater," *MP,* 40 (1942), 147-59.

³¹LaTourette Stockwell, *Dublin Theatres and Theatre Customs (1637-1820)* (Kingsport, TN., 1938), pp. 1-3; William S. Clark, *The Early Irish Stage* (Oxford, 1955), pp. 30-31.

³²Nason, *Shirley,* p. 94; Dyce, *Works,* I, lxxxii-lxxxix.

³³Stevenson, "James Shirley and the Actors at the First Irish Theater," *MP,* 40 (1942), 153-54.

³⁴Stevenson, p. 156.

³⁵Stevenson, p. 155.

³⁶Bentley, *JCS,* II, 350, 615-16; III, 679-80; Stevenson, "James Shirley and the Actors at the First Irish Theater," pp. 149-52; Clark, *The Early Irish Stage,* p. 27.

³⁷Armstrong, *Poems,* pp. 29-33.

³⁸Arber, *Stationers,* IV, 385.

³⁹Robert S. Forsythe, *The Relation of Shirley's Plays to the Elizabethan Drama* (New York, 1914), pp. 213-20.

⁴⁰Though the merchants in this play have no peculiar Dublin customs, LaTourette Stockwell (*Dublin Theatres*), has suggested that the subplot is based on Dublin life, pp. 11-12.

⁴¹*Claricilla,* by Thomas Killigrew, was presented by Queen Henrietta's Men at the Phoenix in 1636; *Aglaura,* by Sir John Suckling, was staged at the Blackfriars theatre in February 1638 and at the Cockpit theatre in April of that year. The date for Suckling's play tends to place the writing of Shirley's play earlier than 1636 and also points to a rewriting of *The Coronation.* Bentley, *JCS,* V, 1201-07; IV, 698-700.

⁴²Forsythe, *The Relation of Shirley's Plays to the Elizabethan Drama,* pp. 231-33.

⁴³The only Shirley play that suggests by its title a similar subject is no longer extant—*The Tragedy of St. Albans,* entered in the Stationers Register on February 14, 1640. Arber, *Stationers,* IV, 472. See the prologue and others written to plays produced in Ireland by Shirley and Ogilby in Dyce, *Works,* VI, 490-96 and Armstrong, *Poems,* pp. 29-33.

⁴⁴Hugh MacMullen, "Sources of Shirley's *St. Patrick for Ireland,*" *PMLA,* 48 (1933), 806-14. MacMullen describes Shirley as merely ex-

ploiting tradition and high moral drama for novelty and gimmickry. See also his "Note on Source Studies of *St. Patrick for Ireland*," *PMLA*, 51 (1936), 302; William K. Magee, *Anglo-Irish Essays* (Dublin, 1917), pp. 64, 66; John P. Turner, Jr., *A Critical Edition of James Shirley's 'St. Patrick for Ireland'* (New York, 1979). On the distinction between the Anglo-Irish Catholic aristocracy and the New English Protestant hierarchy, see J. C. Beckett, *A Short History of Ireland* (New York, 1968), p. 65.

[45]Turner, *St. Patrick,* pp. 162-73.

[46]Turner, *St. Patrick,* pp. 194-203.

[47]Turner, *St. Patrick,* p. 244. Albert Wertheim, "The Presentation of James Shirley's *St. Patrick for Ireland* at the First Irish Playhouse," *N & Q,* 14 (June 1967), 212-15; Peter Kavanagh, *The Irish Theatre* (Tralee, 1946), pp. 17-18; Alan H. Stevenson, "Shirley's Dedications and the Date of His Return to England," *MLN,* 61 (Feb. 1946), 80. Presumably some of the Lord Deputy's entourage took part in the play, among them young Henry Osborne; he spent the summer of 1639 in Dublin and at Nass, Wentworth's home.

[48]Dyce, *Works,* IV, 103.

[49]Bentley, *JCS,* V, 1139-40; Arber, *Stationers,* IV, 385, 508; W. W. Greg, *A Companion to Arber, A Calendar of Documents in Edward Arber's Transcript of the Registers of the Company of Stationers of London, 1554-1640* (Oxford, 1967), #538, pp. 676-77.

[50]Stevenson, "Shirley's Publishers: The Partnership of Crooke and Cooke," *The Library,* 25, 4th Ser. (1944-45), 141-46, 155-61. Generally the author lost his rights to his work once he sold a play to an acting company; perhaps Shirley made an agreement with Beeston, head of the Queen's Company, for whom he had written many of his plays.

[51]Arber, *Stationers,* III, 686; IV, 411, 464, 473, 508; Greg, *Bibliography,* III (1959), #588. For a brief outline of Andrew Crooke's career, see Henry R. Plomer, *A Dictionary of the Booksellers and Printers Who Were at Work in England, Scotland and Ireland from 1641 to 1667* (London, 1907), I, 45. See also the listing of Shirley's published works and his publishers in Ruth K. Zimmer, *James Shirley: A Reference Guide* (Boston, 1980). In 1629 Andrew Crooke and in 1630 William Cooke had entered the rolls of the Stationers Company as freemen. Crooke was sworn into the Livery in 1637 and paid the usual fee of £20. *Records of the Court of the Stationers Company, 1602-1640,* ed. William Jackson, Bibliographical Society (London, 1955-56), II, 305.

The Master of the Revels licensed plays and other works and thus granted permission to perform a piece on stage; to publish a work required registration with the Stationers Company. Often a printer worked for a publisher who then turned the result over to a bookseller: thus three persons could take part in publishing a work. Usually the owner of the copy is the stationer who enters the work in the Stationers Register and subsequently publishes it. For an interesting record of the various scraps, indenturing, and general activities of the publishing business during this time, see the Letter Book and the Fine Book in *Records of the Court of the Stationers Company,* ed. Jackson.

[52]Dyce, *Works,* I, lxxxii-lxxix.

[53]Armstrong, *Poems,* p. 40; Bentley, *JCS,* IV, 948-51. Aubrey, *Brief Lives,* II, 101-102; Theophilus Cibber, *Lives of the Poets,* II, 265-67; G[ordon] G[oodwin], "Ogilby, John," *DNB* (1894-95).

[54]Town Depositions, Court of Chancery, PRO MS. C24/732, May 6, 1650, Pt. 2.

[55]Armstrong, *Poems,* p. 40.

[56]The title page of his addition to Sidney's *Arcadia* notes, "Written by R. B. of Lincolnes Inne, Esq." J[ohn] T[homas] G[ilbert], "Bellings, Richard," *DNB* (1885-86).

[57]Aidan Clark, *The Old English in Ireland,* pp. 224-25; Thomas L. Coonan, *The Irish Catholic Confederacy,* pp. 82, 187, 202, 311, 342; Hunter, *Chorus Vatum,* IV, 21.

[58]*Calendar of the Papers of the Marquis of Ormonde,* HMC, 14th R, App. VII, #14, pp. 107, 109. The initial suggestion for Shirley's play, *St. Patrick for Ireland,* may have come from his friend W. Smith, if he is the same man of that name listed in the Warburton Collection as the author of a play no longer extant entitled *St. George for England.* See Hugh MacMullen, "Sources of Shirley's *St. Patrick for Ireland,*" p. 814; Bentley, *JCS,* V, 1177-78.

[59]S. Austin Allibone, *A Critical Dictionary of English Literature and British and American Authors* (Philadelphia, 1891), II. Smith's livelihood probably came from elsewhere than writing. As early as July 1634 the Lord Deputy's Order Book authorizes Mr. Wm. Smith to find out about the bells of the Catholic Church of St. Patrick (fol. 37, BM MS. Harl. 4295). Wm. Smith is listed in the Dublin Assembly Roll for 1636, and a William Smith, gent., was elected sheriff for Dublin in 1637. See the Dublin Assembly Rolls (1636) in a *Calendar of Ancient Records of Dublin* (Dublin, 1892), III, Roll XII, 58b, 321. A Wm. Smith is noted as the author of *Hieronymo* and *The Hector of Germany* in Edward Phillips, *Theatrum Poetarum Anglicanorum: Containing Brief Characters of the*

English Poets Down to the Year 1675, ed. Sir Egerton Brydges, 3rd ed. (Geneva, 1824), No. 31. See also LaTourette Stockwell, "Lirenda's Miserie," *Dublin Magazine* (1930), p. 19. Lirenda is an anagram for Ireland; interestingly enough, in his will Shirley refers to a daughter named Lawrinda. The child was possibly born while Shirley was in Ireland.

60Stevenson, "James Shirley and the Actors at the First Irish Theater," pp. 155-56.

61Bentley, *JCS,* II, 487-90. A ballad about a raid by soldiers on players at the Red Bull in 1655 refers to an actor named Tom Jay. Bentley presumes that this man acted before 1642 as well; yet there is no evidence that he was ever in Ireland (*JCS,* II, 482). See also Clifford Leech, "Jordan's Interregnum Masques," *London Times Literary Supplement,* April 12, 1934, p. 262; Hunter, *Chorus Vatum,* II, 35-38.

62Dyce, *Works,* I, lxxxviii-lxxxix.

63Hunter, *Chorus Vatum,* IV, 565; STC, #5870.

64*Calendar of the House of Lords,* HMC, 4th R, June 28, 1625, p. 3.

65*Cal. SP Ire.,* Ser. 3, 1633-1647, p. 64.

66*Cal. SP Ire.,* 1633-1647, p. 338. The name Captain Jackson appears in records of the 1640's for the Committee for the Advance of Money, with the information that he is of St. Katherine's parish in London and has paid none of his asessed fee of £150. PRO MS. SP 19/69, fol. 53. Several other Jacksons are also noted. See, for example, PRO MS. SP 19/67, fol. 34; PRO MS. SP 19/46, fol. 80; PRO MS. SP 19/65, fols. 53, l08. Finally, a Lt. Col. John Jackson was granted permission to go abroad in 1656. Passes and Warrants, 1656-57, PRO MS. SP 25/114, p.7. It is probable that Shirley first knew Jackson at the Inns of Court, but the name is common and John Jacksons were admitted to Lincoln's Inn, Gray's Inn, and the Inner Temple. See *Students Admitted to the Inner Temple, 1547-1600,* ed. W. H. Cooke (London, 1878), p. 208; "Admissions 1420-1799," *Lincoln's Inn Admission Register* (1896), I, fol. 65b, p. 189; Foster, *Register: Gray's Inn,* fol. 708, p. 140; fol 984, p. 231.

67Dyce, *Works,* I, lxxxvi.

68Register of Petitions to the Earl of Strafford, 1637-38, BM MS. Harl. 430, fol. 99^V, p. 181.

69A William Markham, son of Abraham Markham of Newboro' Abbey is entered. *The Visitations of the County of Nottingham in the Years 1568 and 1614, with Many Other Descents of the Same County,* ed. George Wm. Marshall, Harleian Society (London, 1871), IV, 25-26.

70Peter Young, *Newark and the Civil War,* HM Stationery Office (1964),

p. 94; David Underdown, *Royalist Conspiracy in England 1649-1660* (New Haven, 1960), p. 145.

[71] Venn, *Alumni Cantabrigienses,* I, 390. See also Chapter I of this work.

[72] Foster, *Register: Gray's Inn,* fol. 778, p. 162.

[73] Dyce, *Works,* I, lxxxiv.

[74] *Cal. SP Dom.,* 1633-34, 229, p. 70; 1631-33, July 3, 1632, 220, p. 371.

[75] HMC, 14th R, App. VII, pp. 122, 129; *Cal. SP Ire.,* 1633-37, Ser. 3, 260, pp. 360, 378, 552.

[76] *Cal. SP Ire.,* 1633-47, Ser. 3, 260, p. 378; *The Visitations of Hertfordshire,* ed. Walter C. Metcalfe, Harleian Society, 22 (London, 1886), pp. 29-30.

[77] Dyce, *Works,* I, lxix-cv. A James Mervin of Southampton, age 15, was matriculated at Christ Church College, Oxford, on June 10, 1618. Boase and Clark, *Register: Oxford,* II (Matriculations), Part 2, 369.

[78] Dyce, *Works,* I, 101. Henry Osborne was active in the Royalist cause during the Civil Wars and was in Newark in October 1645. Peter Young, *Newark and the Civil War,* Appendix I, "Royalists in the Newark Garrison," p. 79. A Mr. Henry Osborne was paid by the House of Lords for transporting food and goods. *Calendar of the House of Lords,* LJ, HMC, 5th Report, VI, 231-232, p. 107.

[79] Stevenson, "Shirley's Dedications and the Date of His Return to England," pp. 79-82.

[80] John F. Nims, *James Shirley's 'Love's Cruelty,' A Critical Edition* (New York, 1980), p. 3; Arber, *Stationers,* IV, 491; Greg, *Bibliography,* II, #573, pp. 711-12.

[81] Stevenson, "Shirley's Dedications and the Date of His Return to England," p. 82; Gervas Huxley, *Endymion Porter: The Life of A Courtier, 1587-1649* (London, 1959), pp. 243, 247-50, 253-56, 279-81 and *passim;* Bentley, *JCS,* V, 1129-32; Nims, *James Shirley's 'Love's Cruelty,'* pp. 70-78; Kenneth Allott, *The Poems of William Habington* (London, 1948), pp. 13-14, 165-66.

[82] Dyce, *Works,* III, 369; Stevenson, "Shirley's Dedications and the Date of His Return to England," pp. 82-83, and "Shirley's Years in Ireland," pp. 27-28.

[83] See also Chapter I of this work. Nason, *Shirley,* pp. 117-19.

[84] Armstrong, *Poems,* p. 30.

[85] Armstrong, *Poems,* p. 30.

[86] Armstrong, *Poems*, p. 29.
[87] Armstrong, *Poems*, p. 29.

V

'London is Gone to York': The Newcastle Circle and the Stanley Coterie

In the four years since Shirley began his Irish career, London had experienced startling political changes. At his departure London had been seething with the plague; he returned to a city in a ferment of political antagonisms. The whole country lay depressed: unemployment and heavy taxes increased disillusionment with a King who ruled by "divine right" but with little political wisdom. In London religious sentiment had shifted from the Church of England to Presbyterianism, itself faction-ridden. Religion entered politics, pitting Royalists against Parliamentarians, Presbyterians against Independents, Aldermen against Common Councilmen. The upshot was the ascendancy of the Puritan or Presbyterian forces over the Royalists, and with this the city of London over the rest of the country. Politically powerful, London also had its own military forces, nearly equal to those of Parliament. The trained bands (the rough equivalent of our modern-day national guard), active and strong in London, had long before the Civil Wars become staunchly Puritan, for they came from the citizenry of London in which Puritan merchants were the chief element.[1]

Shirley's first concern would have been to reestablish his reputation in drama. He brought with him from Ireland several plays as yet unpublished, as he noted in his dedication of *The Maid's Revenge.* He also needed to produce these plays on stage, and the death of Philip Massinger in March 1640 landed him the job of playwright for the most prestigious of the private acting groups, the King's Men of Blackfriars theatre.[2] Shirley settled in the parish of St. Giles in the Fields, where the Cockpit theatre was located on Drury Lane. For May 29, 1641, the parish register there lists the christening of "Michaell sonne of James and Elizabeth Sherley." Also living in the parish during these years were a number of actors, William Beeston, the theatre manager, and Richard Brome, the playwright; both names appear in the register for 1641 and 1642.[3] St. Giles was familiar territory to Shirley, a village that once had been separated by broad fields from London and Westminster. It lay farther west of the parish of St. Andrews in High Holborn; from St. Giles, Holborn led to The Bars and Drury Lane led to Temple Bar and Fleet Street, both areas of the Inns of Court. Most of the private theatres were located outside the city limits in Middlesex as was the parish of St. Giles, a safer area for both playwrights and recusants, free from the close scrutiny of the Puritans. Although it was located within the walls of the city, the precinct of Blackfriars was not under the city's jurisdiction; the Blackfriars Theatre was located in a fashionable district near St. Paul's Cathedral.[4]

For the spring fare at the Blackfriars theatre, Shirley probably at first used plays composed and produced in Ireland. But by November 1640, in six months' time, he had completed a new play, *The Imposture,* licensed for presentation on November 10th. In his prologue Shirley comments:

> He knows not what to write;
> fears what to say
> He has been stranger long to the
> English scene (V,181)

He remarks here in this first address after a four-year absence that the tastes of theatregoers have changed and rather sarcastically observes that all of the interest is on a witty prologue. Finally, Shirley offers a rather long comment to the ladies in the audience, assuring them that in his play "no innocence shall bleed in any scene."[5]

Shirley wrote only three more plays that we know of: *The Cardinal* (lic. November 25, 1641); *The Sisters* (lic. April 26, 1642); and *The Court Secret* (never licensed).[6] His last years of active playwriting were foreshortened by the Puritan edict that closed the theatres in 1642.[7] All of the last newly composed plays take place in Italy and Spain, yet remarks included in the plays reveal that Shirley's intentions and interests look to current events and political leaders.[8]

Set in Navarre and following the plot of John Webster's Elizabethan tragedy *The Duchess of Malfi* (1623), *The Cardinal*—the best of Shirley's ventures into his weakest genre—is in part a commentary on the political situation of the times. In the prologue the playwright says:

> We doe believe most of you Gentlemen
> Are at this hour in France, and busie there, . . .
> But keep your fancy active, till you know,
> By th' progress of our Play, 'tis nothing so; . . .
> Think what you please, we call it but a Play.[9]

Shirley invited his audience to reflect that the matter of the play, or at least some of its characters, might be applicable to Englishmen of the time. Charles R. Forker has written in some detail about the likeness of Archbishop William Laud to Shirley's Cardinal. Although Forker does not call the play a political allegory, he suggests several topical references to Laud, his political activities, and his unpopularity with both Puritans and Roman Catholics.[10] In an accusation that the Duchess makes to the Cardinal, Shirley almost explicitly renders him as Laud:

> . . . see those unjust acts
> That so deform you, and by timely cure,
> Prevent a shame before the short haird men
> Do croud and call for justice.[11]

At the time, 1641, the ascending power of the Puritans made the future of play performances uncertain. A play attacking Laud was simply good politics, for Laud awaited trial, a prisoner in the Tower. And any play glancing at current, highly-charged political events was likely, then as now, a box office attraction. What we have, as Forker observes, is a play presumably by a Catholic, who writes to an anti-Catholic audience and attacks Laud, an enemy of recusants—and gets away with it.[12]

The Cardinal was the only tragedy Shirley wrote expressly for the Blackfriars theatre. By the following spring he had turned to a lighter vein, that of romantic comedy, perhaps to relieve the darkening eve of Civil War. The prologue to *The Sisters* reflects quite clearly the pessimism of the time:

> ... the whole town is not well ...
> and, for fear of catching cold, dares not
>   salute this air.
> But there's another reason, I hear say,
> London is gone to York, ... (V,356)

King Charles had reached York on March 19, 1642, and many noblemen followed in the next few months; a private theatre would keenly miss the bulk of its clientele.[13]

In *The Sisters,* Shirley takes a departure from his usual practice, concentrating not only on the nobility but also on the lower class and the criminal element of society. Edgar L. Chapman suggests that the bandits and their organization satirize the various Puritan factions of the time, an internal quibbling between sects. The bandit leader Frapolo and another comic buffoon, Piperollo, manage a great deal of the story, although they supposedly form only the subplot.[14] This last of Shirley's plays performed before the closing of the theatres contains his strongest criticism of manners. He exposes the social affectations of the upper class by assigning them to middle and lower class characters trying to act like their "betters."

Just before the Civil War Shirley completed at least one more play, *The Court Secret*. The dedication that Shirley wrote for the play in its printing of 1653 laments, "it happened to receive birth when the stage was interdicted, . . ." The printed title page states that it was "never acted, but prepared for the scene at the Black-Friars." It was probably the last full play for the theatre that Shirley wrote other than masques or private entertainments for select groups.[15]

The play indicates that Shirley was working under external pressure, knowing the future of the theatre to be uncertain, particularly in London, as the power of the Puritans rose. Perhaps the events of these two years had tired and disillusioned him. The fall of Thomas Wentworth, Earl of Strafford, and his subsequent death by beheading in 1641 must have unnerved a man who had for four years been closely associated with the Lord Deputy's court in Ireland.[16] As early as November 1640, the licenses recusants had to obtain in order to live in London had been revoked. Anti-Catholic riots had raged throughout the summer of 1641. Mobs attacked the houses of the Catholic ambassadors, and Marie de Medici, the Queen Mother of France, left for that country in August 1641 by order of the House of Commons. By the fall of 1642 Puritanism had become so strong that many Royalists were disarmed, arrested, or fined. Shirley must have feared for his own fortunes. *The Court Secret,* at any rate, does not touch on political matters.[17]

With the closing of the theatres and the onset of Civil War, Shirley found solace in poetry and friendship. "A Songe," Shirley's lament on the state of England and particularly the mood in London just before the Civil Wars, shows him in the most partisan political light, making direct references to people and events, a rare departure for one whose style was allusive and indirect. Shirley ridicules the Puritan practice of "inspired" speaking, the tinkers, cobblers, and coopers who preach without education. He claims that he, too, is "possest/with prophesy, or poesy at least." The poem touches on the growing power of the Puritans in the Parliament, their reluctance to give taxes to the King, their eagerness to behead Lord Strafford, the mobbing of the Lords in Parliament by London apprentices in late December 1641. Shirley speaks of the Irish rebellion, the growing antagonism towards bishops and church laws, the preaching against papists and the Pope, the litanies written in profusion. Yet his plea at the end of the poem is that "all be friends and in their witts againe:/. . . all things with the year be new/Except the Church, and but a few/Old officers which yet remain true."[18]

In his prologue to *The Sisters,* Shirley's reference to the King and his entourage "gone to York" is followed by the question, "must we/Be now translated north?" Soon after he did go north.[19] According to Anthony à Wood, "When the rebellion broke out, and he thereupon [was] forced to leave London, and so consequently his Wife and Children (who afterwards were put to their shifts), he was invited by his most noble Patron, William [Cavendish], Earl of Newcastle, to take his fortune with him in the wars."[20] Shirley and Brome both enjoyed the patronage of Cavendish who later became Marquis of Newcastle. This generous supporter of many writers, most notably Jonson, exemplified the secular virtues most often described during his era as the mark of the gentleman: honor, magnanimity, generosity, compassion, humility.[21] Newcastle was the model of civil conversation. This was the man to whom Shirley chose to dedicate his play, *The Traitor,* in 1635. At that time Newcastle had been host to the king and queen on visits they had made to his estates of Bolsover and Welbeck in the English Midlands in 1633 and 1634. Newcastle, having spent over £20,000 for their highnesses entertainment, including the masques Ben Jonson wrote for the festivities, still held no court office of importance.[22] By 1638, however, he was governor to the Prince of Wales and in 1639 a member of the Privy Council.[23] The association with Shirley apparently was inspired by artistic interests and continued on personal terms. For the years 1635 to 1644 when Shirley was acquainted with him, little of Newcastle's personal affairs is known; numerous official letters of the period indicate the extent of the Earl's patronage but not the details. And Shirley himself was away in Ireland during the years 1636 to 1640. What we know from these references is that Newcastle's contemporaries spoke of him as heading a literary coterie during the war years, while people who seemed to have belonged to it also held office in what enemies referred to as his "papist" army.[24]

Shirley joined the Royalist army in northern England commanded by Newcastle from November 1642 until after the Battle of Marston Moor in early July 1644. In a pamphlet listing claimants to a portion of £60,000 granted by Charles II in 1663 for the relief of Royalists who had served the cause in the wars, "Shirley, Jam. Q Gen. in Newark" appears under a listing of quartermasters. We learn that he had been certified for his commission in Nottingham, quite likely by Newcastle. As Quartermaster General, Shirley presumably reported to Newcastle, for he is not listed under any other officer. His son-in-law, Standerdine Sherley (alias Sachell), is entered as a lieutenant to Captain Thomas Taylor in Nottingham. He had been certified in this rank in Surrey.[25]

Records of the wars show the active work of Newcastle in movements all over the North—hardly a time filled with gala entertainment.[26] The Earl, according to Lord Fairfax, the Parliamentary general, commissioned many Roman Catholics as officers against the order of King Charles that no "popish recusant" or anyone refusing the two oaths of allegiance and supremacy could serve. In a letter to the House of Commons dated from Ipswich on December 27, 1642, Newcastle's army was called "the Catholike Army . . . there being six or seven thousand known Papists and Recusants serving therein."[27] It was natural enough, for the Catholic stronghold in England lay in the northern provinces, especially York, Lancaster, and Stafford—an area all under the command of Newcastle. Certainly Catholic families can be identified with the Royalist army, such as the Markhams of Ollerton, the Coopers of Thurgarton, the Goldings of Colston Bassett— all of Nottinghamshire and all friends of Shirley.[28]

Some of the Earl's staff apparently stayed in or near the Royalist garrison at Newark-on-Trent or in the surrounding garrisons at Thurgarton, Shelford, Wiverton, or Belvoir. Some may also have traveled with the Earl during his advances from 1642 to 1644. The pamphlet of 1663 puts Shirley "in Newark," but does not indicate how long he was there. Newark was in a particularly strategic spot; it lay at the topmost point of a large piece of countryside running between Lincolnshire on one side to Derbyshire and Yorkshire on the other—land owned by Royalists.

In December 1642 and January 1643, Newcastle held the main part of the Royalist army under his personal command at Pontefract. Lord Willoughby of Parham, another Parliamentary general, held the Lincolnshire side. By March 1643 Newcastle had retreated to York. He then traveled south, staying for some time at Welbeck. From there his troops scattered over Nottinghamshire during the winter of 1643.[29]

The siege of Newark began with less than two thousand men stationed at that garrison in 1644, for Cavendish had rushed north to save Newcastle-on-Tyne and most of the Newark cavalry had been sent into Leicestershire and Derbyshire. By July the Earl of Newcastle was at Marston Moor. After the battle there on the second of July his regiment was gone and he soon sailed for the continent. Then during the winter of 1644 the Parliamentary generals began their advances on the Royalist strongholds of Belvoir, Thurgarton, and Pontefract castle. By late June 1645, several Royalist strongholds had surrendered and Newark had become the rallying point for the Cavalier forces, the best fortified garrison left for the King.[30]

After the King had conferred on Newcastle the title of Marquis on October 27, 1643, Shirley wrote a poem praising his patron, "Great both in Peace and War," and speaking of the Marquis' literary endeavors, which included books on horsemanship. The poem makes no reference to drama; perhaps the plays of Newcastle were composed later.[31] Yet the Harleian collection includes a manuscript of a play that in altered form would be published in 1649 at The Hague with *The Variety* under the title *Captain Underwit or, The Country Captain*. Internal references to historical events such as Charles I's march to Scotland in 1639 indicate that the play was written after that date and probably before the closing of the theatres in 1642. The version of 1649 has been attributed to the Earl of Newcastle. We may suppose that as a patron and close friend to Shirley he collaborated with the playwright. Albert Wertheim, after examining the style, gives the two main plots to Shirley and the minor Captain Underwit plot to Newcastle. One of the two major plots depicts a situation similar to that of *The Lady of Pleasure* with its reform of illicit lovers and revitalization of existing marriage, while the other involves the reform of a scornful lady, like the correction of Carol in *Hyde Park*. Neither plot has much to do with the Underwit subplot, the gulling of the Captain by a maid. It is probable that Newcastle wrote the Captain Underwit material between 1639 and 1641, but Shirley may have labored on it during 1642-44, working the three plots into the version published in 1649.[32]

During the war years, friends were the subjects of several of Shirley's poems and give us an indication of the membership of the Newcastle circle. One poem directly related to the war is entitled "Upon the Death of G.[errard] D.[alby] Engineere, who died upon service to which he had no command." Apparently Dalby, whose position was that of Master Gunner to Lord Newport, Master of the Ordnance, took charge of a cannon on his own initiative.[33] Another elegy might be especially applicable to the years 1642-1644: "Upon the Death of G.M." R. G. Howarth suggests that G.M. is Gervase Markham, who died in 1637 in St. Giles, Cripplegate. His acquaintance with Shirley's patron Newcastle had derived from their common interest in horsemanship.[34] But a more likely candidate is Gilbert Markham, of the well known Catholic Royalist Markhams of Ollerton in Nottinghamshire, a family that Shirley may have met through Edward Golding at nearby Colston Bassett in the early 1630's.[35] In *England's Black Tribunal,* under a list of those sergeant majors slain appears "S. M. Wilson and M. Gilbert Markham, at Naseby."[36] Ray L. Armstrong observes that the last few lines of Shirley's poem indicate that the subject had been a clergyman. Henry Foley in his *Records of the English Province of the Society of Jesus* notes that Gilbert Markham, brother to Thomas, had entered a Jesuit order in 1638, and adds that Thomas and Gilbert Markham died in the civil wars.[37] Shirley's poem, more intimate than most of his eulogies, seems directed to a close personal friend rather than the more distant yet famous Gervase Markham. The poem itself hints only briefly that G. M. has died in battle: "Be judge you that did want him, while he liv'd,/But more now, since he then your lives repriv'd,/. . ."

"The Common-Wealth of Birds," like "A Songe," is satirical and grieves at the state of England. But the poem could go into

Shirley's published *Poems,* for it alludes to no specific people or events. The piece opens in the manner of a mock epic and may be making some sly allusions to fellow writers Jonson, Donne, and Isaac Walton:

> Let other poets write of dogs,
> Some sing of fleas, or fighting frogs,
> Anothers Muse be catching fish,
> And every Bard cook his owne dish.[38]

He then continues, using the imagery of birds, a familiar image in Shirley's poems. Its setting is London at a time when Puritanism was in the ascendancy and playwriting had been censored: "And no reward from Prose, or Verse,/The Scholars are turn'd wood-peckers." The image of scholars as wood-peckers (li. 43-44) perhaps reflects the slim income for poets and writers of the time; they must figuratively peck at trees to find insects inside. Those in power are birds of prey (buzzards and gulls) or of deceit (starlings, lapwings) or of little sense (cuckoo, bat, daw). Larks and canaries are quite outnumbered and the few honest men are black swans, rare birds. The King, a nightingale, "never . . . goes to rest,/But has a Thorne upon his breast."

"Upon Scarlet and blush coloured Ribbands given by two Ladies" could have been occasioned by the fashion that had developed by 1642 among Royalists of wearing colored bands. An entry for December 13, 1642 appears in the Journals of the Court of Common Council in London commanding "divers ill affected persons" not to wear colors or ribbons or other badges as a means of recognizing one another; such a practice, except for trained bands, burials, and weddings, was forbidden in the city and liberties.[39] Another reference to the practice indicates that the bands Royalists wore were rose-colored.[40] It may be that the two ladies of the poem (the Tufton sisters?) sent the ribbons to Shirley before he left with the Earl of Newcastle for the North in November 1642.

The Newcastle circle, or at least Shirley's place within it, comprised a small group of literati who used poetry and drama as solace during the war. Newcastle himself was said to retire from the field of battle to music and poetry, a release from the frustration and misery of war.[41] Shirley presumably stayed in Newark much of the time between 1642 and 1644, although Newcastle moved from place to place throughout the northern counties of England. The group that he worked with became the literary circle and the subjects of many poems during this time, a group hailing from established Catholic families in the Nottinghamshire area—the Markhams, Coopers, Goldings. It is likely that Shirley endeavored to lighten the burden of the war's responsibilites by the diversion of poetry and drama; that there was collaboration between Shirley and Newcastle is evident from a close examination of the published *Captain Underwit* by Newcastle in 1649.[42] Despite the war and its effect on the lives and fortunes of many noblemen, the usefulness and even necessity of patrons is illustrated by Shirley's service under his patron during the early war years.

Shirley most likely returned to London some time after the summer of 1645. If we assume that the James Shirley listed in the 1646 Recusant Roll is the playwright, we can calculate his return, at least to the parish of St. Giles in the Fields, in November or December 1645. The fee, figured at one shilling per week, indicated absence from church for thirty weeks—from mid-December 1645 until mid-July 1646, the date given on the Roll.[43] Certainly we know Shirley was in London for the publication of his *Poems,* entered in the Stationer's Register on October 31, 1646.[44]

In "A Postscript to the Reader," affixed to the edition of 1646, the poet makes it absolutely clear that he chose the poems and oversaw their publication. Their arrangement is puzzling. They do not appear in chronological order; in fact, there seems to be only a slight attempt to group them by type. The two scholars who have studied Shirley's poetry most thoroughly, R. G. Howarth in an unpublished pioneering and creative study and Ray L. Armstrong in a literary examination of the poetry published in 1941, agree that the work of another poet of the time, Thomas Carew, shows striking similarities to Shirley's. Three of Shirley's poems were included in a collection of Carew's poetry published one year after his death in 1640, and it is often difficult to distinguish Shirley's pieces from Carew's. Armstrong in particular notes their similarity in superficial classicism and in the care and smoothness of their verses.[45]

That Shirley had been away from the city for some time is indicated by the verses his friend George Hill contributed to the publication:[46]

> When th' age groan'd out thou
> and thy Muse were gone,
> And epitaphs each wit was thinking on;
> When to bestrew thy grave, and stick thy hearse
> With herbs, or the more fragrant flowers of verse;
> When to thy worth rich trophies how to raise,
> Our fancies strove; thy cypress then turn'd bays,
> Which on thy brow grac'd with poetic rage,
> Secur'd thee from the thunder of the age.
> Thus the spring's warmth brings back by mild degrees
> Raiment and food to th' leafless, sapless trees;
> Thus the wing'd quire their vocal lutes do string,
> And turtles, having found their mates, do sing;
> Thus, like the quickening sun, thy flames do spread,
> And add new life to us, that fear'd thee dead.

London and the surrounding countryside were so thoroughly under Puritan control that, according to the diary of John Greene, by the spring of 1646 Parliamentary troops had been getting training in Hyde Park.[47]

Wood writes that during Shirley's absence his wife had been on her own with the children.[48] Conceivably she moved to Surrey and lived with the family of Standerdine Shirley (assuming he was commissioned in his home area), but most likely she remained outside the city proper, perhaps in Westminster. There is a tithe ledger for St. Andrew's Holborn that is arranged by street. Under "Holborn" is entered "Sherly vv"; the rest is torn away. Rose Alley, an address of the playwright during the 1630's, is also listed, but no entry for Shirley appears there. Although the ledger is dated 1665, a notation in it states, "Here ends the copy of the Book up to 1643," and this is followed by several blank pages. It is apparent that some Shirley lived in Holborn as late as 1643 when the record stopped.⁴⁹ Yet in 1641 Shirley's son Michael had been baptized in the parish of St. Giles in the Fields, the parish in which the later Recusant Roll places the James Shirley that could be the dramatist.⁵⁰

Much of what we know about Shirley and his family during the years 1642 to 1646 comes to us through his *Poems*. Some were written about the war; others indicate his direct involvement in it. There are in all about nine poems that can be studied for their information about the playwright and the Newcastle circle during the war years.⁵¹

The name "Odelia" seems almost unquestionably to refer to Shirley's wife. It is possibly an anagram making use of her name, Elizabeth, in the construction "Ode [to] Elia."; there is no known classical poetic antecedent for it. At least two poems to her are written during the war years. "To Odelia," an undistinguished love poem, talks of being in the North for several months while she remains in a "Southern clime." The poet asks that she send a sigh: "But be so kind/To send by the next wind,/'Tis far,/And many accidents do wait on War." The content of "To a Mistris in whose Letter some Tears were dropt" suggests that Shirley's wife had written chiding him for forgetfulness and neglect. In the first stanza the poet apparently defends himself: "Think not my dearest Mistris, that I can/Forget my vows to thee, and be a man: . . ." The tear-drops in the letter from his wife physically blur the paper yet make her meaning more clear, and he ends the stanza with a sincere comment: "I would have read thy eyes, and not thy tear."⁵²

"On a black Ribband" is probably one of the last poems Shirley wrote before his poetry was entered for publication. Upon the flight of Charles I from Oxford on April 7, 1646, Shirley's new patron Thomas Stanley had begun to wear a black mourning band to express sympathy with the King's plight. Stanley chose black for mourning but also because the wearing of other colors had been forbidden.⁵³ Others in the Stanley coterie also wore the ribbon. John Hall of Durham includes a Latin piece "Armilla Nigra" in his poetry published in the same year.⁵⁴ Shirley says of the band he is to wear, "I'le be more proud,/then when the fair/*Odelia* once gave me her wreath of hair, . . ." It was sent "From One, whose blood writes noble, but his mind/And souls extraction leave that stream behind: . . ." By the time Shirley entered the Stanley circle, many of his poems had been written and possibly circulated in manuscript form.[55]

Two poems discovered only in manuscript can be attributed to Shirley and appear to be personal expressions of love for his first wife that he apparently did not choose to publish. "The Goodnight," to be found in a British Museum manuscript and signed "James Shirley," does not contain startling, clever, or provoking imagery.[56] But it illustrates Shirley at his lyrical best. The smooth lines that open the first two stanzas help to save the poem from triteness:

> Good night to her, who when she sleepes,
> the world in sable Darknesse keepes; . . .
> Good night to her, who makes ye Bed
> wch doth enfould her Maydenhead

Again, Shirley elaborates on the senses of sight, smell, taste that the lady evokes to their perfection. He closes the poem with a prayer for her rest:

> May pleasing slumbers, wch invite
> thy Beauteyes to repose, delight
> thy sences charmd by silent sleepe; Goodnight,
> > thou Magazine of all perfection,
> > my heart, by Loves Election,
> > is left to thy protection.

The other poem, in the Rawlinson manuscript, is the only clue we have to the date of the death of the poet's first wife, Elizabeth Gilmet.[57] If we can safely suppose that the manuscript poems were earlier versions of the published poems rather than revisions for some future publication, we can conclude that she died before October 1646. The poem is simple and brief, quite unlike some other epitaphs Shirley composed. It is entitled "Vpon M:E:S: Epit.[aph]":

> If to maintain the vse, I must
> Say here Lyes, Here Lyes the Dust
> Of one, that added to the Graces,
> Whose memorie noe Death defaces,
> Not she herself, to Heauen fflowne,
> Earth hath nothinge but her owne,
> She cannot be, it is most true,
> Heere, and in Heauen an Angell too.

Another version, slightly changed, appears in the British Museum manuscript containing "The Good Night." It is titled, "Epitaph on ye most faire & vertuous Lady, E: S:"[58]

The well-known dirge that Shirley wrote for a private group was set to music several times.[59] Even during the poet's lifetime, Edward Coleman wrote music for the poem, and it is said that the poem was sung by Robert Bowman to King Charles I when he was imprisoned at Oxford.[60]

> The glories of our blood and state,
>   are shadows, not substantial things,
> There is no armour against fate,
>   Death lays his icy hand on Kings,
>   Scepter and Crown
>   Must tumble down,
>   And in the dust be equal made,
> With the poor crooked sithe and spade.
>
> Some men with swords may reap the field,
>   and plant fresh laurels where they kill,
> But their strong nerves at last must yield,
>   They tame but one another still;
>   Early or late,
>   They stoop to fate,
>   And must give up their murmuring breath,
> When they pale Captives creep to death.

> The Garlands wither on your brow,
>   Then boast no more your mighty deeds,
> Upon Deaths purple Altar now,
>   See where the Victor-victim bleeds,
>   Your heads must come,
>   To the cold Tomb,
>   Onely the actions of the just
>   Smell sweet, and blossom in their dust.

The idea of death as leveler of all is of course not original. It is the stateliness of the poem, the strong metaphors well sustained, that gives it distinction.

Shirley included with the publication of his *Poems* in 1646 a masque entitled *The Triumph of Beauty*. He says, "it was personated by some young gentlemen, for whom it was intended, at a private recreation."[61] No clue indicates the date of composition or for what young gentlemen Shirley composed the piece. Perhaps it was performed during the 1630's, the heyday of masques. Or Shirley may have written it for performance during the war years in Newark, as a reprieve for Newcastle. Another possibility is that Shirley composed the piece in Ireland to be given before the Lord Deputy. F. G. Fleay thinks that the antimasque at the beginning is a satire on the Lord Mayor's pageants, aimed indirectly at Thomas Heywood, the principal writer. Fleay notes the talk of pageants by sea and land, which was frequent in the Lord Mayor's shows.[62]

The inclusion of *The Triumph of Beauty* also suggests that Shirley may have composed the piece just prior to the publication of his *Poems* in 1646, possibly for the group gathering around young Thomas Stanley. One of a half dozen friends who wrote commendatory verses to Shirley on the publication of his *Poems*,[63] Stanley had come from a well-to-do family whose country home was in Cumberlow Green, Hertfordshire. When he assisted Shirley (and many others—so much so that he later was in financial difficulty), he had just returned to England after the usual tour of Europe, probably traveling with his tutor, William Fairfax. He took up residence in London, entered the Middle Temple, and into his rooms there came many young and old writers and poets, including Shirley. Stanley was more than a sometime patron to Shirley: according to Wood, he kept the playwright from poverty after his return to London after the wars; Shirley's own dedications and poems to Stanley support this assertion. And Stanley's reference to Shirley as "dearest Friend" in his commendatory poem is sincere and personal. His poem follows the arrangement of Shirley's pieces, first praising the love poems which give Odelia "the prize of beauty,/Thee of wit." He notes that the poet then unties "all the mystick chains of love" and finally returns "To sing thy softer numbers o'er again" in *Echo and Narcissus*.[64]

That there were still others with whom Shirley kept acquaintance or made friends during the war years we know from his literary work, especially the poems. Among those who wrote verses commending Shirley's poems at their publication include Thomas May, an old friend from the Gray's Inn group Shirley knew in the late 1620's and early 1630's. That they remained close friends is clear from May's verses.[65] May became an advocate of the Parliamentary cause and Historian to the Parliament. The theatre "is fitly silenc'd by the Lawes," says May, and now Shirley's poems will be read by those with skill and taste, not viewed by ignorant spectators. George Bucke, who calls Shirley "dear James" and had known him probably since the Gray's Inn days, writes a fulsome poem of praise, centering on *Echo and Narcissus*. Bucke himself had reprinted Sir George Buc's *Eclog* in 1635 and wrote verses in 1647 on the Beaumont and Fletcher folio.[66] Francis Tuckyr had written a poem to Brome on the publication of *The Northern Lasse* in 1632 and another on Shakerley Marmion's *Cupid and Psyche* in 1637. He may have had a connection to the Inns of Court during the 1630's. In his verses he refers to the "dearth of art," the antagonism of the Puritans to any kind of writing other than prose. He had known Shirley as playwright and refers to the time when "the scene/Obey'd thy powerful empire."[67] The commendatory verses by Edward Powell reflect on the love poems and Odelia. We know little about Powell, and the name is common in the records of the time. An Edward Powell signed verses on the Beaumont and Fletcher folio edition, and

Dyce quotes from Gildon that an actor in 1698 named George Powell was son of an actor, "an ancient player, lately dead."[68] He does not appear to be Sir Edward Powell, one of the Masters of the Court of Requests, for in his lines to Shirley he refers to "thy worthier friends their flowers bring . . . ." It seems probable that Shirley's friend was one of the ten actors who put together the Beaumont and Fletcher folio in 1647.

George Hill wrote two commendatory poems to Shirley's publication, one in Latin and one in English. He talks of the rebirth of Shirley as poet. That a "G. Hills" wrote verses for Beaumont and Fletcher the following year indicates that Shirley's friend was in London, as does his poem to Shirley. On the back of Shirley's *Six New Playes,* published by Humphrey Moseley in 1653, is a catalog of the books Moseley had for sale. It includes "The Odes of Casimire, translated by Mr. George Hills of Newark, in 12º."[69] The George Hill of the commendatory verses, then, may have been associated with Shirley in Newark during the wars. According to Hunter's *Chorus Vatum,* the Hill(s) translation was dedicated to Bernard Hyde in 1646, the same man to whom Shirley offered his volume of *Poems.*[70] In the Catholic records at Westminster, a letter of political news in a volume covering the years 1637 through 1640 mentions a schoolmaster named Hill "who teacheth children both Catholics and Protestants," and a George Hill was schoolmaster of the Magnus School in Newark from 1650 to 1655.[71] So it would appear likely that Shirley's friend was a fellow schoolmaster. Many clergymen and schoolmasters were turned out of their livings during the 1640's, and perhaps it was for want of employment that Hill came to London.[72]

Shirley addressed his *Poems* to Bernard Hyde and says they "in themselves [are] not worth your eye" but until he can offer something better he would be encouraged by Hyde's acceptance of them.[73] Hyde represented the wealthy merchant class; during the Civil Wars the Committee for Advance of Money had assessed the family £ 1,000.[74] Shirley's dedication shows clearly that he did not know Hyde but would like to become acquainted. He presumably was aware of his potential patron, for Hyde had been admitted to the Middle Temple in 1629.[75] Or perhaps Shirley had met Hyde through Stanley just before publication of the *Poems*. It is even more likely that Shirley's new publisher, Humphrey Moseley, who was to do much of his publishing thereafter, suggested Hyde as benefactor. Moseley's will, dated April 30, 1660, leaves bequests to Bernard and Humphrey Hide.[76] Their father, also Bernard, was a London merchant who came to London from Kent and lived, at least for a time, in the parish of St. Dunstan's in the East.[77] What was the composition of this new group and Shirley's association with its membership? And what was their influence on the direction he was to take in his career?

A good indication of Stanley's inner core of friends is given in a series of nine poems written by Stanley called the "Register of Friends."[78] These people, however, cannot all be considered a part of the Stanley coterie during the late 1640's; some were intimate friends he made later, such as the Reverend Thomas Salmon, who probably met Stanley in the 1670's, or guests of Stanley's at Flowre, his in-laws' country retreat in Northamptonshire, such as Sir Justinian Isham and perhaps Robert Bowman. The rest quite possibly formed the coterie which met in Stanley's rooms at the Middle Temple: his tutor William Fairfax, William Hammond, John Hall of Durham, Richard Lovelace, Robert Herrick, Edward Sherburne, and James Shirley. No direct connection has been made between Shirley and Stanley's uncle, William Hammond, but it seems reasonable to believe that Shirley wrote "To the Painter preparing to draw M.M.H." to Mary, William Hammond's sister and the mother of Thomas Stanley.[79] When Shirley revised his poems for publication, he deleted many initials which might have been too personal for his readers. For instance, the poem to Sir George Calvert's lady takes all references to any particular woman out. Interesting, too, is that the original version of that poem and the one to "M.M.H." in the Rawlinson manuscript make no reference to a "virgin" though that word is used in both of the published versions of these poems. The "M.M.H." poem refers to the lady's "virgin sweetness." It seems likely here that Shirley, in honor of William Hammond, his patron Thomas Stanley, and the lady, Mary Hammond, kept the initials in the poem intact. Certainly Shirley could have known Stanley's parents earlier, through William Hammond. He knew of young Thomas earlier, for he remarks in his dedication of *The Brothers* to Stanley that he had considered dedicating the play to him "after its birth" when the young man had made known his "fair opinion, when it was represented." The play was first acted in 1641.[80]

Other of Stanley's intimates, such as William Fairfax, Shirley probably met through his patron. Possibly Shirley had known the poet Richard Lovelace earlier; Lovelace was imprisoned for some time for his Royalist activities and not released until 1649. A cousin of Stanley's, Lovelace lost money and health in the King's cause and Stanley supported him after he left prison.[81] Edward Sherburne, like Lovelace, had been imprisoned, Sherburne for not issuing munitions to Parliament while Clerk of the Ordnance in 1642. In the Civil Wars he was in Nottinghamshire, serving as Commissary General of the King's artillery, and after the Battle of Edgehill he went with King Charles to Oxford. In 1646 he returned to London an impoverished man, afterwards living near his cousin, Thomas Stanley, in the Middle Temple.[82] Shirley may have come to London in Sherburne's company, though Wood says that the playwright "retired obscurely" to London after "the King's cause declined" and "among other of his noted friends, he found Thomas Stanley, Esq. who exhibited to him for the present."[83] Perhaps it was Sherburne who brought the two together.

Sherburne was a poet and translator, mostly of Seneca, and, if his later correspondence with Wood is an indication, something of a snob. In the 1670's and 1680's he wrote frequently to Wood, giving him information about a number of people he had known. In 1683 Sherburne received an English translation of Bonarelli della Rovere's *Filli di Sciro,* a work that "J.S. Gent" had published in 1655. Sherburne, who had written two poems praising Shirley's grammar *Latinam Linguam,* said of the translation, "the worke of a very Artlesse Undertaker, and therefore may well beare the Name of J. S. whether James Shirley or other such like.... You know the Proverb 'Similes habent Labra Lactucas.'" In another letter to Wood dated January 18, 1679, Sherburne remarks, "As to Mr. James Shirley, I had a familiar acquaintance with him," but adds little to our knowledge of him except to say that Shirley's "last Employ" had been in grammar teaching and that he had been told that Shirley was buried in St. Bride's Churchyard.[84]

Shirley wrote several poems to Stanley before he dedicated his play, *The Brothers,* to him in 1652. "Friendship" seems to have been written just before the 1646 volume appeared. It was a response to verses presumably sent to Shirley by Stanley, who had written them to his mistress—possibly Dorothy Enyon, whom he would marry in 1648. Shirley begins by regretting his own farfetched compliments to women and suggests to his friend that his mistress ". . . be fair/With her owne beauty. . . ." He goes on to declare that he can "love a man/With Honour, and Religion; Such a one/As dares be singly virtuous gainst the Town;/A man that's learned too, and for his parts/Is held a Prodigie of all the Arts; . . ."—high praise to a young man of twenty-one. In a poem written in anticipation of Stanley's publication of his own poetry, Shirley again praises the accomplishments of young Stanley: "Thou early miracle of Wit and Art. . . ." Shirley places Carew, the "oracle of Love," second now to Stanley, whose poems are innocent and chaste. Yet he also tells the young poet that youth has as yet kept his poetry from its perfection.[85]

When Stanley married Dorothy Enyon on May 8, 1648, Shirley wrote an epithalamium, a formal stanzaic poem that begins "Good Morrow" and, like Spenser's famous poem, traces the day's activities through to "Goodnight." It is a poem in the convention, making comparisons of sunrise with the blushing cheek of the bride. Shirley urges the sun, "childe of Time and Nature," to hurry, for the bridegroom is anxious, yet the sun is reminded to "ope the Curtains [eyelids]" of the bride from behind or it will think it is meeting another daybreak. Like Shakespeare in his sonnets to his young man, Shirley rejoices that there will now be hope of more like Stanley. The poet closes with the usual mention of the names of the lovers, wishing them children in the metaphor of a tree bearing flowers and fruit.[86]

But Shirley, with a large and strong body of work to his name, did not confine himself to the role of client. In these years he was remembering the writings of friends and encouraging others. Most of Shirley's commendatory verses appeared in the 1640's and 1650's, when the theatres were closed and he and his friends turned to publishing for a livelihood. Shirley wrote a brief but well-regarded introduction to the works of Beaumont and Fletcher, published in 1647 with 36 commendatory verses by others appended in honor of the famous playwrights. The folio came about when ten actors, in an effort to raise money after being turned out of their jobs by the Puritan edict against stage performances, gathered together the plays. Asked to write the preface for this folio edition, Shirley makes a fine statement of the instructive use of poetry and drama, whether on stage or in print. He notes that the Beaumont and Fletcher plays are "the greatest monument of the scene that time and humanity have produced. . . ." Drama, says Shirley, can educate as well as foreign travel and helps to explain pleasurably what often is lost in the "sourer ways of education." Shirley also wrote some verse on this publication, turning from the plays and their authors to make a prophecy for "peace in the kingdom"; "A Balme unto the wounded Age I sing,/And nothing now is wanting but the King."[87]

At least twice during these years Shirley wrote commendatory poetry in circumstances that illustrate Catholic sympathies. Walter Coleman, alias Christopher of St. Clare, a Franciscan imprisoned from 1641 until his death in 1645, had been convicted with other priests, among them John (or Augustine) Rivers alias Abbot, who is said to have been the author of a play attributed to Shirley called *The Traitor*. Shirley wrote in praise of Coleman's *La Danse Macabre or Deaths Duel,* dedicated to Queen Henrietta Maria.[88] Commendatory verses also appear in the fourth edition, published in 1646, of a translation from the French that Francis Hawkins, a boy of eight, had made of a book of manners that he called *Youths Behaviour*. The original work was by pensionnaires at the Jesuit College of La Fleche. Young Hawkins himself became a Jesuit in 1649 and lived abroad, teaching later at Liege.[89]

During 1646 Shirley also wrote poems to another member of the Stanley coterie, John Hall of Durham, who published in that year a little volume of essays called *Horae Vacivae*. At that time Hall was only nineteen, and he later became, like May, a partisan of the Parliamentarian cause. From April to August of 1648 Hall wrote a Parliamentarian pamphlet called *Mercurius Britannicus*. John Berkenhead, an acquaintance of Stanley, wonders at "Jack Hall of Cambridge" when he writes in the Royalist pamphlet, *Mercurius Bellicus* (1648): "let not money so farre sway thee, as to forfeit thy Loyaltie and honesty. . . ." Hall had come to London in early 1647, where he entered Gray's Inn and lived near Stanley; he left in 1648 when he began writing *Mercurius Britannicus.* So his daily association with the coterie can be clearly dated. Yet his friendship with Shirley continued. He wrote verses on the publication of *The Cardinal* in 1652, calling Shirley the fourth greatest playwright, surpassed only by Jonson and Beaumont and Fletcher.[90]

The letters of Hall are instructive about the man but also about his friends and associations. Writing to his friend Hartlib, he speaks of a plan for an Academy of "sixty elected gentlemen of blood and coat-armour." Apparently Stanley, of whom Hall frequently speaks, was offered second place in the proposed Academy, that of Orator, but refused because of a design—"Armilla Nigra." (This apparently refers to the Order of the Black Ribbon.) Hall's plans did not reach fruition, or not at his own hands. But perhaps Stanley and Hall helped Shirley to set up a school. The playwright's next work is a Latin grammar, *Via ad Latinum Linguam,* possibly written in anticipation of such an Academy as Hall had projected.[91]

Shirley was part of a cluster of friends rallying to the cause of poetry amid war. There was some capacity for putting poetry and friendship above politics, as shown by the exchange of poetry between Shirley and the later Parliamentarians May and Hall. Shirley's association with Stanley continued most likely until, and possibly after, the young man returned to his country estate at Cumberlow Green in Hertfordshire, where he turned to a serious study of the classics and subsequently to the history of philosophy. The bent of Stanley towards serious scholarly work in poetry and translation presumably influenced Shirley to return to teaching, and his subsequent dramatic efforts confined themselves to rather formal masques based on classical sources. In part, of course, the continued suppression of public play performances required him to seek other means of supporting himself and his family. He was helped substantially by Stanley but could not expect the young man to be his entire means of support indefinitely. Publication of plays and masques served to supplement his income; the combination of patron in the historic sense and publisher as the new patron helped the dramatist to survive financially.

Shirley remained in London and began the task of "setting up as a schoolmaster" in an effort to improve his situation. But the Stanley coterie proved a necessary link in the survival of poetic and dramatic works during the war years. And other similar small groups formed around other patrons willing to support and encourage the literary efforts of bereft playmakers and dramatists. No longer dominated by a Court with sovereigns who had specific tastes, the theatres closed, these writers concentrated on nondramatic publication, translation, and poetry. The younger, affluent gentry who had escaped from the financial and physical scourge of the wars returned to offer support and encouragement to the struggling writers. It was perhaps soon after the war took a disastrous turn in April of 1646 that Shirley began to think of taking up his old profession of schoolmaster. His friends would support him—morally or financially—as he gave his efforts to his grammars and his teaching career in the 1650's.

Notes

[1] Perez Zagorin, *The Court and the Country: The Beginning of the English Revolution of the Mid-Seventeenth Century* (London, 1969), p. 350; John J. Schroeder, "London and the Civil Wars," Diss. University of Wisconsin 1954, pp. 225, 393-96. "Independents" were mostly Congregationalists.

[2] Dyce, *Works,* I, 101; Bentley, *JCS,* I, 108; see also 64, 67, 131; T. W. Baldwin, *The Organization and Personnel of the Shakespearean Company* (New York, 1927), p. 65; Hanson T. Parlin, "A Study in Shirley's Comedies of London Life," *Bulletin of the University of Texas,* No. 371 (Nov. 15, 1914), p. 48.

[3] "Christenings, 1638-1650," St. Giles in the Fields, Holborn, Parish Register, fol. 17^V (in the keeping of the Rector). It is likely that during these years two other children were born to Shirley and his wife Elizabeth, but there is no extant record of their christenings. See Bentley, "Players in the Parish of St. Giles in the Fields," *RES,* 6 (1930), 149-66, and *JCS,* II, 344, 364-70, 387, 390, 525, 607 and *passim.*

[4] Joseph Quincy Adams, *Shakespearean Playhouses* (New York, 1917), pp. 183-84, 229.

[5] Herbert, *Dramatic Records,* p. 39. Twelve years later in his dedication to Sir Robert Bolles, Bart., at the play's publication, Shirley asserts it to be one of his best and most successful plays. He also reveals that he himself directed its publication. See Dyce, *Works,* V, 179.

[6] Herbert, *Dramatic Records,* p. 39.

[7] The official ordinance closing the theatres is dated September 2, 1642. See *An Excellent Collection of All Remonstrances, Ordinances, Proclamations, . . . between the Kings Most Excellent Majesty, and His High Court of Parliament beginning . . . in December 1641 . . . until March the twenty-first, 1643* (London, 1643).

[8] Patrick J. Canavan, "A Study of English Drama as a Reflection of Stuart Politics from 1603 to 1660," Diss. University of Southern California 1950, p. 185.

[9] See *The Cardinal,* ed. Charles R. Forker (Bloomington, 1964), p. 6.

[10] Forker, "Archbishop Laud and Shirley's *The Cardinal,*" *Transactions of the Wisconsin Academy of Sciences, Arts and Letters,* 47 (1958), 242-248; see also Patrick J. Canavan, "A Study of English Drama," pp. 133-35.

[11] *The Cardinal,* ed. Forker, p. 46.

¹²Forker, "Archbishop Laud and Shirley's *The Cardinal,*" pp. 249-51.

¹³Samuel R. Gardiner, *History of England, 1603-1642* (1883-84; rpt. New York, 1965), X, 178-96; Bentley, *JCS,* V, 1148; Herbert, *Dramatic Records,* p. 39. See the play in Dyce, *Works,* V, 353-424.

¹⁴Edgar L. Chapman, "The Comic Art of James Shirley: A Modern Evaluation of his Comedies," Diss. Brown University 1964, p. 113; James Howell, "The Rogue in English Comedy to 1642," Diss. University of North Carolina 1941, p. 399 and Appendix A, pp. 561-67. The character of Piperollo comes fresh from *The Imposture* in the similar character role of Bertholdi. It suggests that Shirley needed to provide two regular comic actors with roles here, presumably one played by Pollard, who spoke the epilogue to *The Cardinal,* and the other, William Robbins, from Shirley's old Cockpit group.

¹⁵See the play and dedication in Dyce, *Works,* V, 428-29, 431-514; also see Linda Kay Ward Ellinger, "A Critical Edition of James Shirley's *The Court Secret,*" Diss. University of Iowa 1979. Greg, *Bibliography,* II, #724, pp. 840-41.

¹⁶Melvin C. Wren, "London in the Revolution of 1648," Diss. Iowa State University 1939, pp. 183, 222, 243 245; Perez Zagorin, *The Court and The Country,* pp. 329-50 and *passim.*

¹⁷John J. Schroeder, "London and the Civil Wars," p. 142.

¹⁸For detailed analyses of this poem, see Armstrong, *Poems,* pp. 77-78, 100 and R. G. Howarth, "Some Unpublished Poems of James Shirley," *RES,* 9 (1933), pp. 277-80. Howarth dates the piece a New Year's poem, December 1641, from the phrase "May all things with the yeare be new," but this may mean near to March 25, 1642. Howarth found the poem in BM MS. Harl. 6918, fol. 28; the poem understandably was not printed with Shirley's *Poems* in 1646 but appears in the following additional manuscripts: Oxford University Bodl. MS. Ashmole 36, fol. 127; BM MS. Rawl. Poet 26, fol. 140 and Rawl. Poet. 62.

¹⁹Dyce, *Works,* V, 356; Nason, *Shirley,* p. 136.

²⁰Wood, *Athenae,* III, 737.

²¹Yet Newcastle's abandonment of the King after the defeat at Marston Moor in July 1644 appears to be out of the character of a Cavalier gentleman. His enemies saw him as a defector. The loss of the battle owed to Prince Rupert's lack of coordination and consultation with the other aristocratic generals. But among his fellow Royalists Newcastle's reputation remained intact throughout his career. After the Restoration he returned from abroad and acted as patron to Hobbes, Gassendi, and

arlier he had helped Jonson, Shirley, and Davenant. Jay A. Gertzman, "Some Biographical Accounts of Two 17th-Century Gentlemen: Ideals of Aristocratic Conduct Vs. the Personal Motives which Determine Behavior," *Selected Papers from the West Virginia Shakespeare and Renaissance Association,* 5 (1980), 25-30; Douglas Grant, *Margaret the First: A Biography of Margaret Cavendish, Duchess of Newcastle, 1623-1673* (Toronto, 1957), pp. 58, 60-62.

[22] Anne Barton, "Harking Back to Elizabeth: Ben Jonson and Caroline Nostalgia," *ELH,* 48, No. 4 (Winter 1981), 706; Geoffrey Trease, *Portrait of a Cavalier: William Cavendish, First Duke of Newcastle* (New York, 1979), pp. 66-70; *The Traitor,* ed. John Stewart Carter (Lincoln, 1965), p. 2.

[23] Trease, *Portrait of a Cavalier,* pp. 76-84; Theophilus Cibber, *The Lives of the Poets of Great Britain and Ireland to the Time of Dean Swift* (London, 1753), II, 169-75; David Nichol Smith, *Characters from the Histories and Memoirs of the 17th Century* (Oxford, 1918), no. 29, pp. 116-19, 283. Smith uses Clarendon's *History of the Rebellion* (1888), ed. Macray, III, 380-83, among other sources. See also Sir Henry Craik, *The Life of Edward Earl of Clarendon* (New York, 1911), I, 195.

[24] "Certain Information . . ." No. 42, 30 Oct.—6 Nov. 1643, p. 326; *Mercurius Civicus, Londons Intelligencer,* No. 24, Nov. 2—9, 1643, p. 188, Thomason Tracts, BM E75; Bentley, *JCS,* IV, 142-45; Trease, *Portrait of a Cavalier,* pp. 65, 95-96; Grant, *Margaret the First,* pp. 46-65. Another contemporary account assessing Newcastle reads quite differently: "And for Newcastle, he is but a counterfeit marquis; at the best but a playwright; one of Appolo's whirligigs; one, that, when he should be fighting, would be fornicating with the nine muses, or the Dean of York's daughters; a very thing; a soul traducted out of perfume and compliment; a silken general, that ran away beyond sea in a sailor's canvas: He, with his tinder-box of authority, first lighted the fire in the north, yet was so kind to see it quenched again, ere he left us." "The Character of an Oxford Incendiary," (1643), in *Harleian Miscellany; or, A Collection of Scarce, Curious, and Entertaining Pamphlets and Tracts* (London, 1810), V, 345.

[25] Charles II issued a proclamation in February 1663 which endeavored to reward those who had served the Royalist cause during the civil wars. PRO MS. SP Dom 29/68, fols. 122, 154. When Standerdine Sachell alias Shirley married Shirley's daughter Mary is not certain, but "Marie," the dramatist's daughter, was born in 1619 and would have been 23 years old by 1642.

[26] Trease, *Portrait of a Cavalier,* pp. 105-39.

[27] For contemporary references to the papist element in Newcastle's army, see *An Excellent Collection of all Remonstrances, Ordinances, Proclamations,* pp. 510-11, 799, 813-14, 902; John Vicars, *England's Worthies: under whom All the Civill and Bloudy Warres, since Anno 1642 to Anno 1647 are related* (London, 1647), p. 22 in addition to sources cited in footnotes 21 and 24.

[28] *The Nottinghamshire County Records, Notes and Extracts,* comp. H. Hampton Copnall (Notts, 1915), list in Appendix A "Popish Recusants Presented." They include Wm. Dalby from Boale (1636-38); Wm. Smith and wife from Boughton (1630-39); Edw. Goulding of Colston Bassett (1622-42); Geo. and Thos. Markham of Ollerton (1615-42); Edw. Willoughby's wife from Cossall (1633-41); and another Wm. Smith from No. Collingham (1640-42).

[29] See maps which show Newcastle's advances and the strategic position of Newark-on-Trent and the surrounding garrisons in Alfred Wood, *Nottinghamshire in the Civil War* (Oxford, 1937), Map I, p. 65; Map IV, p. 105, and pp. 14, 27, 29-30, 37, 60, 83, 87-89, 94, 208. See also Perez Zagorin, *The Court and the Country,* p. 338. Edward Golding fought alongside Wm. Staunton at Edgehill in 1642; both Standerdine Shirley and John Hall were under Staunton's command. Newcastle was given the title of Marquis on October 27, 1643, by the King; David N. Smith, *Characters,* p. 116.

[30] Wood, *Nottinghamshire in the Civil War,* pp. 62-83, 94, and *passim;* Zagorin, *The Court and the Country,* p. 338.

[31] See the poem in Armstrong, *Poems,* p. 11.

[32] The manuscript, primarily a domestic comedy, is in the same hand as the Worcester College manuscript of *The Court Secret;* both make frequent use of contractions, which are common in Shirley's plays. Bullen, in his edition of the Harleian manuscript, describes a number of parallels between the piece and Shirley's work. Sir Richard Huntlove and his Lady resemble the Bornwells in *The Lady of Pleasure.* A line in the play appears word for word in *A Bird in a Cage:* "That snorts at Spaine by an instinct of Nature." The play satirizes the affectations of gallants, as does *The Lady of Pleasure* and, like *The Witty Fair One,* it mentions scholars who write plays and take no money. The play is printed in *A Collection of Old English Plays,* ed. A. H. Bullen (London, 1883), II; 315-16, 324, 350, 409 and *passim.* Bullen's version is based on BM MS. Harl. 7650; it differs considerably from the play printed with *The Variety.* Albert Wertheim, "The Dramatic Art of James Shirley," Diss. Yale University 1966, pp. 226-31.

[33] Armstrong, *Poems,* p. 68. Reference is made to a Gerald Dalby in BM MS. Sloane 1200. Gunners, according to Armstrong, were called engineers then.

[34] Howarth, "Poems," pp. xi, 250; Armstrong, *Poems,* pp. 14, 67.

[35] See the entry under "Recusants" in the Quarter Sessions Minute Books of the County of Nottinghamshire for reference to Thomas Markham of Ollerton. Notts County Record Office, QSM, XII (c. 1640-42), 68.

[36] *England's Black Tribunal,* 6th ed. (London, 1737), p. 275; "Lt. Col. Thos. Markham of Ollerton" was slain along with "Col. Dalby, that excellent Engineer, kill'd at Wingfield manor in Derbyshire," pp. 272-73.

[37] Armstrong, *Poems,* p. 15; Henry J. Foley, S.J., *Records of the English Province of the Society of Jesus* (London, 1880), V, 784. Another Markham, Sir Robert, Bart., of Sedgebrook, Lincs., was the King's Commissioner for Lincoln and Notts and a resident in the garrison of Newark in January 1644. *Newark on Trent: The Civil War Siegeworks,* The Royal Commission on Historical Monuments (London, 1964), Appendix I, 94.

[38] Armstrong, *Poems,* pp. 9, 62-63, 93; Howarth, "Poems," pp. 235-38. The poem appears in BM MS. Harl. 6918 and Bodl. MS. Rawl. 88.

[39] "Journals of the Court of Common Council, 1640-49," Corporation of London Records Office MS. 40, fol. 44; *Cal. SP Ven.,* 26, p. 181.

[40] John J. Schroeder, "London and the Civil Wars," p. 140.

[41] See the discussion earlier in this chapter and notes 26 and 27.

[42] See a discussion of this collaboration earlier in this chapter and note 32.

[43] Shirley's likely identity with the Jacobus Shirley listed in the Recusant Roll is discussed in Chapter II of this work. The roll is in the Pipe Series of records, PRO MS. E377/49.

[44] *A Transcript of the Registers of the Worshipful Company of Stationers; From 1640-1708,* ed. Geo. E. Eyre and Chas. R. Rivington, 3 vols. (London, 1913-14), I, 250. Hereafter cited as Eyre, *Stationers Transcript.*

[45] Armstrong, *Poems,* pp. xix-xxi, xvii-xxvi, 56-57; Howarth, "Poems," pp. xxix, 232-36. On Carew's poetry, see Edward I. Selig, *The Flourishing Wreath: A Study of Thomas Carew's Poetry* (New Haven, 1958), pp. 29-30, 32, 35, 66, 76-80; F. E. Schelling, "Poems of Shirley Attributed to Carew and Goffe," *MLN,* 11 (1896), 137-39.

[46] Dyce, *Works,* I, xcvii, n. l; xcviii. Dyce suggests this is the same man who signed his name "G. Hills" to the Beaumont and Fletcher folio edition printed in 1647, for which Shirley wrote the preface.

47"The Diary of John Greene," ed. E. M. Symonds, *EHR,* 43 (1928), 385-94, 598-604, and *EHR,* 44 (1929), 107.

48Wood, *Athenae,* III, 737.

49Tithe ledger, St. Andrews, Holborn, Guildhall MS. 9588, fol. 30.

50St. Giles in the Fields, Parish Register, fol. 17^V. No records of the christenings of Lawrinda, Christopher, or James, Jr., have been discovered.

51Armstrong's *Poems* and Howarth's "Poems," give much information, both biographical and literary, concerning Shirley's poetry.

52The poems do not always use the name of Odelia, but it is clear that they are written to his "mistress" and while separated from her. Other poets, such as Thomas Stanley, refer to Shirley's Odelia, and we may assume that this was his poetic name for his wife. See Dyce, *Works,* I, xcii-xcviii; Armstrong, *Poems,* pp. 1, 5.

53Howarth, "Poems," pp. 247-49.

54Howarth, "Poems," pp. 247-49; *The Poems and Translations of Thomas Stanley,* ed. Galbraith Miller Crump (Oxford, 1962), Introduction, pp. xxv-xxvii.

55The holograph Rawlinson manuscript comprises a number of poems most likely privately circulated by Shirley among his friends; when he publicly printed the poems, many personal references and initials were deleted. Bodl. MS. Rawl. 88.

56Armstrong, *Poems,* pp. 36, 77; Howarth, "Poems," p. 276.

57Bodl. MS Rawl. 88; Armstrong, *Poems,* p. 34.

58The manuscript which contains these poems is BM Addl. MS. 33,998; the BM version is included in Armstrong, *Poems,* p. 100.

59Armstrong, *Poems,* pp. 54, 85-86. The piece appears in the final scene of Shirley's masque *The Contention of Ajax and Ulysses for the Armour of Achilles* and was first printed in 1658, originally written for a "private Entertainment of some persons of Honour" and "nobly represented by young Gentlemen of quality." The masque is printed in Dyce, *Works,* VI, 369-97.

60Dyce notes that a manuscript note in Langbaine's *Account of the English Dramatick Poets* (Oxford, 1691), p. 495, states that Bowman sang the dirge to King Charles and to the writer, William Oldys. Dyce, *Works,* VI, n.1, 397.

61For the masque, see Dyce, *Works,* VI, 315-41.

[62]Fleay, "Annals of the Careers of James and Henry Shirley," *Anglia,* 8 (1885), 409-10. Felix E. Schelling suggests Shirley wrote the *Triumph of Beauty* for a Lord Mayor's pageant in 1637; but the notation on the title page would probably claim that if so. *Elizabethan Playwrights* (New York, 1925), p. 250. Alfred H. Harbage suggests Shirley wrote the piece for students at his school. *Cavalier Drama* (1936; rpt. New York, 1964), p. 205.

[63]See the commendatory poems to Shirley in Dyce, *Works,* I, xcii-xcviii.

[64]For Stanley's works, see Margaret Flower, "Thomas Stanley; A Bibliography of His Writings in Prose and Verse," *Trans. of the Cambridge Bibliographical Society,* I, No. 2 (1950), 139-72 and *The Poems and Translations of Thomas Stanley,* ed. Crump, p. xxv. Wood, *Athenae,* III, 738.

[65]Allan Griffith Chester, *Thomas May: Man of Letters 1595-1650* (Philadelphia, 1932), pp. 6-11, 40-41; see also Chapter I of this work.

[66]Dyce, *Works,* I, xcv. A George Bucke was admitted to Gray's Inn on November 21, 1627. Foster, *Register: Gray's Inn,* fol. 846, p. 183. His name appears in the parish register of St. Bride's by Fleet Street as early as 1636, the parish where Shirley was later to reside. That register also lists the burial of "George Bucke late of the parish of St. Bridgitte als. Bride's, near Fleet Street, city of London," on December 2, 1647. "Baptisms," St. Bride's Parish Register, Guildhall MS. 6536; "Burials," St. Bride's Parish Register, Guildhall MS. 6538. See also the Prerogative Court of Canterbury (PCC), Wills, 172 Coventry, PRO; PCC Administrations, 1647, fol. 172, PRO.

Mark Eccles in two articles places Sir George Buc, one time Master of the Revels, as the author of the verses on both Shirley's *Poems* and the Beaumont and Fletcher folio. Although Sir George died in 1645, Eccles believes the verses were printed posthumously. The younger George Buck he believes to be a grandnephew of Sir George. See Eccles, "Brief Lives: Tudor and Stuart Authors," *SP,* 79, No. 4 (Fall 1982), 18-19, and "Sir George Buc, Master of the Revels," in C. J. Sisson, *Thomas Lodge and Other Elizabethans* (Cambridge, MA, 1933), pp. 499-503. See also Bentley, *JCS,* IV, 1066 and Hunter, *Chorus Vatum,* I, 384.

Sir George Buc's *An Eclog treating of Crownes and of Garland,* first published in 1605, was revised and reprinted in 1635 by "Geo. Buck, Gent" under the title of *The Great Plantagent, or a continued success of that royal name.* W. W. Greg, *Pastoral Poetry and Pastoral Drama* (London, 1905), p. 116.

[67]In 1634 a Francis Tucker, second son of Elizabeth Sedley and George Tucker appears in the *Visitations of Hertfordshire,* ed. Walter C. Met-

calfe, Harleian Series, 22 (London, 1886), p. 91. He may have been a student of Shirley's at St. Albans. In addition, in 1619 a Francis Tucker is entered in the Pilgrim Book of the English College at Rome. Foley, *Records of the Society of Jesus,* VI, 598. The only original writing attributed to a "Fr. Tucker, MA of St. John's College, Oxford" appears in the Thomason Tracts for April 4, 1661: "The Divine Dirge of a dying Swan," signed by the widow of a Francis Tucker who says her husband was an active Cavalier. Thomason Tracts, No. 12, BM MS. E1068. Possibly Shirley met Tucker at Oxford.

⁶⁸Dyce, *Works,* I, xcvi-xcvii; Bentley, *JCS,* II, 535. In the parish register of St. Dunstan's in the West an entry appears for the baptism of Ann, daughter of Edward Powell in Fleet St. on December 20, 1642. Guildhall MS. 10,344. An Edward Powell is entered in the *Visitation of London* for 1633-34, naming him of London, gent., second son of Robert Powell of Parkhall, esq. *Visitation of London,* ed. Jos. Jackson Howard, Harleian Society, 17 (London, 1883), II, 175. And in the Middlesex Sessions Rolls on December 4, 1641, "Edward Powell, gentleman" of "St. Andrews in Holborne co Midd," was indicted for recusancy. Jeaffreson, *Middlesex Records,* III, 150. Whitelocke's *Memorials* give several references to a "Col. Powel." In 1648, reference is made by Prince Rupert in a letter to Ld. Gen. Fairfax, asking that moderation be used towards "Col. Powel." He was referred to be tried with others that same year and was sentenced to death in 1649, then pardoned; finally, an "Order for £ 20 for the burial of Mr. Powel, a reduced officer" is noted in 1649. Sir Bulstrode Whitelocke, *The History of England, or, Memorials of the English Affairs* (London, 1713), II, 384, 553; III, 13, 28, 93.

⁶⁹The Victoria and Albert Museum copy 25.E.37.38 contains the Moseley catalog of books published in Shirley's *Six New Playes;* see sig. A4.

⁷⁰Hunter, *Chorus Vatum,* III, 555.

⁷¹The letter of political news that mentions Hill as schoolmaster is item #133, "A" Series Archives, 29 (1637-1640), 429-30, Westminster Cathedral MS. Collection. In a letter received from Mr. John Morley, Librarian of Gilstrap Public Libraries, Newark-on-Trent, Notts Record Office, he writes that "a George Hill" was "the schoolmaster of the Magnus School, Newark, from 1650-1655." Letter dated November 15, 1968. Shirley's acquaintance with Hill may have originated at Oxford, for on June 3, 1614, a George Hill signed the Subscription Book. Boase and Clark, *Register: Oxford,* II, Pt. 2, "Matriculations," ii, 333. A George Hill married Elizabeth Sawtige on June 30, 1623, according to the Newark-on-Trent parish register. *Nottinghamshire Parish Register, Marriages,* ed. W. P. W. Phillimore and John Standish (London, 1898), IV, 72.

⁷²Hill was still living in 1655, for in the Visitation Books of Derby, a Mr. George Hill is entered with *"liber cleri"* (including schoolmasters) for the Town of Breadsall. He may not have become schoolmaster there until 1662, following John Harpur, for the Visitation Books entered Hill at Breadsall in Castlemarie, Derby, and in Rependon and Ashburne in September 1662. Visitation Books, Lichfield Country Record Office MS. B/V/1/67, fol. 18^V, 20^r. Under the Chesterfield Diocese a man of that name appears as early as 1639 as the curate of Barley in a listing of *liber cleri* on March 21, 1639. Lichfield Country Record Office MS. B/V/1/62 (1639). The same man's will was proved by his wife on July 25, 1667. He named his wife executor, giving all to her except his books, which he bequeathed to his grandson George. An "Inventory of Goods" gives only the notation of 294 books valued at £ 52 with no titles named. Perhaps Hill returned to teaching as early as 1650 but not to the work of parish priest until after the Restoration.

⁷³Dyce, *Works,* VI, 403.

⁷⁴Assessments, Committee for Advance of Money, PRO MS. SP 19/63, fol. 158^V, 159; alphabetical list by name, PRO MS. SP 19/46.

⁷⁵"Bernard Hyde, son and heir of Bernard Hyde, of St. Dunstan's in the East, London, esq." on February 9, 1629; "Humfrey," a second son, also was admitted at this time. Sir Henry F. Macgeagh and H. A. C. Sturgess, comp., *Register of Admissions to the Honorable Society of the Middle Temple* (London, 1949), I, 122.

⁷⁶The connection between the publisher Moseley and Hyde was made by Howarth, "Poems," p. 215. Humphrey Moseley "of the parish of St. Gregories in Paules Churchyard London Stationer of the age of 29 or thereabouts" gives testimony on October 7, 1634, regarding a suit between John Powell, merchant, and Bernard Hyde, Esquire. Town Depositions, Court of Chancery, PRO MS. C24/60l, Pt. II.

⁷⁷Town Depositions, Court of Chancery, Deposition dated December 15, 1626, PRO MS. C24/529, Pt. II, #76.

⁷⁸The discovery of Stanley's "Register of Friends" was made by James M. Osborne. See his interesting account in "Thomas Stanley's Lost 'Register of Friends'," *Yale University Library Gazette,* 32 (1958), 122-47. The original manuscript can be seen in Box 58, No. 26 of the Osborne Collection, Yale University Library.

⁷⁹Howarth, "Poems," pp. 223-24; Armstrong, *Poems,* p. 50. Robert Bowman, along with Robert Herrick, may have joined the group after being ejected from their parish livings in 1648. By 1651, however, Bowman was given a fellowship at Clare Hall, Cambridge. See *The Poems of Thomas Stanley,* ed. Crump, Intro., pp. xxiv-xxv, n.3.

[80] *A New Miscellany of Original Poems, Translations and Imitations,* ed. by Anthony Hammond and published in 1720, asserts that M.M.H. is Mrs. Mary Hammond and that the poem was "Written by Mr. James Shirley, in the year 1634." This later version calls the lady "Lucinda," and perhaps the poem was amended by another and addressed to another lady entirely. See the dedication to Stanley in Dyce, *Works,* I, 191.

[81] Lovelace's famous poem, "To Althea, from Prison," has prompted many critics to attempt to identify Althea. She may have been a poetic substitute for a lady, as was Shirley's Odelia. But in the parish register of St. Giles in the Fields, an entry in 1666 notes the burial of "Althea Cartwright als Lovelace," on June 11th. This lady may have been Lovelace's Althea; Lovelace sold his property in 1649 to regain funds lost in the Cavalier cause and this property later was purchased by the actor, Edward Cartwright. Interestingly, Cartwright describes a portrait (still extant) as "Althea's pictur. her hare descheull on 3 quarters clouth." Lovelace, only 40 years old when he died in 1658, may have had a wife or mistress named Althea Cartwright who, in turn, most likely was the daughter of the younger William Cartwright who lived in the parish of St. Giles in the Fields. Parish Register, St. Giles in the Fields, Holborn (in the keeping of the Rector). See Cyril H. Hartmann, *The Cavalier Spirit and Its Influence on the Life and Work of Richard Lovelace, 1618-1658* (London, 1925), pp. 45, 76, 120-22; Bentley, *JCS,* II, 402-05; IV, 720-22; *The Poems of Richard Lovelace,* ed. Cyril H. Wilkinson (Oxford, 1930), pp. xliii-xlv.

[82] On Sherburne's imprisonment, see House of Lords Calendar, LJ, V, 308, p. 43, HMC 5th Report. His activities in the wars are noted by F. J. Van Beeck, author of *The Poems and Translations of Sir Edward Sherburne* (Assen, 1961), pp. xvii-xix, xxii-xxv. He also outlines Sherburne's relationship with Stanley (pp. xxvi-xxvii) and notes that Sherburne gave Wood a good deal of information on Carew, Shirley, Stanley, Charles Aleyn, and Lovelace.

[83] Wood, *Fasti,* Part II, IV, col. 30, 31. The year after Sherburne's release from prison, the Sequestration Committee took his goods. Committee on Sequestration, #292, fol. 333, PRO MS. SP 28/212. Wood's reference to the decline of the King's cause most likely refers to the surrender of Oxford in June 1646. Coupled with the fact that Stanley did not return to England from France until that time and could hardly have aided Shirley earlier, the probability is strong that Shirley stayed in Newark after Marston Moor, at least until November or December of 1645. Margaret Flower, "Thomas Stanley; A Bibliography," I, 142-43; Wood, *Athenae,* III, 737-38.

84Van Beeck, *The Poems and Translations of Sir Edward Sherburne,* p. xlii; Wood MSS, BM MS. Wood, F44 (see especially fol. 234). One critic says Sherburne himself has been suggested as translator of the *Filli di Sciro;* Sherburne wrote a preface to the play after 1660. W. W. Greg, *Pastoral Poetry and Pastoral Drama* (1906; rpt. New York, 1959), p. 249. See also BM MS. Sloane 836, fol. 76^V and Sloane 857, "Papers Relating to the Glass-sellers Co," fol. 182-94, 195^V. Sherburne's reference to Shirley's death is on fol. 234^r and 235^r of BM MS. Wood, F 44. Sherburne adds that Shirley died with some "[illegible] of his namesak-House." This is a bit puzzling, for Shirley never lived in St. James Clerkenwell so far as we know, and Wood is probably more accurate in placing Shirley at the parish of St. Dunstan's in the West near Fleet St. for part of his life. The will itself states that Shirley lived in Whitefriars. Prerogative Court of Canterbury (PCC) Wills, Mico 170, PRO.

85Dyce, *Works,* I, 189; Armstrong, *Poems,* pp. 9, 16.

86The wedding poem is entitled "Epithalamium: Or a Congratulatory Ode to the happy Marriage of Thomas Stanley Esq; and Mris Dorothea Enyon (May 8, 1648)." Armstrong, *Poems,* pp. 37-38. See also Gerald Eades Bentley, "James Shirley and a Group of Unnoted Poems on The Wedding of Thomas Stanley," *Huntington Library Quarterly,* II (1938-39), 212-32.

87Dyce, *Works,* I, xlvi-xlix; Eyre, *Stationers Transcript,* I, 244.

88"To the Author [W. Colman] vpon his Poem," in Armstrong, *Poems,* p. 79. See Richard Challoner, *Memoirs of Missionary Priests . . . from the Year 1577 to 1684,* ed. J. H. Pollen (Dublin, 1874), I, 400-02, 442, 445; Foley, *Records of . . . The Society of Jesus,* V, 217-18, 220; Joseph Gillow, *A Literary and Biographical History, or Bibliographical Dictionary of The English Catholics* (London, 1885-1902), p. 537.

89"In laudem Authoris [Francisci Hawkinsii]," in Armstrong, *Poems,* p. 40. See J. E. Mason, *Gentlefolk in the Making; Studies in the History of English Courtesy Literature and Related Topics from 1531 to 1774* (Philadelphia, 1935), pp. 259-60; Arthur C. F. Beales, *Education Under Penalty; English Catholic Education From the Reformation to the Fall of James II, 1547-1689* (London, 1963), p. 196; T[hompson] C[ooper], "Hawkins, Francis" *DNB* (1891).

90Armstrong, *Poems,* p. 40. Certainly Hall is one of the more interesting figures of the period. He also dedicated his *Poems* to Stanley, writing from St. John's College in Cambridge, and notes that he first became indebted to Stanley at Durham. John Hall, *The Advancement of Learning,* ed. A. K. Croston (Liverpool, 1953), pp. v-viii; Hunter, *Chorus*

Vatum, III, 56-57. Berkenhead is quoted in Raymond L. Schults, "The Civil War Press, 1641-1649," Diss. University of Calif. Los Angeles 1957, pp. 128-29. Hall was admitted to Gray's Inn on June 7, 1643, "John Hall of the city of Durham, gent," Foster, *Register: Gray's Inn,* fol. 1003. His verses to Shirley are printed in Dyce, *Works,* I, xc.

[91] G. H. Turnbull, "John Hall's Letters to Samuel Hartlib," *RES,* N.S. 4, No. 15 (1953), 230-33. See also Howarth, "Poems," pp. 247-49; George Saintsbury, *A History of English Prosody from the 12th Century to the Present Day* (London, 1923), II, 206. Hall's own father was a schoolmaster in the grammar school at Durham. Hunter, *Chorus Vatum,* III, 57. That Hall disappointed Stanley is evident from a poem written apparently after the death of Hall in 1656. The poem is in the "Register of Friends" manuscript. Stanley mourns the change of allegiance in Hall from Royalist to Parliamentarian and also notes his interest for a time in Deism; Hall died when only 29 years old. Osborne, "Thomas Stanley's Lost 'Register of Friends'," pp. 122-47.

VI

The Last Years: 1649-1666

Nearly everyone, Shirley announced in the dedication to his *Via ad Latinam Linguam Complanata* in 1649, was publishing grammar books, in part because public play-acting had been forbidden and writers were busily penning "instructive" works, translations, romances, or revamping plays for printers. The grammar book is a work for young scholars, "The Rules composed in English and Latine Verse: For the greater Delight and Benefit of Learners."[1]

William Herbert, to whom Shirley dedicated the *Latinam Linguam,* came of an illustrious family: he was son of Philip, Earl of Pembroke and Montgomery, the Lord Chamberlain (who, as one author put it, "insulted genius by patronizing it") and nephew of William, Earl of Pembroke, whom Shirley calls "the ornament of the court and kingdom." At this time, young William was only nine years old, the prime age for such a book. Perhaps Shirley was not seeking a patron, but he refers to the Lord Chamberlain as one "whose name is worthily affixed a *Patron* to more generous wit than our *Nation* must hope to see again in all *future Ages,*" and was casting about for a position as tutor and hoped to get a Herbert's recommendation.[2]

The seller of the book, John Stephenson, had his shop "at the sign of the Sun on Ludgate-Hill," a street that terminates by running into Fleet, not far from St. Bride's parish where Shirley was living some time before 1651. Again, the commendatory verses written for the grammar book's publication give an indication of his circle of friends. Shirley was still clearly associated with the Stanley coterie, and the grammar was appropriately saluted by Thomas Stanley and Edward Sherburne. Both wrote poems in Latin, and Sherburne wrote a second poem in English, "To my Worthy, and Ingenious Friend . . ." lauding the author for simplifying and clarifying Latin grammar.[3] As late as 1654, Stanley was still living in London, according to a deposition dated January 22, 1654, in which Stanley gives testimony, stating he is "of Symons Inn, London, gent, aged 30 yeares or thereabouts."[4]

Five other friends also inscribed verses. The poem of Shirley's long time associate John Ogilby laments the dreariness and difficulty of most grammars for the young: "For only here and there a boy, that can/Eat stones like the Italian, proves a man." Yet Ogilby continued to risk new ventures in printing and play production. In 1660 he was granted a license for 31 years to print mathematical books in "the letter and character now used at the Louvre in France." He received the following year a patent that named him Master of the Revels in Ireland.[5] Edward Saltmarsh writes praises with conventional images in which the author's work, in its melodious and clear rendering of Latin grammar into verse, replaces Lilly's. Saltmarsh reflects, as do Sherburne and Ogilby, on the "scholar's labyrinth" of grammar, "Those cloudy parts of speech" that Shirley has made shining "as the orient morn."[6]

Francis Lang(s)ton apparently made Shirley's acquaintance during the 1630's in the Inns of Court days. He had seen the playwright's plays on the stage, for he refers to the time "when you [Shirley] steer'd the souls of men/With your harmonius scenes and graceful dress. . . ." A Francis Langston was admitted to the Middle Temple in 1634, the seventh son of Anthony Langston of County Worcester.[7] In a deposition dated July 10, 1644 in the Court of Chancery, a Fra: Langston gives testimony in a case regarding "divers and sundry sorts of goods and valuable merchandise to be dispersed and transported beyond the Sea into Russia by way of Traffique" amounting to about £1500. This man notes that he is "late of Elmeley Castle in the Countie of Worcester but nowe of the parish of St. Brides als Bridgett, London, gent, aged 38 yeares or thereabouts."[8]

On some slim evidence, we can suggest that George Blakeston, author of another of the commendatory poems, met Shirley during the war years in the North. The name of George Blakeston, Lt. of Horse to Sir Frances Cobbe in County York under Prince Rupert, appears in the list of claimants to the compensation offered by Charles II in 1663 to Royalist supporters in active service.[9] A letter dated from Westminster on September 9, 1645, from John Blakiston, M.P., to Sir Henry Vane, includes the remark, "I give you hearty thanks for the honour and respect you showed to my brother George and for your favours to myself and friends in those parts, which are under many distresses."[10] Possibly this brother George is the same man who penned verses to Shirley.

But it is Alexander Brome who gives Shirley the most elaborate praise: "We shall have swaddling scholars; infants now/May shake their Grammar with their coats away." Brome, Edward Phillips reports in his *Theatrum Poetarum* (which he dedicated to Stanley and Sherburne), worked as an attorney of the Mayor's Court and liked wine and mirth: "of so jovial a strain . . . among the sons of Mirth and Bacchus . . . ."[11] Brome had entered Gray's Inn in 1648 and in 1659 was admitted to Lincoln's Inn.[12] A comedy, *The Cunning Lovers,* is attributed to him, and Phillips notes that Brome also translated the *Odes* of Horace.[13] But in 1649 Brome was occupied with poems that satirized the Roundheads and with political ballads that used a dialect of West England. Most of his songs, published after the Restoration, refer with bitterness to the money-raising committees of the Puritans such as the Committee for the Advance of Money and the Committee for Compounding with Delinquents. "A La Mode," written around August 1647 when London submitted to the Parliamentarian Army, notes that if the opposition's general, Lord Fairfax, brings back the King, "Tom May shall all his acts write downe. . . ."[14]

On October 30, 1650, Brome stated in a Chancery Court deposition regarding lands in Kilkenny, Ireland, that he was 28 years old.[15] Some years later, in 1662, in testimony given regarding judgments involving Thomas Whitaker of St. Paul's Churchyard, London, and his father, Richard Whitaker, both deceased, Brome calls himself "gent" and gives his address as the parish of St. Stephen, Walbrooke, London and his age as "40 yeares or thereabouts."[16] Brome was apparently involved in this case because of his wife, Martha. She was the widow of Thomas Whitaker, a bookseller. And Shirley had used Richard Whitaker as the publisher of two of his Dublin plays. Alexander Brome also collected several plays of Richard Brome for publication in 1653; access to the plays may have come about through his wife's earlier connections in the bookseller's market.[17]

This group of friends who launched Shirley on his new venture in publishing grammar books lived or worked in the Inns of Court area, some old acquaintances from the heyday of the thirties, a few possibly fellow activists on the Royalist side in the Civil Wars in the northern provinces, and newer friends whose work and interests drew them once again to London, the center of writing, publishing, and business affairs. And for Shirley there remained the Catholic associates, still an underground group yet maintaining ties within England and abroad. If Shirley did travel abroad during these years, he presumably visited Catholic centers. His religious preference, as always, remained subdued and private, and illustrated by the indirect reference in his holograph will.

Shirley's other support during these years was his publisher. Increasingly, his work was directed towards the reader, and booksellers willingly offered old plays with new dedications to the literate public anxious for entertainment. His friends also reveal the clientele of the reading public—frequently men connected with business and law. While not all dramatists during the Interregnum chose to teach and to write grammars, most refurbished old plays and published them with new dedications. These new dedicatees were frequently the Royalist sons of the old gentry and nobility who survived the financial strains of the war.

Shirley's publishing activities during the Interregnum reflect the enormous growth of the printing industry during his career. That he could raise substantial funds through dedicating his earlier works to potential patrons and sell his plays for profit shows the continuing interest in the drama. Since public productions were forbidden, reading plays became even more popular. Unlike the younger Davenant and Killigrew, Shirley did not busy himself writing new plays and plan for the reopening of the public theatre. He was 55 years old in 1651 when he apparently was teaching again, and the influence of the Stanley coterie weaned him away from drama towards more scholarly pursuits. Stanley himself, at first attracted to poetry, gradually turned to translation and philosophy. Others in the coterie who wrote concentrated on translation or poetry. And once Shirley established himself as a schoolmaster, he became involved in writing Latin grammars (and perhaps some translating at well) and chose not to thrust a comfortable living aside for the vagaries of the stage. Coupled with this is the recognition that an old rival, Davenant, remained the rising star once the theatres reopened at the Restoration. That Shirley could prepare formal masques or presentations as occasional pieces is clear from his publications during these years. But his associations gradually strayed from the professional dramatists; those most closely associated with him had died.

The publication of his *Via ad Latinam* suggests that Shirley was teaching again. His school was in the precinct of Whitefriars. Thomas Dingley, who during the reign of Charles II compiled a book on teaching in London, recorded James Shirley as "a famous Poet my Schoolm^r" at Whitefriars in the war years.[18] Anthony à Wood notes that some time after 1651 and before 1660 David Whitford was Shirley's usher (assistant) "in the White-friars near Fleet-street in London." Wood names John Lackenby as another usher in Shirley's employment. Concerning Lackenby, who had been made B.A. from Magdalen College in 1643, we get information that bears on Shirley's religious sympathies during this time. Originally from County Durham, Lackenby had lived at St. Edmund's Hall as a student until the garrison surrendered in 1646. Then, Wood says, he went abroad, "perceiving the English church tottering . . . changed his religion, and was entered into the English coll. at Doway." He later returned to England and served as usher to Shirley "when he [Shirley] taught in the White Fryers at London in the time of Oliver. . . ."[19] The Vestry Minutes for the parish of St. Bride's notes that on May 14, 1652, there was an "order for ye buildinge of a Schoolehouse in ye spare place in ye backe churchyard" on the south side; a note is entered, stating that it would "bring in a handsome rent for laying out a small sum. . . ."[20] Perhaps this was to be Shirley's school. The business of the precinct of Whitefriars, which had no parish church, was included in registers for St. Bride's. And in 1651 Shirley testified before the Committee on Compounding that he lived in the parish of St. Bride's.[21]

The parish and precinct where Shirley would spend the last fifteen or more years of his life was a relatively small area with many inhabitants—at least until the Great Fire in 1666. According to the parish Vestry Minutes, a survey taken in 1651 showed that St. Bride's parish contained 510 able families, 870 poor families, 1160 poor children, and 168 "families that receive." Even before the fire, the plague would take the lives of thousands. By the summer of 1665 plague that had begun the previous winter in the parishes northwest of the city had spread over a broad area, bringing the total number of deaths up to 7,000.[22]

When Shirley came before the Committee on Compounding on February 4, 1651, he gave no reference to his occupation; he called himself "gent," presently living in St. Bride's. He admitted adhering to the Royalist cause and assisting in it. Officially he petitioned to compound, noting that he had never been sequestered. That was probably because he had no goods or property valued above £100. He claims to be worth only £6, including household goods and wearing apparel. The typical fee, one-sixth of a man's estate, would mean a fine of £1 and that is the fee Shirley entered and paid the following day. His entry, numbered 3039, he duly recorded and signed. He was thereby free of all further fines.[23]

Shirley appears a poor man, yet when he made his will in 1666 he had acquired a comfortable living, as his bequests indicate.[24]

Some time before 1655, Shirley married Frances Blackburne. No entry for the marriage has been found in the extant parish registers. Beginning in 1653 civil marriage ceremonies were solemnized by the Protectorate and a fee charged for entry of the ceremony in a parish register.[25] It is probable that Shirley, as a Roman Catholic, would have used a priest of that faith to perform any religious ceremony that may have been added to the civil one. The situation supports the suggestion that the marriage took place between 1653 and 1655. Frances was sister to John Blackburne, a citizen and merchant taylor of London. Shirley had again chosen for a wife a woman from the mercantile class. And again the family appears affluent—Frances perhaps brought to the marriage a comfortable dowry—showing the effects of a good income. John Blackburne's will, dated April 29, 1655, bequeathed his seal ring (which had been his father's) to his nephew and £400 to Richard Poulton, husband of his daughter, Mary, and left money for the poor of two London parishes. It was Mary Poulton who was named to prove the playwright's will after the death of Shirley and his wife. Frances Shirley was a witness to her brother's will and was given 20s. to buy a ring. The will was probated in London on June 19, 1655.[26] Because the playwright is not named, we can suppose that they had not been married long or that Frances was not in financial straits.

Some years later, on June 6, 1660, Frances Shirley was called upon to give testimony in a Chancery Court case involving a dispute over houses situated in "Googe Alley in Shoolane in the parish of St. Bridgett als Brides London." In her deposition, she states that she is the "wife of James Shirley of the Precinct of Whitefryers London, gent, aged 60 years and upwards." Most interesting is her revelation that she was the widow of one Richard Ellis when a judgment was awarded to the defendents in the current case, Bradshaw and Ashurst, against the personal estate of Richard Ellis, valued at around £34. The interrogation refers to houses or tenements in Googe Alley sold by Arthur and Ursula Knight in 1651 to John Rickman, but Bradshaw and Ashurst had gotten possession of the tenements through a judgment won in court against Knight, Richard Ellis, and Richard Brett. Rickman began the suit against Bradshaw and Ashurst in 1659; it was resolved in 1662.[27] Francis Blackburne Ellis apparently was a widow some time after 1651 and had lived in the parish of St. Bride's for several years. Perhaps her estate consisted of property in the area, for the deposition indicates that Richard Ellis was not a rich man. Again, it suggests that the Blackburne side of the family was the more comfortable financially.

During this period, Shirley not only wrote and published grammar books while teaching but also published private masques and dramatizations written earlier. While the public theatre was closed, publication of plays was permissible, and there were private presentations. *Honoria and Mammon,* printed in 1652, was an extension of a piece called *Honour and Riches* that Shirley had published in 1633 with a dedication to Edward Golding.[28] The later version has none of the conventional marks of a masque—music, song, scenery, dance. It seems as close to a play as Shirley could get without calling it one. Despite the allegorical names given to some of the characters, Shirley manages to make their conversation and persons more realistic than a strict allegorical personification would allow. The moral remains the same in both versions: Honor (Lady Honoria) bestows herself on the true scholar (Alworth), and money (Lady Mammon) is paired off with power (Conquest). In his preface "to the candid reader," Shirley declares: "It . . . is like to be the last, for in my resolve, nothing of this nature shall, after this, engage either my pen or invention."[29] Can we presume that Shirley kept to his resolution and that all the dramatic pieces that appeared in print after 1652 had been written at an earlier time? The composition of another masque, *Cupid and Death,* published in 1653 and, according to the title page, presented before the "Embassadour of Portugal, Upon the 26 of March, 1653,"[30] could have fallen on either side of 1652. A copy of a manuscript version accompanying another private presentation, at the Military Grounds in Leicesterfields in 1659, belonged to Matthew Locke—later composer for Charles II—who together with Christopher Gibbons had composed music for the Leicesterfields showing, so the manuscript informs us. It notes that the story of the masque had come from John Ogilby's version of Aesop's *Fables,* published in 1651.[31] Shirley was familiar with Ogilby's translation, for he wrote commendatory verses when the work was published. The version that the Portuguese ambassador witnessed could therefore have been written at any time between 1651—or before, if Shirley had seen Ogilby's work in manuscript or discussed it with him—and 1653. Shirley consented to a second printing of the masque because, he says, no sooner was the first out than another version appeared "with an addition before it . . . by another hand. . . ." This implies that the edition of 1659 "corrected" some other version published soon after 1653.[32]

In the story of *Cupid and Death,* as taken apparently from Ogilby's work, the arrows of Death are switched with those of Cupid without the knowledge of either. This little masque depicts a world gone wrong, with love causing death and death turning enemies into lovers. If the masque is primarily an occasional piece, its moral commentary crosses political lines. Shirley attacks the nobility for its folly and yet, at a time when Cromwell and the citizenry are in power, denounces a world out of order. The character of Nature laments that tradition and natural rule are gone; Mercury comes to set it right. Shirley then returns to lecture the nobility when he urges that it be guided by will rather than capriciousness. The piece represents Shirley's habit of balancing his moral judgments.[33]

The dramas in *Six New Plays,* published in 1653 by Humphrey Moseley and Humphrey Robinson jointly, were among the plays written earlier that Shirley put out during the 1650's, possibly to raise money for his school and surely to support his family. All of the plays in the volume display individual title pages dated 1652 except for *The Court Secret,* "Never Acted, But prepared for the Scene at Black-Friars," which carried the date of 1653. The other plays, *The Imposture, The Brothers, The Sisters, The Doubtful Heir,* and *The Cardinal,* all had been performed at the private Blackfriars playhouse. Each play carries a separate dedication.[34]

It is puzzling that the dedication of Shirley's finest tragedy, and a play he asserted to be "the best of my flock," was to a man identified only as "G.B., Esq." Presumably he was well known to those who would read the plays and needed no other identification. His identity now can only be conjecture. Charles Forker, in his edition of *The Cardinal,* suggests George Buck, who wrote verses to Shirley on the production of his *Poems* in 1646.[35] Yet the dedication implies that Shirley had only recently met G.B.; and by 1653 the George Buck of the commendatory verses had been Shirley's friend for at least seven years, or, if the George Buck who had lived in St. Bride's parish in the 1640's, he had been dead since 1647.[36] Since all of the other people the playwright chose to receive dedications are of impressive lineage, "G.B., Esq." would more likely represent the son of a nobleman who could expect to inherit his father's title. The only person of known association with Shirley whose name matches those initials is George, Lord Berkeley, well known as a patron, to whom Shirley had dedicated *The Young Admiral* in 1637. That dedication makes it clear that the playwright did not know Lord Berkeley, although he would like to. A "Geo. Berkly Esq. the Lord Berkeley his son" is entered in 1646 as owing £300 to the Committee for Advance of Money. Clearly G.B. was a man of some importance with whom Shirley hoped to establish a profitable association.[37]

Shirley's dedication of *The Imposture* to Sir Robert Bolles, Bart., speaks of Sir Robert's tastes in learning and in music. The author asserts that the play "may march in the first rank of my own compositions; . . ." and so dedicates it to Bolles "as acknowledgment of your late obligation upon me . . . ."[38] Possibly Bolles had acted as patron to Shirley. Sir Robert, holder of an M.A. from Cambridge, Baronet since 1648, had been assessed £800 by the Committee for Advance of Money in 1646, but apparently his estate was "vacated" by order of the Committee the following February.[39]

The dedication of *The Sisters* to William Paulet, Esquire, was the result perhaps of an earlier acquaintance with Lady Jane Pawlet, Marchioness of Winchester, about whom Shirley had written an elegy on her death in 1631. Lady Jane was the daughter of Thomas, Viscount Savage and related to Henry, Earl of Holland, both some time patrons of Shirley.[40] Since Shirley refers to Paulet's "name that continues bright and impassible among the constellations in our sphere of English honour . . . ,'' we can assume he is related to that noble family.[41] A William Paulett, son of Thomas, second brother of the Marquis of Winchester, is listed in the Visitations of Somersetshire in 1623 with a notation that William was the only child living of his father's issue.[42] He is listed among those claiming to the funds that Charles II gave for the relief of officers who had supported the Royalist cause in the Civil Wars.[43] He had apparently served in the counties of London and Westminster, so possibly Shirley did not meet him until after the wars in London. Several Wm. Paulets were admitted to the Inns of Court. In his dedication, Shirley refers to other noblemen who had lost their fortunes in the civil wars, especially those who went abroad—possibly an allusion to the Marquis of Winchester.[44]

Shirley may have taught Sir Edmund Bowier when Bowier was a child if we are to take his remark literally in his dedication of *The Doubtful Heir* that Shirley had "read excellent characters of you when you writ but a small letter . . . ,'' but has not seen Sir Edmund since and is not certain that he ever saw the play performed.[45] Shirley, then, seems to be talking about an acquaintance before the Civil Wars and the cessation of stage performances. In 1633 Bowier had been knighted and succeeded to his uncle's estate at Camberwell, Surrey.[46] His property, along with that of others, was sequestered in 1648 "to be used for support and payment of guards of horse attending Parliament until £5000 could be raised." In that same year an order for his apprehension was issued for being in arms against the Parliament.[47] A case was brought against "Sir Edmond Bowyer, Knight,'' and others in the Court of Chancery on November 24, 1652. The case concerned the terms of the will of Joyce Byne regarding lands in Newington, Surrey, and the rents. The bill does not give the address of Sir Edmund but Chancery cases generally were heard in Westminster. Shirley may have met Sir Edmund through Richard Lovelace, part of the coterie group, since Lovelace's brother, who published the poet's *Lucasta* a second time, inscribed a copy to Bowier as "the worthiest of friends . . . ." Bowier had written verses for the first edition of *Lucasta*.[48]

Shirley dedicated *The Court Secret,* included as one of the *Six New Plays* gathered together for publication, to William Wentworth, Lord Strafford's only son. He had known the young man as a child; William was ten years old when Shirley arrived in Ireland. John Evelyn in his diary mentions visiting Wentworth at his lodging in the Middle Temple in 1653,[49] so Shirley may have renewed his acquaintance with the young man through associations he kept through membership in the Stanley circle. Earlier, Wentworth had been abroad in France; Evelyn mentions visiting him at Calais in 1650.[50] An entry appears in *Mercurius Politicus* for the week of July 14-21, 1653, dated from Copenhagen on June 25: "My Lord Wentworth is here at present from his pretend Monarch, Charles Stuart, with great applause and state."[51] By August he was back in England, according to the entries in Evelyn's *Diary.*

Shirley's premier patron during these years, Thomas Stanley, received the dedication of *The Brothers.* When "I considered my obligation to your favours," says the gratified playwright, "I was still deterred by their greatness and number. . . ." He had intended to dedicate the play to Stanley "after its birth," but only now has gotten the boldness to do so.[52] Bentley argues that this claim of having considered an earlier dedication to Stanley helps to identify *The Brothers* with *The Politique Father*, licensed in May 1641, for in 1626 when another *Brothers* was licensed Stanley would only have been one year old.[53] Shirley was more indebted to Stanley than to anyone else during these lean years for financial support and for enabling him to meet many potential patrons. From 1646 onward through at least 1654, Stanley kept chambers in the Inns of Court and many of the people to whom Shirley dedicated his plays lived in or near the area and presumably knew Stanley.[54]

What might have been the point of Shirley's writing separate dedications for each of six plays bound and issued together in one volume? The time and circumstances of the playwright argue that he was seeking not merely patrons but funds. A person to whom a poem or play was dedicated might pay the author of the work twenty to thirty pounds. In some instances, however, dedicating a play was the only means the playwright had to acknowledge publicly his obligations and indebtedness to those who had befriended him so handsomely.[55] It is likely that those to whom he dedicated his plays had contributed to his school, making it possible for him to write and teach once again.

John Ogilby, one of Shirley's oldest and closest associates, was one of several writers for whom Shirley was writing commendatory poems. It is said that David Whitford, one of Shirley's ushers at his school in Whitefriars, had taught Ogilby Greek. In the 1640's Ogilby began translations from Latin and Greek, and in 1651 he published his translation of the *Fables* of Aesop. Shirley's verses refer to his late blooming: "whilst thou emergent from the night,/Like Days new Soveraign, has discover'd more,/ Than all their revolutions shew'd before." Shirley exhorts Ogilby to "Awake that Poem, born from thy own flame," but we have no evidence that Ogilby ever published his own work.[56]

A passage in Shirley's poem for Richard Brome's *A Jovial Crew: or, The Merry Beggars,* published in 1652, suggests (along with other friends who wrote commendatory verses for the piece) that the Stationers Company created some problems with its publication:

> This Comedy . . . without a praise
> Begg'd by the stationer, who, with strength
>   of purse
> And pens, takes care to make his book
>   sell worse . . . .[57]

Shirley predicts that the play will endure and that "he,/That dares despise, may after envie thee." It appears, at any rate, that the play had come under criticism, directed perhaps at the author's lack of formal education, for Shirley insists that it is knowledge of humankind that makes a good playwright, not whether the author has studied the arts. Brome's wit, he says, is made of stronger metal, while the small minds who make a loud noise go out like faggots in a quick-burning fire. This poem, which expresses so strongly the antagonism Shirley felt towards attacks on his friend, may reveal as well antagonism on his own part towards newer writers—or perhaps the more popular Davenant and Killigrew.

Two acquaintances not known to have been connected earlier with the dramatist also had verses from Shirley commending their published work. It may have been the personal situation of Major Wright, who translated the Bishop of Bellay's history and published it in 1650 as *Loving Enemie,* that inspired Shirley to write verses for him. The title page of the piece asserts that Wright did the work while imprisoned.[58] A Captain Wright, in fact, was imprisoned in Pendennis Castle in June 1649 after being taken at sea, where he was "bound for Ireland to serve the enemy." The following August, a Major Wright and others were committed to Newgate for levying war against the Commonwealth.[59] So we may assume that Shirley's Major Wright was active in the Royalist cause; perhaps he was a fellow Catholic. In 1655 he published *The Civil Wars of Spain,* a translation from P. de Sandoval.[60] Edmund Prestwich published in 1651 his translation of Seneca's story of Hippolitus. Shirley's verses to him remark that when Prestwich writes his own love poetry, he is even better.[61] This friend also wrote a play called *The Hectors, Or False Challenge,* printed in 1656, which contains specific references to events of the time.[62] Prestwich may have been a part of the little group of Royalist poets and writers who gathered together in the darkest years of the Civil War and later received encouragement and support from Thomas Stanley.

In 1655 Shirley published two plays he had written for the Queen's company at the Salisbury Court theatre, *The Gentlemen of Venice* and *The Politician.*[63] On a Houghton Library copy of the two plays bound together is the notation that *The Gentleman of Venice* was "Acted at Salisbury Court 30 Oct. 1639." Probably the play was written and acted in Dublin before that year. The dedication in 1655 is to Sir Thomas Nightingale, Baronet. In it Shirley refers to the play "upon the first return home..." which rather clearly indicates that it been missing (at least from his possession) for some time.[64] Sir Thomas became a Baronet in l645 and perhaps was living in London then. Two letters written by Nightingale are in the manuscripts of George Alan Lowndes, Esq. Both give no date but the content implies each was written during the war years. In the second he complains of high levies (fifth part of men's estates in lands and a twentieth part of goods) and refers to his sons, one at sea and the other at the Inns of Court.[65] Some years later, on May 26, 1663, one of those sons had succeeded to the title, for a Sir Thomas Nightingale gave testimony in a Chancery case, giving his address as Clavering Park in the County of Essex, "Baronet aged 32 yeares and upwards." The interrogation refers to "Edward Nightingale, late of Greys Inn in the county of Middlesex, gent," and his part in securing a lease for a group of gentlemen in County Surrey.[66] It was perhaps the elder son who was the recipient of Shirley's dedication.

Another bid for patronage was directed to Walter Moyle, Esquire. In the dedication of *The Politician,* Shirley commends Moyle for his love of drama unstained by profanity or "impudence." Just as when he published *Honoria and Mammon* in 1652 he had vowed to write no more dramatic pieces, so Shirley in this dedication asserts, "For my own part, this is the last which is like to salute the public view in this kind; and I . . . conclude with so judicious a patron."[67]

On a Houghton Library copy of *The Politician,* a leaf is inserted with a note in modern hand which states: "Arthur Moyle was the son of Robert Moyle, Esq. of the inner temple; and died the 24th of May 1660 at the age of 31 and was buried in the church of west Twyford in Middlesex, where there is an inscription in his memory."[68] In the State Papers for 1635-36 a letter from the King to Attorney General Bankes directs a bill to be prepared in behalf of Robert Moyle, third prothonotary at the Court of Common Pleas, assuring the office to Walter Moyle, eldest son of Robert.[69] Again, Shirley's acquaintance seems to have been related to the Inns of Court. The connection between the playwright and Walter Moyle becomes more concrete with the revealing testimony of Standerdine Shirley in a court case brought to the Court of Chancery on October 8, 1667. Standerdine Shirley "of the parish of St. Andrews, Holborn, London, gent, aged 50 years or thereabouts" states that he knew Walter Moyle for around ten years before his death on May 24, 1660.[70] In his profession as barber surgeon, Standerdine Shirley undoubtedly met many people to whom the dramatist was also introduced. Perhaps Standerdine Shirley served as Moyle's physician.

The Constant Maid, originally published in 1640 and probably written in Ireland, appeared in a second printing in l66l with the title *Love Will Finde Out the Way.*[71] The edition gives the author as "T.B.," which possibly refers to the actor Theophilus Bird. This mistaken attribution of the work to Bird, according to Andrew Reimer, results from an epilogue the actor added to the work; the compositor saw this and carried the initials to the title page, since preliminary matter customarily was set in type last.[72] Richard Whitaker, the publisher in 1640, gives no information about the company who performed the piece; there is no record of its being acted in London or owned by the Queen's Men, and Whitaker published it with *St. Patrick for Ireland,* which we know to be a work Shirley did for Ireland, indicating the 1640 edition was a Dublin play. But Theophilus Bird, so far as is known, did not venture to Dublin, and by 1640 he was a member of the King's Company in London. Perhaps the play had been readied in London to be performed during the time Shirley was in Ireland and Bird had written an epilogue for that expected performance; the 1661 publisher, Samuel Speed, may have been using a prompt copy carrying Bird's addition. This later edition asserts that the actors were the Queen's Men, performing at the Phoenix in Drury Lane.[73] Can we suspect that since the 1640 edition had no apparent connection with that company there was an even earlier version, perhaps with the title *Love Will Finde Out the Way?* Andrew Reimer thinks so. He notes a number of variations between the 1640 edition and that of 1661. The character of Sir Pol Davis appears only in the later version and some lines are identical to lines in *The Lady of Pleasure,* which was written in l635. Did these materials come from a script preceding *The Constant Maid?* It is possibly for this version, we may add, that Theophilus Bird, perhaps then a member of the Queen's Men, wrote the epilogue. Reimer suggests that the plague and the use of a mock king kept the original *Love Will Finde Out the Way* from being performed. Shirley may have taken it with him to Ireland and there turned it into *The Constant Maid or, Love Will Finde Out the Way.*[74]

Another dramatization appeared in print in 1659, *The Contention of Ajax and Ulysses for the Armour of Achilles.* Based on material in Ovid's *Metamorphoses,* it apparently was an occasional piece. The author notes that it was ". . . nobly represented by young Gentlemen of quality, at a private Entertainment of some persons of Honour."[75] The work probably was written and presented at the request of a patron such as Thomas Stanley or the Earl of Newcastle. Nothing in the piece gives a clue to events of the time that could suggest a date of composition. Shirley follows Ovid rather closely, but the introductory material—the quarrel between the servants of the two antagonists vying for Achilles' armour—is original, as is the comic relief interspersed within exchanges between Ajax and Ulysses, notably in the person of Thersander, a member of the council of Greeks, who falls asleep and confuses the two antagonists. Shirley also puts Ajax into an exchange concerning the outcome of the decision to give the armour to Ulysses. Shirley's best known poem, "The glories of our blood and state. . ." concludes the piece.[76]

The Contention, bound with *Honoria and Mammon,* includes an interesting engraving of Shirley dated 1658. Perhaps the engraver, R. Gaywood, knew the portrait of Shirley that Wood in the 1690's would refer to as hanging in the Bodleian Library. The engraving, at any rate, seems clearly based on the Bodleian portrait. An engraving dated 1646 that appeared with the publication of Shirley's *Poems* was by W. Marshall. It is unlike the portrait and the later engraving: Shirley wears no cap, the clothing is a loose robe with a wide, white collar, and the work includes no coat of arms, as do the later engraving and portrait. Both engravings, however, show a mole, unlike the portrait. The 1653 volume of *Six New Plays* again shows the Marshall engraving. This suggests that the Bodleian portrait and the Gaywood engraving both were executed after 1653 and before or in 1658. Had the portrait or the later engraving been available in 1653, surely the earlier engraving would not have been used in that volume.[77]

Shirley issued two more grammar books during this last period, in 1656 *The Rudiments of Grammar* and in 1660 *Manductio,* an enlargement. Both were published by Richard Lowndes, whose shop was in St. Paul's Churchyard.[78] Obviously written for his students, they are added evidence that Shirley was actively engaged in schoolteaching. As late as 1662 he was designated a schoolmaster. On August 18 of that year he assented in his own hand to the Bill of Uniformity, which required all preachers and teachers to subscribe to everything contained in the Book of Common Prayer. The entry reads: "Jacobus Shirleuis^{MA}: olim admissus ad exequendum officium Ludimagistri, im Whitefryers London."[79]

There is also a possibility that during the 1650's Shirley went abroad. The State Papers for January 1658 include a notation that *"The Foresight* in Margate Road [Kent] has seized 5 very suspicious persons from Holland; . . ." The message comes from *The London* at Downs, located on the Coast about ten miles north of Dover; it is directed to the Admiralty Commissioners and written by Sir Richard Stayner. Two days later Stayner gave more details: "I have sent up the Hawk ketch as high as the Tower, with Hen. Finch, related to Lord Finch, Jas. Shirley, Albertus Twing, Jno. Wainwright, and Geo. Kempt, who were seized as suspicious persons on coming from Flushing; . . ."[80] On April 27, 1655 Shirley's eldest son, Mathias, had been granted a pass to go to Holland.[81] Many young men who were Catholic crossed the sea, some of them posing as merchants' factors or sailors, and frequently they left no official records of their whereabouts or activities.[82] If Mathias Shirley went to Europe, possibly the playwright visited him there. It is possible, of course, that James Shirley the dramatist went abroad with pupils or with patrons, visiting Catholic centers and Royalist exiles, notably his old patron, the Earl of Newcastle. We know, however, from the preface to the reissue of *Cupid and Death* in 1659 that he consented to the printing, and we may presume that he was then in London.[83]

Hen[eage?] Finch, one of the people apprehended with "Jas. Shirley," had gotten on May 13, 1656 a warrant to go to Holland with one servant. He was related to the more famous Sir John, Lord Finch of Fordwich, who had become Lord Keeper in April 1640 and upon his impeachment eight months later fled to The Hague, staying abroad until the Restoration. Sir John was a friend of the Earl of Newcastle and Endymion Porter and had many dealings in Spanish foreign affairs.[84] George Kempt (Kempe), another passenger on the ship that carried "Jas. Shirley," was a known Catholic. Educated at St. Omer's and ordained at the Roman College at Rome in 1651, he worked as a Catholic agent and as agent for continental Royalists. Kempt, who took many aliases, was the son of John and Lucy Kempe of London, middle-class Catholics. At age 19 he had become a Jesuit, taking his oaths in 1646.[85] A man by the name of John Wainwright appears in the subsidy rolls as early as 1625 under both St. Dunstan's (East) and St. Bride's parish, assessed in lands £10/60 and £10/40. Probably he was the John Wainwright from County Derby, included among claimants to Charles II's grant of compensation for Royalist service, who may have known Shirley during the dramatist's stay in Nottinghamshire. If he comes from County Derby, that John Wainwright had been excommunicated for nonconformity. Capt. Stayner seems to have come upon a party of Catholics and Royalists who had been abroad perhaps to promote the cause of monarchy and Catholicism in England.[86]

English Catholics were often transported from secret points to Calais. Younger ones might go to St. Omer's or Douai for their education. Many, perhaps most, upper-class Catholic Royalists in the Civil Wars had studied or traveled abroad in their early years, and Flanders with its Catholic colleges and seminaries was a gathering place for this important minority within English society. Walter Montague, prominent in the court and activities of Queen Henrietta Maria before the Civil Wars, for example, headed a religious house north of Paris and maintained a Catholic faction of Royalists during the Civil Wars.[87]

Shirley would find himself during the 1650's in a familiar if precarious position because of his Royalist and Catholic sympathies. As early as 1650 the Long Parliament required all persons over eighteen to take an oath of loyalty to the Commonwealth. Money was the great problem for Royalists and for Catholics in the face of numerous fines: sequestration for adhering to the King, weekly fines for non-attendance at church (recusancy), levies for the support of the militia. Even the Act of Oblivion on February 24, 1652, did not cancel fines for delinquency. In 1655 all Cavaliers worth over £100 in property a year were required to pay one tenth of their income to support new militia. The sequestration of property created a new gentry of citizens, soldiers, and public creditors, who were often paid in lands and goods seized from Royalists' estates.[88] Even in 1663, it seems Shirley had been assessed for the militia tax in the precinct of Whitefriars. The list includes his name along with three other familiar ones: Mr. Powell, Mr. Stanley, and Mr. Hall. Shirley apparently owned some property at this time, for he was assessed 5/6d. for lands and 1s. as an inhabitant of the precinct.[89]

Towards the end of the 1650's, some public entertainment began again. The diarist John Evelyn, for instance, notes that on his way to London in September 1657 he saw the famous Turkish rope dancer and a bearded lady. In May of 1659 he attended a new opera with recitative music and scenes but was much disappointed with it.[90] The following year a Thomas Lilleston had been required to answer a charge of acting a public stage play on February 4 at the Cockpit in Drury Lane.[91] But in July 1660, after the return of Charles Stuart, a vast entertainment was staged for the King, the Duke of York, the Duke of Gloucester, and the Lords and Commons of Parliament. The city of London, as sponsor, paid about £ 5,000 for the show.[92] Shirley was not a part of this revival, and few of his plays were featured in the repertories of William Davenant's new company (the Duke's Men) or Thomas Killigrew's troupe (the King's Men). These new owners of acting companies took the plays held by earlier acting groups and selected those to their taste for presentation.[93] On December 12, 1660, August 20, 1668, and January 12, 1669, Davenant and William Beeston drew up ownership lists of plays, each list designating some of the plays as belonging to Davenant and some as Killigrew's.[94] In the 1660 list Davenant included among his plays the dramas the Cockpit had owned in 1639, and three of these are by Shirley; the catalog of August 1668 adds another of Shirley's plays, and the list dated several months later picks up still another.[95]

A book of epigrams published in 1651 by Samuel Sheppard contains a reference to Shirley as bowing to the popularity of "the most excellent Poet, Sir Wm. Davenant." and reads in part:

> What though some shallow Sciolists dare prate,
> And scoffing thee; *Apollo* nauseate:
> What *Venus* hath snatch'd from thee, cruelly,
> Minerva, with advantage doth supply:
> *Johnson* is dead; let *Sherly* stoope to Fate,
> And thow alone, art Poet Lawreate.[96]

In the Restoration Shirley, the representative of an age preceding the era of heroic tragedy and comedy of manners, was in fact again passed over for the honor of poet laureate. His publications in the later years are earlier pieces; and he asserts in prefaces to his publications in 1652 and 1655 that he will write no more. *Amores,* a volume of poems that Philip Jenkins published in 1660, includes verses lavishly praising Shirley:

> ...Thou has reedified the falling stage,
> And once more built the theatre with thy pen,
> In spite of foes, hast made it live again; ...[97]

But these lines were composed quite likely back in 1652, to be included as commentary verses with the publication of Shirley's *Six New Plays.*

Possibly the last poem Shirley wrote was an ode composed "Upon the Happy Return of King Charles II to his Languishing Nations, May 29, 1660."[98] After welcoming King Charles, he turns to address the people. He treats in turn the Dutch, indifferent to the politics of England, so long as they can fish in the coastal waters; the Irish, who did not join the rebellion; the Scots, considered traitors for surrendering Charles I to the Parliamentary forces; the Welsh, remaining true to the crown; and last the Spanish, now at peace with England, opening the way for freedom of trade and of the seas.

Still, Shirley's fortunes improved with the return of the monarchy. That his school was large enough to include two assistants on its staff suggests that he was now able to support himself as schoolmaster. And he probably received a share of the recompense planned for those Royalists who had served as officers in the wars. His will gives further indication that his finances had improved.

Dated July 1666, the original draft was written most probably in Shirley's own hand. The copy will, with a number of deletions and changes, was entered in the probate records on November 3, 1666.[99] A reference to Shirley's daughter, Lawrinda, in the holograph will as "now wife of" Edward Fountain, has been struck out and "relict" inserted above it, which would mean that Edward Fountain died some time between July and early November. A portion that would pass on to Lawrinda one piece of plate marked and three silver spoons is crossed out, as is a section providing for Shirley's son Christopher to receive one piece of plate marked and the remainder of the playwright's wearing apparel in addition to £100, and a provision leaving six silver spoons to his daughter Mary. A section forgiving Mary's husband Standerdine Shirley alias Sachell all former debts is pared down to one particular debt of £50 and "all former debts." And there is a larger portion of the draft that has been deleted in transferring this amended holograph will to the copy entry:

> I give to Mstrs. Mary Poulton now wife of Mr. Richard Poulton of Epney [Upney] in Essex [left blank] to buy her a ring. I give to Mr. Robert Sturges of Whitefryers the summe of [left blank] I give to the poore of the parish of St. Dunstan's in the West five pounds to be disposed and distributed according the prudence of my executrix. And further my will is that I do give and bequeath that all the residue of my estate and whatsoever shall remaine in any kind whatsoever herein not disposed of and not bequeathed by me formerly in this my present will bequest first being paid shall remaine with my loving wife Frances . . . (after the discharge of my debts, funerall charges, and payment of my the bequests abovesaide).

This holograph will has a broad "†" at the top of the first page, a common mark of a cross made on such documents, especially by Catholics.[100] There are no witnesses named to the will or to the document as corrected. Changes made on the holograph, such as the word "relict," showing Lawrinda a widow, appear to be in a different hand.

Do the changes mean that Shirley's generosity waned? Circumstances offer a likelier explanation. The overwhelming event was the Great Fire of early September. On the night of September 2, 1666, a Sunday, a fire began in Pudding Lane. It spread to East London, blotted out most of the city inside the walls, and worked its way to Shirley's area of Fleet Street. The conflagration raged for over three days. Evelyn in his *Diary* describes what he saw when he went on horseback on September 4 to survey the devastation: "all Fleetstreete, old baily, Ludgate Hill, Warwick Lane, Newgate, Paules chaine, Wattling-streete now flaming & most of it reduc'd to ashes . . . ." Three days later he traveled afoot "with great difficulty" because the ground was so hot it burned the soles of his shoes "& put me all over in Sweate . . . ."[101] By the time the fire subsided, 436 acres had been burned and 89 churches, along with over 13,000 houses, reduced to ashes.[102] The flight of Shirley and his wife to escape the fire which destroyed his goods and property was the primary reason for changes in the will. The will makes no mention of property other than movable goods. Yet Shirley was assessed in 1663 for a Whitefriars militia tax as "landlord."[103] Mary Poulton, who administered Shirley's will, could not carry out the bequests that had vanished; and mention of her bequest too is crossed through.[104]

Some of the people other than relatives mentioned in the will are friends not known to have been earlier associates of Shirley. Robert Sturges of Whitefriars, whose name is given and then eliminated, died before Shirley's will was in probate and before the playwright himself: "for burial of Robert Sturgis in the Churchyard [of St. Dunstan's in the West] the Churchwardens gave...the ground" on August 5, 1666, entering a fee of 1s.[105] Probably Shirley and Sturges were friends for many years. As early as November 1652 in a Chancery Court case Robert Sturges identified himself as "of High Holborne in the County of Middlesex gent aged 63 yeares or thereabouts." And on June 28, 1665, he again testified in a court case, noting that he was "of White fryers London gent aged 80 yeares or thereabouts."[106]

John Vincent Cane, Shirley's "loving friend," to whom the will leaves £20, had studied for a few years at Cambridge, travelled to Europe, and entered a Franciscan monastery at Douai. In 1661 he published *Fiat Lux,* arguing for England's return to the Roman Church, and an enlarged edition appeared the following year. Cane spent much of his life in London. As was common among Catholic activists, he had several aliases: Bodwill, John Baptist, or simply "JVC" among them. In an article on Shirley's connection with Cane, Aline M. Taylor suggests that Cane was Shirley's confessor. Shirley omitted "John" from his name, perhaps as a legal safeguard, and referred to him as "Mr.," a customary public use among Catholics. The vagueness of the description of the bequest may imply some religious use that Shirley deemed unsafe to mention: "to be Disposed by him according to a former agreement betwixt Us."[107]

John Warter of the Inner Temple was a close enough acquaintance for the will to speak of him as Shirley's "worthy friend." Perhaps Shirley's "Epithalamium to Mr. I.W." is to John Warter rather than to the angler, Izaac Walton, although there is a marriage entry for Walton to Ann Keen of St. James, Clerkenwell, County Middlesex in 1647.[108] Two pieces of court testimony by Warter place him as Shirley's friend. In November 1660, he notes his address as the Inner Temple and identifies himself as a gentleman aged 40; similarly, on January 18, 1663, he gives the same information prior to his testimony, noting his age as "43 years or thereabouts."[109]

All of the friends mentioned were presumably connected with the business of the Inns of Court, long time associates who shared with Shirley his scholarly and literary interests. Striking, too, is the narrow circumference of place in which most of Shirley's world and his activities was centered, a tiny and crowded section just outside the city of London. Despite his travel and the wide range of his associations, his memberships in the various literary circles and coteries, most of his friendships and work ultimately can be traced to the area where he began his literary career—the Inns of Court.

Shirley's family continued within the prosperous burgher class that had given him birth and upbringing, a class that his plays with their aristocratic audience can view satirically and yet with critical openness toward its more virtuous representatives. In a will dated October 7, 1678, Standerdine Shirley—there is no reference to "Sachell"—does not mention his occupation of barber-surgeon, calling himself only "gent." The playwright's son-in-law gives generously to the poor of three parishes—Whitefriars, Islington, and Clerkenwell. He also bequeaths rings or money to both James and Christopher Shirley, whom he names his brothers-in-law, and mentions "james Shirley the younger" who was to be given £20 and to enter an apprenticeship when he came of age.[110] The will of the playwright's son Christopher, dated January 29, 1697, states that he is a barber-surgeon and lives in the parish of St. Andrews, Holborn. He bequeaths £80 to his niece Elizabeth Whitehead and to his other niece Sarah Shirley £20.[111] James, another of Shirley's sons, had been apprenticed to Standerdine Shirley in 1653, as had Christopher.[112] That two of Shirley's sons should enter that employment can be explained by Standerdine's rather profitable living in it. It was also an occupation that attracted many Catholics, since it was one of the professions that did not require a university degree and no Catholics were granted degrees from the universities.[113] For information touching on Mathias we have only his pass to go to Holland, granted in 1655; perhaps he entered religious orders and stayed in Europe. Wood's notation that he gleaned information about Shirley from the playwright's son, "the butler of Furnival's inn, in Holborn, near London,"[114] has not led to any records concerning his name. Certainly when Wood published his work in 1691 Christopher Shirley was still alive, but not, apparently, any other children. At least he does not mention them in his will. James Shirley, the barber surgeon, gave testimony in a Chancery Court case on June 1, 1685, giving his address as "Stonecutter Steete in Shoe Lane in the parish of St. Brides London," and noting that he was a barber "aged 40 years or thereabouts."[115] Such a reference indicates that Elizabeth Shirley must have been living as late as 1645, since none of Shirley's children was the issue of his second wife, Frances.

Wood, who has been proven accurate in much of his account of Shirley, says that the playwright was ". . . overcome with affrightments, disconsolations, and other miseries occasion'd by that fire and their losses, . . ."[116] We may presume that the school, his livelihood, had been burned and with it his home along with manuscripts and other valuables. Both Shirley and his wife "died within the compass of a natural day; whereupon their bodies were buried in one grave in the yeard belonging to the said Church of St. Giles's on the 29 of Octob. . . ."[117] At the time of his death Shirley was seventy years old. The burial entry in the parish register simply states: "Mr. James Sherley" and "Mris. Frances Sherley his wife."[118]

Shirley's death in the aftermath of the Great Fire is fitting to a life that intersected with momentous and calamitous events in the history of England. Born in the last years of the reign of Elizabeth I, he came into a glorious time of literary and commercial achievement; his early years in one of England's finest grammar schools, Merchant Taylors, gave him a grounding in history, language, and literature that was enriched by his years at Cambridge and at Oxford. He suffered the defeat of the Royalist cause, experienced a period of rule by the merchant class in the Commonwealth years, and with a poem greeted the return of a monarch. And while his works seldom refer in detail to political events, they are a commentary on the cultures and manners that attended and further exacerbated the great political conflicts of the age.

Notes

¹The dedication appears in Dyce, *Works,* I, li. The complete title of the grammar is *Via ad Latinam Linguam Complanata. The Way made plain to the Latine Tongue* (London, 1649).

²John H. Jesse, *Memoirs of the Court of England During the Reign of the Stuarts, Incl. the Protectorate* (Philadelphia, 1840), I, 241-43. Philip, given the title Earl of Montgomery, died early in 1650. William's uncle, William, Earl of Pembroke, allegedly had Catholic sympathies; his wife was a known Catholic. See Violet A. Rowe, "The Influence of the Earls of Pembroke on Parliamentary Elections, 1624-41," *EHR,* 50 (1935), 354. A Sir William Herbert appears in a list of suspected recusants dated May 8, 1628. HMC, l3th R, App. I, Portland I, Nalson MSS, 1628-1683, p. 2. In the Diocesan Archives at the Archbishop's House, Westminster, a William Herbert is mentioned frequently as giving money to various priests during the year 1638. Westminster Cathedral MS. "A" Series, 29 (1637-44), Nos. 39, 57, 79; pp. 153, 201, 259.

On the family geneaology, see G. E. C[okayne], *The Complete Peerage* (London, 1910-1959), 10 (1945), 421-22.

³W. W. Greg, *Some Aspects of London Publishing between 1550 and 1650* (Oxford, 1956), pp. 85, 106, 108, 112, 116-17.

⁴Dyce, *Works,* I, xcviii-cv. Town Depositions, Court of Chancery, PRO MS. C24/782, Pt. 2, #23.

⁵Docquet Book, Signet Office Records, PRO MS. IND 6813. According to one early biographer, Ogilby died in 1676 and was buried in St. Bride's. Theophilus Cibber, *The Lives of the Poets of Great Britain and Ireland to the Time of Dean Swift* (London, 1753), II, 266-67; see also Aubrey, *Brief Lives,* II, 99-104 and Bentley, *JCS,* IV, 948-50.

⁶Saltmarsh himself is obscured by a heavy cloud, for although he might be the son of a Saltmarsh family from East Riding in Yorkshire, there is no concrete evidence of such a man living in London in 1649. One Captain Edward Saltmarsh served the Parliamentary cause, and a Mr. Saltmarsh of the Duke's Place was assessed in 1645 for £100 but did not pay the Committee for the Advance of Money. Committee for the Advance of Money, PRO MS. SP19/69, fol. 7. The Yorkshire Saltmarsh family had Catholic leanings; Capt. Edward Saltmarsh later became a Catholic and settled in North Riding, and two of his sons became priests. Hugh Aveling, *Northern Catholics: The Catholic Recusants of the North Riding of Yorkshire 1558-1700* (London, 1966), p. 211. In November 1648, Capt. Saltmarsh petitioned the House of Lords in behalf of his son-in-law, asking that his land not be sequestered for he could not pay.

House of Lords Calendar, HMC, 7th R, Part I, p. 63a. But other than these bits and pieces, it is hard to place the man in a literary context.

[7]The name is variously spelled Langton and Langston. Sir Henry F. Macgeagh and H. S. C. Sturgess, comp., *Register of Admissions to the Honorable Society of the Middle Temple* (London, 1944), I, 129. A Francis Langton was admitted sizar at age 19 to St. John's College, Cambridge, in 1638, son of a yeoman from E. Haddon, Northants. Venn, *Alumni Cantabrigienses,* III, 46. Another with that same name and spelling taught at Magdalen College, Oxford, in the early 1630's. *Cal SP Dom.,* 214, March 19, 1632, No. 84, 290.

[8]Langston may have been a lawyer who was involved in the case of James Corke, plaintiff, and John Dickons, defendant, businessmen involved in shipping cloth, among other merchandise. Town Depositions, Court of Chancery, PRO MS. C224/683, Pt. 2.

[9]SP Dom., PRO MS. SP 29/68, fol. 111.

[10]*Cal. SP Dom.,* 510, 1645-47, 123-24.

[11]Phillips, *Theatrum Poetarum,* ed. Egerton Brydges, 3rd ed. (Geneva, 1824), #51.

[12]"Admissions, 1420-1799," *Lincoln's Inn Admission Register* (1896), I, fol. 24, p. 280; Foster, *Register: Gray's Inn,* fol. 1040, p. 249.

[13]Phillips, *Theatrum Poetarum,* #51.

[14]*Political Ballads Published in England During the Commonwealth,* ed. Thomas Wright, Percy Society Collections, III (London, 1842), I, 67 and *passim.* See also S. Austin Allibone, *A Critical Dictionary of English Literature and British and American Authors* (Philadelphia, 1874), I, 67; Hunter, *Chorus Vatum,* III, 33.

[15]Cuthbert vs Ogle, Town Depositions, Court of Chancery, PRO MS. C24/740.

[16]Town Depositions, Court of Chancery, PRO MS. C24/874, #134, Pt. I.

[17]Bentley, *JCS,* III, 47-48.

[18]Dingley, *History from Marble (Being Ancient and Modern Funeral Monuments) Comp. in the Reign of Charles II,* ed. John Gough Nicholas, Camden Society, I (London, 1866), xiii, 25. Dingley cited Shirley's coat of arms: "paly of 6 or and azure a Canton-/quarter/ermine," an indication that Shirley customarily used his coat of arms or that Dingley had seen the portrait or engraving of Shirley which displays a coat of arms.

[19]Wood, *Fasti,* Part II, IV, col. 57, pp. 101, 229. For his reference to Shirley's school in Whitefriars, see Wood, *Athenae,* III, 738. On Shirley as Catholic schoolmaster, see A. C. F. Beales, *Education Under Penal-*

ty; *English Catholic Education from the Reformation to the Fall of James II, 1547-1689* (London, 1963), p. 207.

[20] Vestry Minutes, 1644-1665, St. Bride's Parish Register, Guildhall MS. 6554/1, fol. 124.

[21] *Calendar of the Proceedings of the Committee for Compounding &c. 1643-1660*, ed. M. A. E. Green (London, 1892), Part IV, p. 2703; see also SP Dom. (Interregnum), PRO MS. 23/321, fols. 55, 56, 60.

[22] Vestry Minutes, 1644-1665, St. Bride's Parish Register, Guildhall MS. 6554/1, fol. 120^V; see also P. H. Boynton, *London in English Literature* (Chicago, 1913), pp. 85-86.

[23] *Calendar . . . Committee on Compounding*, ed. Green, Part IV, p. 2703; Part V, p. lx-lxxxiii and *passim*. See also John J. Schroeder, "London and the Civil Wars," Diss. University of Wisconsin 1954, pp. 204, 209.

[24] See the copy will under Mico 170, PRO. The more detailed holograph will is filed separately but with the same reference.

[25] W. E. Tate, *The Parish Chest* (Cambridge, 1960), pp. 46-48.

[26] John Blackburne's will is under the Prerogative Court of Canterbury (PCC), PRO MS. Aylett 264; the Probate entry is PRO MS. Prob. 11/248.

[27] Rickman vs Bradshaw and Ashurst, Town Depositions, Court of Chancery, PRO MS. C24/845.

[28] Robert S. Forsythe, *The Relation of Shirley's Plays to the Elizabethan Drama* (New York, 1914), pp. 393-98; Enid Welsford, *The Court Masque* (Cambridge, 1927), p. 285.

[29] Dyce, *Works*, VI, 1-84; Bentley, *JCS*, V, 1118-19.

[30] The 1653 copy was printed by T.W. for J. Baker and J. Crooke, booksellers in St. Paul's Churchyard, but a later edition, published in 1659, was issued by Crooke, still in the same location, and Playford, whose shop was located in the area of the Inner Temple. See W. W. Greg, *A List of English Plays Written Before 1643 and Printed Before 1700* (1900; rpt. New York, 1969), #713, p. 829; Bentley, *JCS*, V, 1102-04.

[31] BM Addl. MS. 17,799; see also copies of the masque in the Victoria and Albert Museum, #9136, 9137.

[32] Dyce, *Works*, VI, 343-67; R. G. Howarth, "Shirley's *Cupid and Death*," *TLS*, November 15, 1934, p. 795.

[33] Mary-Joe Purcell, "Political-Historical Bearings in Original Interregnum Drama from 1649 to 1660," Diss. University of Missouri 1959, pp. 102-04, 187-88.

³⁴All of the plays appear in Dyce, *Works,* V; see Greg, *A List of Plays,* #723-728, pp. 837-41; Bentley, *JCS,* V, 1082-88, 1100-02, 1105-07, 1123-25, 1147-49.

³⁵Forker, ed., *The Cardinal* (Bloomington, 1964), p. 3.

³⁶See the discussion of George Buck in chapter V, n.66 of this work.

³⁷George Berkeley succeeded his father as Lord Berkeley in 1658 and in 1679 was created Viscount Dursley and Earl of Berkeley. Any other number of G.B. Esq.'s could be proposed but with nothing to base the association with Shirley. Committee for Advance of Money, PRO MS. SP 19/71 (1645-49), fol 24. In 1643 Lady Berkeley was assessed £125, PRO MS. SP 19/46, fol. 15. Evelyn mentions visiting or dining with Berkeley on three occasions in 1658 and 1659 after he was created Lord Berkeley. *Diary and Correspondence of John Evelyn, F.R.S.,* ed. Wm. Bray (London, 1862-3), III, 220, 230, 231. See chapter IV of this work for a discussion of the dedication of *The Young Admiral.*

³⁸Dyce, *Works,* V, 179.

³⁹Sir Robert, of Scampton, Lincolnshire, matriculated at Cambridge in 1634 and was made a Master of Arts in 1636. Venn, *Alumni Cantabrigienses,* III, 192. On his assessments during the war years, see the Committee for Advance of Money, PRO MS. SP 19/71 (1646-49), fols. 45^V, 46. The "estate vacated per order Feb. 10, 1646" indicates he failed to produce the desired sum assessed. Sir Robert's will, dated 1663, is in the Prerogative Court of Canterbury (PCC); it was entered for probate in 1664. PRO MS. PCC #1965, fol. 104.

⁴⁰Lady Jane may have been William Paulet's aunt. Two letters from Jane, Marchioness of Winchester, to Henry, Earl of Holland refer to their kinship. *Cal. SP Dom.,* 1629-31, #102, 103, p. 463. Armstrong, *Poems,* pp. 35, 77; Howarth, "Poems," II, 276-77.

⁴¹Dyce, *Works,* V, 355.

⁴²Shirley attributes noble pedigree to William Paulet. He shows no other titles perhaps because he was son of a younger son; traditionally, the first-born son inherited the land and titles and other sons were left to "shift for themselves" by entering the clergy or law. In the Pedigree of Portman in the Visitations of Somersetshire for 1623 is an entry for Elizabeth Portman who married Thomas Pawlett, the second brother of the Marquis of Winchester. A note added at the bottom indicates that William was the only child still living in 1646. *The Visitation of the County of Somerset,* ed. Frederic Thos. Colby, Harleian Society, XI (London, 1876), 127.

⁴³SP Dom., Feb. 1663, Charles II, PRO MS. 29/68, fol. 154; see also chapter V of this book.

⁴⁴Wm. Paulet, son of Wm. Paulet of Edington, Wilts, knight, deceased, was admitted to the Middle Temple on November 12, 1632. *The Middle Temple Bench Book,* ed. J. Bruce Williamson (London, 1937), p. 137. A William Pawlett is named in a draft ordinance clearing several people of delinquency in the *Calendar of the House of Lords* in 1647. HMC, 6th R, 1646-47, p. 178b. The fifth Marquis of Winchester had survived his two older brothers and thus, although a third son, inherited the title. He also had younger brothers, and his loss of goods, lands, and near fortune during the civil wars is described dramatically in the *DNB:* G[ordon] G[oodwin], "Paulet, John, fifth Marquis of Winchester," *DNB* (1895-96).

⁴⁵Dyce, *Works,* IV, 277.

⁴⁶Venn, *Alumni Cantabrigienses,* III, 194. Bowier (Bowyer) was knighted on July 4, 1633, at Dunfermline by Charles I.

⁴⁷*Cal. SP Dom.,* 116 (1647-49), 305; the order that he be apprehended is noted on July 11, 1648, p. 184.

⁴⁸Town Depositions, Court of Chancery, PRO MS. C24/762, Pt. 2, #21. On the relationship with Lovelace, see Hunter, *Chorus Vatum,* II, 203. Evelyn's *Diary* includes entries noting that he visited or dined with Bowyer several times during 1657 and 1658. See III, 197, 211, 488, 490.

⁴⁹Linda Kay Ward Ellinger, "A Critical Edition of James Shirley's *The Court Secret,*" Diss. University of Iowa 1979, pp. 102-06. Evelyn, *Diary,* III, 16, 30, 35, 39, 91; Bentley, *JCS,* V, 1100-02. William had been restored to all of his father's honors; he matriculated in 1641 at Christ Church, Oxford. *Alumni Oxonienses,* ed. Joseph Foster (Oxford, 1891-92), IV, 1599.

⁵⁰Evelyn, *Diary,* III, 16, 30, 35; see also "Passes & Warrants, 1653-56," SP Dom. (Interregnum), Feb. 27, 1655, PRO MS. SP 25/112, p. 277.

⁵¹Thomason Tracts, BM MS. E705, #27, p. 2589.

⁵²Dyce, *Works,* I, 189.

⁵³Bentley, "James Shirley and a Group of Unnoted Poems on the Wedding of Thomas Stanley," *Huntington Library Quarterly,* II, No. 2 (Jan. 1939), 221, and *JCS,* V, 1082-84.

⁵⁴Stanley gives testimony in two depositions, stating he is "of Symons Inn in Chancery Lane," gent, in 1647 ("aged 24 yeares or thereabout") and in 1654 ("aged 30 yeares or thereabouts"). See Town Depositions,

Court of Chancery, PRO MS. C24/709, #42; C24/782, Pt. 2, #23. For further discussion on Stanley, see chapter V of this work.

⁵⁵Henry B. Wheatley, *The Dedication of Books to Patron and Friend* (London, 1887), p. 34.

⁵⁶On Ogilby's later career, see Bentley, *JCS,* IV, 948-51; Wood, *Athenae,* III, 742. Verses to Ogilby are printed in Armstrong, *Poems,* p. 41. Earlier discussion of Shirley's acquaintance with Ogilby appears in chapter IV of this work.

⁵⁷Armstrong, *Poems,* p. 41. See the discussion of the theatre wars in chapter II of this work.

⁵⁸Armstrong, *Poems,* p. 40.

⁵⁹*Cal. SP Dom.,* 1649-50, pp. 216, 284. In 1636 the Visitation Books for Lichfield include a notation that John Wright and Rosamund, his wife, of Hatherhage, County Derby, were excommunicated "for having their daughter baptized after a popish minister." Visitation Books, Lichfield Record Office MS. B/V/1/59.

⁶⁰S. Austin Allibone, *A Critical Dictionary,* III (1878).

⁶¹Armstrong, *Poems,* p. 41.

⁶²Edward Phillips, *Theatrum Poetarum,* #85. He probably was the Edmund Prestwich admitted to Brasenose College in September 1642. *Brasenose College Register, 1509-1909,* ed. C.B. Heberden (Oxford, 1909), I, 179. On the political references in *The Hectors,* see Mary-Joe Purcell, "Political-Historical Bearings," p. 188.

⁶³Bentley, *JCS,* V, 1112-14, 1137-39.

⁶⁴Dyce, *Works,* V, 3; see the BM copy C12f18.

⁶⁵HMC, 7th R, Nos. 699, 766, pp. 559b, 563. See also Venn, *Alumni Cantabrigienses,* III, 259. The Committee for Advance of Money assessed a Lady Nightingale in Bishopsgate Ward £300; nothing directly connects her with the Baronet, however. PRO MS. SP 19/69, Nov. 3, 1645, fol. 102.

⁶⁶Town Depositions, Court of Chancery, PRO MS. C24/878, Pt. 2.

⁶⁷Shirley's remarks can be read in Robert J. Fehrenbach, *A Critical Edition of 'The Politician' by James Shirley* (New York, 1980), pp. 2-4; Dyce, *Works,* V, 91.

⁶⁸Houghton Library copy EC65/Sh662, 655p.

⁶⁹*Cal. SP Dom.,* 309, 1635-36, #10, p. 56. There is a court case, Lyon vs Gifford and Gateman, in which Walter Moyle Esquire testified on February 16, 1653, giving his age, 24 years, and his address, West Twyford in Middlesex. PRO MS. C24/776, Pt. 2. An entry in the parish register for St. Giles in the Fields records the reading of the bans three times for the marriage of "Walter Moyle of Twiford in Co. Middlesex Esq and Mrs Mary Stapleton of this parish." The entry notes that they were married Feb. 20, 1654. The register is in the keeping of the Rector of the parish.

⁷⁰In this case, Henslow vs Moyle *et al.,* we learn that Moyle's wife Mary later married Thomas Henslow and that Standerdine, at the direction of Mary Henslow, paid several debts of Walter Moyle after his death. PRO MS. C24/921, Pt. 2, #42. In another case, Standerdine testified on September 28, 1667, in a suit regarding the manor and lands called West Twiford in Middlesex owned by Walter Moyle and Robert Moyle. Giving his age as 48 "or thereabouts" and his address as St. Andrews, Holborn, Shirley stated that Moyle had no money of his own and borrowed several sums before his marriage, which brought £1500 from Mary as dowry. In addition Shirley noted that Walter Moyle had traveled abroad to France and Italy and had stayed there about a year and a half. Town Depositions, Court of Chancery, PRO MS. C24/916, Pt. 1.

⁷¹Bentley, *JCS,* V, 1095-96.

⁷²Andrew P. Reimer, "A Study of the Life and Works of James Shirley," Diss. University of London 1963, I, 141-42.

⁷³For various editions, see Nason, *Shirley,* pp. 408, 414. See also Forsythe, *The Relation of Shirley's Plays to the Elizabethan Drama,* pp. 379-80; Bentley, *JCS,* II, 378.

⁷⁴Reimer, "Life of Shirley," I, 146-55.

⁷⁵Dyce, *Works,* VI, 369-97; Bentley, *JCS,* V, 1097-98.

⁷⁶Shirley wrote little for public presentations such as the traditional Lord Mayor's pageants, and he used masques infrequently in his plays. F. G. Fleay believes Shirley satirized the techniques and devices of popular masque writers such as Thomas Heywood in this piece. See "Annals of the Careers of James and Henry Shirley," *Anglia,* 8 (1885), 409-10 and *A Biographical Chronicle of the English Drama, 1559-1642* (London, 1891), II, 238, 244-45, 299. This article has been rather convincingly refuted by Forsythe, *The Relation of Shirley's Plays to the Elizabethan Drama,* pp. 391-92, 400-01. Shirley typically shied away from exaggerated antimasques and concentrated on the presentation, setting, and poetry of the piece, yet all are exemplified in his masque, *The Triumph of Peace.*

Enid Welsford, *The Court Masque* (Cambridge, 1927), p. 226. Felix E. Schelling suggests Shirley wrote both *The Triumph of Beauty* and *The Contention of Ajax* for Lord Mayor's pageants, but their title pages make it clear that they were written for private entertainment. Schelling assigns 1637 as the date of composition for *The Triumph of Beauty* and 1649 for *The Contention of Ajax*. *Elizabethan Playwrights* (New York, 1925), p. 250. See also F. W. Fairholt, *Lord Mayors' Pageants,* The Percy Society, Part I (London, 1843), II, 56-57; Gerard Langbaine, *An Account of the English Dramatick Poets* (Oxford, 1691), p. 485.

[77] See Nason, *Shirley* for a discussion of the portrait and engravings. Frontispiece and pages facing pp. 139, 151.

[78] Nason, pp. 412-13. Copies of Shirley's grammar books can be seen at both the British Museum and at the Victoria and Albert Museum (#9135, 9139).

[79] Shirley's assent to the Bill of Uniformity appears in records of the Diocese of London, Lib. Subscr., Suppl., 1662-64, Guildhall MS. 9539C, fol. 5^V. See also Sir Henry Craik, *The Life of Edward Earl of Clarendon* (New York, 1911), II, 138-40.

Some other names associated at various times with Shirley whose signatures also are entered include Richard Owen, clericus, rector St. Swithin, and William Symth, teacher in the parish of St. Sepulchre, London. Guildhall MS. 9539C, fols. 3, 9^V. In James Howell, *Familiar Letters,* ed. J. Jacobs (London, 1892), Book I, Section IV, 582-83, a "J.S., Esq. at White-Friars" is asked to criticize a tract written by the Duke of Esperon; the request is dated from London, Jan. 2, 1655 (?). Very possibly the J.S. is Shirley, who as schoolmaster was presumed to offer his services in reviewing contemporary books.

[80] *Cal. SP Dom.,* 179 (Interregnum), 254-55. The original papers concerning the "suspicious persons" are in the manuscripts on the Navy Papers—Interregnum, PRO MS. SP 18/179, Jan.-Feb. 1658, p. 4, 4^V. See also Reimer, "Life of Shirley," I, 32-33.

[81] "Passes & Warrants, 1653-56," PRO MS. SP 25/112, p. 135.

[82] John Walter Stoye, *English Travellers Abroad, 1604-1667* (London, 1952), p. 379.

[83] Dyce, *Works,* VI, 345.

[84] "Passes & Warrants, 1653-56," PRO MS. SP 25/112, p. 306. On Hen. Finch's uncle, Sir John Finch, see C. V. Wedgwood, *The King's Peace, 1637-1641: The Great Rebellion* (New York, 1955), pp. 312, 322, 381; Craik, *Life of Clarendon,* I, 90n.

⁸⁵For the Catholicism of George Kempt (Kempe), see Henry Foley, S.J., *Records of The English Province of The Society of Jesus* (London, 1880), VI, 364; *Liber Ruber: Venerabilis Collegii Anglorum DeVrbe,* ed. Wilfrid Kelly, Catholic Record Society, 37 and 40 (London, 1940-41), *"Nomina Alumnorum, 1631-1783,"* #827, p. 35; "Roman Transcripts," English College at Rome, 1656-59, PRO MS. 31/9-10.

⁸⁶John Wainwright is listed in the Subsidy Rolls on April 1, 1625, PRO MS. E179/147/537. In County Derby one John Wainwright was excommunicated for nonconformity: Visitation Books, 1636, Lichfield Record Office MS. B/V/1/59; Mabel G. W. Peacock, comp., *An Index of The Names of the Royalists Whose Estates Were Confiscated During the Commonwealth* (London, 1879), pp. 156, 212.

After February 3, 1657/8, when Capt. Stayner reported that the *Hawk* ketch had now six suspicious men aboard—he identified only five by name—and that Captain Ashford was charged to remain with them until further notice, we hear nothing more of the entire affair. The records seem bare of information on Albertus Twing, the other man Stayner named; quite possibly his was an assumed name. SP Dom., Interregnum, PRO MS. SP 18/179, fols. 4, 4^V; Reimer, "Life of Shirley," I, 32.

⁸⁷Stoye, *English Travellers Abroad,* pp. 265-70, 273-77, 394-96, 432-37.

⁸⁸C. H. Firth, "The Royalists Under the Protectorate," *EHR,* 52 (Oct. 1937), 637-42.

⁸⁹On Shirley's assessment, see "Assessment for the Militia," Whitefriars Assess.-Militia Tax, c. March. 1664 (assessment made April 5, 1663), Corporation of London Records Office MS. Assess. 18/MS14.

⁹⁰Evelyn, *Diary,* III, 198, 229.

⁹¹The case of Thomas Lilleston appears in the Middlesex Sessions Rolls, Jeaffreson, *Middlesex Records,* III, Feb. 24, 1660, 282. In March Charles II proceeded to give out warrants to recover lands; the palace at Whitehall was crowded with petitioners for preferment and places about the Court, including clergymen seeking to return to their livings from which they had been ejected during the Commonwealth years. See the letters of W. Smith to Mr. John Langley, dated June 30, July 28, and August 4 and 7, 1660. *Manuscripts of the Duke of Sutherland,* HMC, 5th R (1876), pp. 205-06.

⁹²The King's entertainment by the City of London is described in Alfred Harbage, *Cavalier Drama* (1935; rpt. New York, 1964), p. 237.

⁹³On the plays owned by the acting companies and those performed during the 1660's that were written by Shirley, see Edmond Malone, *The*

Plays and Poems of William Shakespeare and An Enlarged History of the Stage, III (London, 1821), 272-76.

[94] Allardyce Nicoll, "The Rights of Beeston and D'Avenant in Elizabethan Plays," *RES,* I (1925), 85-89; W. W. Greg, "Theatrical Repertories of 1662," *Gentlemen's Magazine,* 301 (1906), 71; William Van Lennep, "The Death of the Red Bull," *TN,* 16, No. 4 (Dec. 1962), 134.

[95] Gunnar Sorelius, "The Rights of the Restoration Theatre Companies in the Older Drama," *Studia Neophilologica,* 37 (1965), 77-78, 182-84.

[96] Samuel Sheppard, *Epigrams: Theological, Philos., and Romanticke,* Six Books (London, 1641), Lib. 3, Epig. 6, p. 39. In line three is a familiar reference to Davenant's disfigured nose, the result of his venereal disease. Gebhard J. Scherrer, "James Shirley's Reputation, 1642-1833," Master's Essay Brown University 1948, pp. 17, 21-22. Scherrer notes that Edward Howard published in 1671 a tragi-comedy called *The Woman's Conquest* in which he listed the five best tragedies, two of which were by Shirley.

[97] Dyce, *Works,* I, xci.

[98] Armstrong, *Poems,* pp. 18-19, 78-79.

[99] Shirley's copy will is PRO Mico 170; the original holograph will, which gives us perhaps the largest sample of the dramatist's own hand, is filed separately at the PRO but with the same reference. The administration of the will was entered in the Prerogative Court of Canterbury in November 1666. PRO MS. PCC Admons., Nov. 1666, fol. 203. Upney is in the former parish of Barking.

[100] According to Martin J. Havran, author of *The Catholics in Caroline England* (Stanford, 1962), "Catholic wills usually also have † throughout, the sign of the cross, which again is circumstantial but at least more evidence." Letter to the author from Martin J. Havran, April 5, 1967.

[101] Evelyn, *Diary,* III, 454, 458.

[102] Boynton, *London in English Literature,* pp. 83-89; Walter G. Bell, *The Great Fire of London in 1666* (1923; rpt. London, 1951), pp. 177, 336.

[103] Corporation of London Records Office MS. Assess. 15, 2nd Atr. 29, Chas. II. Shirley may have tranferred ownership or a long-term lease to his son-in-law Standerdine. In 1677 Standerdine was assessed in Whitefriars one shilling as landlord and one-half pence for water tax. Corporation of London Records Office MS. Assess. 61.26.

[104] Mary Poulton is identified in the Administration Act Book as the niece of Frances Shirley's *sister.* This has led to considerable difficulty in tracing Frances' maiden name. She was in fact the daughter of Frances Shirley's

brother, John Blackburne. A check of "Blackburne" yielded John Blackburne's will, which led to Frances Blackburne Shirley's identity. The parish register of All Hallows, London Wall, contains a marriage entry for Mary Blackburne to Richard Poulton in 1646. Alhallowes in the Wall Parish Register, Marriages, Guildhall MS. 9776, March 16, 1646, p. 259. See also the typescripts of Percival Boyd on Marriages, "Middlesex (G-P)," p. 278 in the offices of the Society of Genealogists, London. On the 20th of March 1648, "Blackburne, sone of Richard Poulton & Marye his wife" was baptized in the parish church of St. Michael Cornhill. *St. Michael Cornhill, 1546-1754,* ed. Jos. L. Chester, Harleian Society Registers, 7 (London, 1882), 135.

[105] St. Dunstan's Churchwardens' Accounts, 1666-1681, Guildhall MS. 2968/5. Another possible reference to Robert Sturgis (Sturges) is an entry for his marriage to Katherine Hastings on Feb. 14, 1616, in County Middlesex. See Consistory Court of London, Vicar-General Books, London County Hall MS. DL/C341, fol. 22.

[106] Town Depositions, Court of Chancery, PRO MS. C24/762, Pt. 2 and C24/906.

[107] On Cane, see the *Necrology of the English Province of Friars Minor of the Order of St. Francis, 1618-1761,* ed. Richard Trappes-Lomax, Catholic Record Society, 24 (London, 1922), p. 269; Allibone's *Dictionary,* I; Aline M. Taylor, "James Shirley and 'Mr. Vincent Cane,' The Franciscan," *N & Q,* VII (1960), 31-33; Westminster Cathedral MS. "A" Series, 27 (1633-34), 19; 28 (1635-36), 526; 31 (1655-59), 263; John B. Dockery, *Christopher Davenport, Friar and Diplomat* (London, 1960), pp. 112, 116, 132. Cane's *Fiat Lux* notes on the title page: "By Mr. JVC a friend to men of all Religions"; the preface mentions writing the *Reclaimed Papist* (p. 7). The work possibly was published abroad since no place of publication is given.

[108] Ambrose Heal, *The English Writing-Masters and Their Copy-Books, 1570-1800; A Biographical Dictionary and Bibliography* (London, 1931), has the following entry: "John Warter (fl. 1712) Adver. inserted in No. 377 of the *Spectator,* 13 May 1712: 'Mr John Warter who formerly taught the Court Hand in the Queen's Bench Office in the Inner Temple, now continues to teach . . . at his Chambers three pair of Stairs over Prothonotary Barret's Office in the Temple Walke. . . .'" (p. 111). The marriage entry for Izaac Walton is included in Boyd's Marriage Register, "Middlesex - London, Q-Z" in the office of the Society of Genealogists, London.

[109] Town Depositions, Court of Chancery, PRO MS. C24/848 and C24/884, #167.

[110] Standerdine Shirley's will, under the Commissary Court of London, is Guildhall MS. 9171/36. It was probated November 1678. Commissary Court of London, Cal. 1675-79, Vol. 6, Guildhall MS. 9173A/13.

[111] Christopher Shirley's will, under the Archdeaconry Court of London, is entered in Guildhall MS. 9050/17, Act Book 17, p. 50; the will itself is Guildhall MS. 9052, Box No. 32. There is a manuscript index to the Archdeaconry Court records from 1393-1807, Guildhall MS. 9054/3. Christopher's will was probated by John Plat[e] in January 1697. A Christopher Shirley and Ann Smith were married on August 12, 1661, according to the *St. James Clerkenwell Parish Register,* ed. Robert Hovenden, Harleian Society, 13, *Marriages, 1551 to 1754,* III (London, 1887), 197. In the St. Dunstan's in the West Parish Register is an entry for "James Shirley and Susan Tempest married the 27th of November 1666 by Banes." "Marriages 1656-1739," Guildhall MS. 10347/6. Later entries for the birth and death of the children of James Shirley and his wife appear, including a daughter Mary (Aug. 15, 1671) and a son Standerdine (Jan. 23, 1669). These entries indicate that the younger James lived in Fetter Lane in the St. Dunstan's parish. "Baptisms—Burials, 1669-1709," St. Dunstan's in the West Parish Register, Guildhall MS. 10348/7.

[112] Both Christopher and James Shirley were admitted to their freedom in the Company of Barber Surgeons on April 3, 1666. In the "Audit Book" of the Barber Surgeons, two entries appear: 1652-53, "Of Standerdine Satchill b for James Sherley 2s6d." and in 1657-58, "Of Standerdine Sherley als Sachell for Christopher Sherley 2s6d." Guildhall MS. 5255/1. Under "Admittances of Freemen" for 1665-66 is "Of James Shirley als Sachell 3s4d." and "Of Christopher Shirley als Sachell 3s4d." Guildhall MS. 5255/2, fol. 565. Probably more information could be gleaned by checking further Shirley's sons under their alias of Sachell. A more detailed entry of Admissions to Freedom, covering the years 1665-1704, reads: "Jacob Sherley Appr Standerdine Sherley als Sachill Barb adv [per] servitur 3tio die April 1666 et Jurat" and "Christopherus Sherley Appr Standerdine Sherley als Sachill Barb adv [per] Servitur 3tio Aprilis 1666 eet Jurat." Guildhall MS. 5265/2, fol. lv.

[113] Havran, *The Catholics in Caroline England,* p. 15.

[114] Wood, *Athenae,* III, 737.

[115] PRO MS. C24/1091. Standerdine Shirley also gives £20 to "James Shirley the younger" who was to be apprenticed when he came of age. Guildhall MS. 9171/36.

[116] Wood, *Athenae,* II, 262.

[117] Wood, *Athenae,* III, 740.

[118] St. Giles in the Fields Parish Register, 1638-68, under entries for October 1666. The Register is in the keeping of the Rector. See also Nason, *Shirley,* who prints a facsimile of the entry on the page following 162.

List of Works Frequently Cited

Arber, *Stationers* — *A Transcript of the Registers of the Company of Stationers of London: 1554-1640,* ed. Edward Arber, 5 vols., 1875-94; rpt. New York, 1950.

Armstrong, *Poems* — *The Poems of James Shirley,* ed. Ray L. Armstrong, New York, 1941.

Aubrey, *Brief Lives* — John Aubrey, *Brief Lives,* ed. Andrew Clark, 2 vols., Oxford, 1898.

Bentley, *JCS* — Gerald Eades Bentley, *The Jacobean and Caroline Stage,* 7 vols., Princeton, 1941-68. [I, II (1941); III, IV, V (1956); VI, VII (1968)]

Boase and Clark, *Register: Oxford* — *Register of the University of Oxford,* eds. C.W. Boase and Andrew Clark, Oxford Historical Society, vols. 1, 10-12, 14; Part 2 (1571-1622), Oxford, 1885.

Cal. SP Dom. — *Calendar of State Papers, Domestic, 1547-1625,* eds. Robert Lemon and M. A. E. Green, 12 vols., London, 1856-72; *1625-1649,* eds. John Bruce, W. D. Hamilton, Mrs. S. C. Lomas, 23 vols., London, 1858-97.

Cal. SP Ire. — *Calendar of State Papers, Ireland, 1625-1670,* ed. Robert Pentland Mehaffy, 8 vols., London, 1900-10.

Cal. SP Ven. — *Calendar of State Papers, Venetian,* ed. Rawdon Brown, G. C. Bentinck, H. F. Brown, and A. B. Hinds, 35 vols., London, 1864-1935.

Dyce, *Works*	*The Dramatic Works and Poems of James Shirley,* eds. William Gifford and Alexander Dyce, 6 vols., 1833; rpt. New York, 1966.
Foster, *Register: Gray's Inn*	*The Register of Admissions to Gray's Inn, 1521-1889,* ed. Joseph Foster, London, 1889.
Greg, *Bibliography*	W. W. Greg, *A Bibliography of the Engish Printed Drama to the Restoration,* Bibliographical Society, 4 vols., Oxford, 1939-59. [II (1951), Plays 1617-1689, #350-836]
Herbert, *Dramatic Records*	*The Dramatic Records of Sir Henry Herbert,* ed. Joseph Quincy Adams, New Haven, 1917.
Howarth, "Poems"	Robert G. Howarth, "An Edition of the Poems of James Shirley," Non-Collegiate Thesis, 2 vols., Oxford, 1931.
Hunter, *Chorus Vatum*	Joseph Hunter, *Chorus Vatum Anglicanorum*, 6 vols., BM Addl. MS. 24487 (I, 1838); 24488 (II, 1843); 24489 (III, 1845); 24490 (IV, 1848); 24491 (V, 1851); 24492 (VI, 1854).
Jeaffreson, *Middlesex Records*	*Middlesex County Records,* ed. John Cordy Jeaffreson, 4 vols., London, 1886-92.
Knowler, *Strafford's Letters*	*The Earl of Strafford's Letters and Dispatches,* ed. William Knowler, 2 vols., 1739.
Nason, *Shirley*	Arthur H. Nason, *James Shirley Dramatist,* 1915; rpt. New York, 1967.

S. Mary Woolchurch Transcript	*Transcript of the Registers of the United Parishes of S. Mary Woolnoth, S. Mary Woolchurch, Haw, 1531-1760,* eds. G. M. S. Brooke and A. W. C. Hallen, London, 1886.
STC	A. W. Pollard and G. R. Redgrave, *A Short-Title Catalogue of English Books 1475-1640,* Oxford, 1926.
Venn, *Alumni Cantabrigienses*	*Alumni Cantabrigienses, A Biographical List of all Known Students, Graduates, and Holders of Office at the University of Cambridge from the Earliest Times to 1900,* comp. John Venn and J. A. Venn, 10 vols., Part I (To 1751), 4 vols., Cambridge, 1922-54.
Venn, *Matriculations: Cambridge*	*The Book of Matriculations and Degrees: A Catalogue of those who have been Matriculated or been Admitted to any Degree in the University of Cambridge from 1544 to 1659,* comp. John Venn and J. A. Venn, Cambridge, 1913.
Williams, *Dedications*	Franklin B. Williams, Jr., *Index of Dedications and Commendatory Verses in English Books Before 1641,* London, 1962.
Wood, *Athenae*	Anthony à Wood, *Athenae Oxonienses, An Exact History of All the Writers and Bishops who have had their Education in the University of Oxford,* London, 1691-92, ed. Philip Bliss, 5 vols., London, 1813-20.

Wood, *Fasti* — Anthony à Wood, *Fasti Oxonienses or Annals of the University of Oxford,* ed. Philip Bliss, 3rd ed., 4 vols., Part I, London, 1815; Part II, London, 1820.

INDEX

Abbott, John. *See* Rivers, John (Augustine)
Abington, William. *See* Habington, William
Advance of Money, Committee for, 118, 170, 179, 186
Albovine. See Tragedy of Albovine, King of the Lombards, The
Acting companies: payments to authors, 42; rivalries, 67-70. *See also* Theatres; Queen's Men; King's Men
Actors: lists, 65; in Ireland, 118-19
Aglaura, 71-72
Aldermen, 139
Aleyn, Charles, 16, 47, 49, 52, 53, 69
Allen, William, 119
Allot, Kenneth, 50
Allot, Thomas, 123
Amyntas, 52
Annesly, Francis. *See* Mountnorris, Francis Annesly, Lord
Antipodes, The, 72
Armiger, Edward, 119
"Armilla Nigra." *See* Order of the Black Ribbon
Armstrong, Ray L., 23, 147, 149-50
Atkins, Will, 54

Ball, The, 55, 62-64, 89
Baltimore, George Calvert, Lord, 23-24, 42
Bancroft, Thomas, 15-16
Bartholomew Fair, 92
Bas, Georges, 68, 69, 70
Battailes of Crescey and Poictiers, The, 47, 49, 53
Baugh, Albert C., 20, 22
Beaumont, Charles, 53, 160
Beeston, Christopher, 42, 47, 73
Beeston, William, 140, 196
Believe as You List, 63
Bellings, Richard, 124-25
Bentley, Gerald Eades, 48, 52, 54, 65, 188
Bergeron, David M., 85
Berkeley, George, 8th Baron Berkeley, 117, 118
Berkeley, George ("G.B."), 185-86
Berkenhead, John, 161
Bird, Theophilus, 192
Bird in a Cage, The, 93, 101
Bishop, Sir Edward, 99
Bishop, Lady Mary (Tufton), 99, 148
Bishops' Wars, 71
Blackburne, Frances Ellis. *See* Shirley, Frances
Blackburne, John, 183
Blackfriars Precinct, 140
Blackfriars Theatre, 49, 65, 72, 94, 140
Blakeston, George, 179
Bodleian Library, portrait of Shirley at, 6

Bodwill, John Baptist. *See* Cane, John Vincent
Bolles, Sir Robert, 186
Bondman, The, 61
Booksellers, 178, 180. *See also* Shirley, James
Bowier, Sir Edmund, 187
Bowman, Robert, 153
Bowyer, Michael, 119
Bowyer, Sir Edmund. *See* Bowier, Sir Edmund
Boyle, Richard. *See* Cork, Richard Boyle, lst Earl of
Brereton, Sir William, 113
Britannia Triumphans, 91
Broken Heart, The, 49
Brome, Alexander, 179-80
Brome, Richard, 54, 56, 57-58, 64-65, 67, 72, 73-74, 140, 180, 189
Brothers, The, 158-59, 188
Buc, Sir George, 155
Bucke, George, 155
Buckingham, George Villiers, Duke of, 61
Bushell, Sir Edward, 97, 100
Butler, Elizabeth. *See* Ormonde, Elizabeth Preston, Countess of
Butler, Francis, 127
Butler, James. *See* Ormonde, James Butler, 12th Earl and 1st Duke of

Calvert, Anne (Mynne), Lady, 23-24

Calvert, Sir George. *See* Baltimore, George Calvert, Lord
Cambridge University: curriculum, 10, 14; Shirley at, 11-12; dispensations for study, 13; political influence, 13; Synod of Dort, 14; official entertainment, 14, 17; Puritan influence, 14-15
Cane, John Vincent, 199-200
Captain Underwit or, The Country Captain, 146-47, 149
Cardinal, The, 141-42, 161, 185-86
Carew, Thomas, 66, 67-68, 69, 70, 86, 149-50
Carlell, Lodowick, 65
Carlisle, Lucy Percy, Countess of, 88, 98
Castara, 50, 52
Catholic Court Coterie: members of, 52, 53; Shirley's dedications, 97-99; Catholic revival, 97-101. *See also* Roman Catholics
Cavaliers, 96-97. *See also* Royalists
Cavendish, William. *See* Newcastle, William Cavendish, Earl (later Marquis) of
Changes, or Love in a Maze, 7, 99
Chapman, Edgar L., 142

Chapman, George, 63-64
Charles I, King of England: royal edicts, 45; patron of the arts, 85-86; *The Gamester,* 89; masques, 92; *The Triumph of Peace,* 94-96; to York, 142
Charles II, King of England, 179
Chetwin (Chetwyn, Chatwin), Katherine. *See* Shirley, Katherine
City Madam, The, 62
Civil Wars: and universities, 13, 14; mentioned, 139-62; Catholic stronghold in, 145; Catholics in, 145, 147, 149; and Earl of Newcastle, 144-47; Royalist cause, 182
Clarendon, Edward Hyde, 1st Earl of, 44, 49
Claricilla, 120
Clark, Hugh, 119
Cockpit Theatre, 42, 43, 54-55, 65, 67, 69, 72, 73, 94. *See also* Queen's Men
Coleman, Edward, 153
Coleman, Walter, 160
Colles, Edmond, 22-23, 48
Common Council, Court of, 148
"Common-Wealth of Birds, The," 147-48
Compounding with Delinquents, Committee for, 179, 182

Constant Maid, The, 119, 123, 192
Contention for Honour and Riches, A, 100-01, 184
Contention of Ajax and Ulysses, The, 192-93
Cooke, Thomas, 119
Cooke, William, 52, 53, 118, 119, 123
Cooper, Drury, 126-27
Cork, Richard Boyle, 1st Earl of, 114, 116, 117
Coronation, The, 120
Cotes, Thomas, 123
Councilmen, 139
Court Beggar, The, 56, 73-74
Court coterie, 53, 65, 66, 72, 85-103 *passim. See also* Catholic Court Coterie
Court Secret, The, 142-43, 185, 187
Craford, Thomas, 68
Crooke, Andrew, 118, 123-24
Crooke, Edmund, 123
Crooke, John, 123
Cupid and Death, 184-85
Curson, Lady Diana (Tufton), 41, 99
Curson, Sir Robert, 99

Dalby, Gerrard, 147
Davenant, William, 44, 49, 56, 66, 67, 70-73, 88, 91, 98, 196
Deserving Favourite, The, 65
Devereux, Dorothy. *See* Shirley, Lady Dorothy

Digby, Sir Kenelm, 50, 51, 52
Digby, Sir Robert, 115
Dirge, 153-54, 193
Doubtful Heir, The, 56, 119-20, 187
Drapers' Company, 4, 11
Drury Lane, 41, 43. *See also* London
Dublin, 113, 119
Dublin Court Circle, 124-28; mentioned, 113-30 *passim*
Duchess of Malfi, The, 141
Duke's Mistress, The, 59-60
Dunn, T. A., 66
Dyce, Alexander, 8

Echo and Narcissus, 15, 100
Education, of arisocracy and merchant class, 9-10
Ellis, Frances Blackburne. *See* Shirley, Frances
Ellis, Richard, 183, 184
Emperor of the East, The, 61, 70
England, Church of, mentioned, 115, 131. *See also* Laud, William
Enyon, Dorothy, 159
"Epithalamium," 89, 159
Evelyn, John, 188, 196, 199
Example, The, 58

Farnaby, Thomas, 9, 47
Fairfax, William, 157, 158
Finch, Heneage. *See* Finch, Henry
Finch, Henry, 194-95

Finch, Sir John, Lord, 194
Fitzgerald, George, 16th Earl of Kildare. *See* Kildare, George Fitzgerald, 16th Earl of
Fleay, F. G., 154
Fletcher, John, 47, 53, 160
Foley, Henry, 147
Ford, John, 48-49, 53, 59, 65, 67
Forker, Charles R., 141, 185-86
Fountain, Edward, 198
Fox, John, 68
"Friendship," 159
Frith, Thomas, 11

G.B., Esq. *See* Berkeley, George
Gamester, The, 89-91, 121
Gaywood, R., 193
Gentlemen of Venice, The, 119, 121, 190-91
Gibbons, Christopher, 184
Gilmet, Elizabeth. *See* Shirley, Elizabeth
Gilmet family, 18-19
Gilmet, Richard, 19
Gilmet, Robert, 19
"Glories of our blood and state, The," *See* Dirge
Golding, Sir Edward, 97, 100-01, 147, 184
Goldsberry, Margarett, 47
"Goodnight, The," 152
Grateful Servant, The, 50, 66, 67-68, 69, 72, 98
Gray's Inn, 43, 46, 71. *See also* Inns of Court

Gray's Inn Circle, 47, 48, 52, 53-54, 65-66; mentioned, 41-75 *passim*
Great Duke of Florence, The, 60, 61
Great Fire of London, 3, 182, 199

Habington, William, 48, 50-52, 53, 69, 88, 97-98, 128-29
Hall, H. R. Wilton, 23
Hall, Jo., 52, 68
Hall, John, 47, 52, 53
Hall, John (of Durham), 151, 157, 160-61
Hammond, Mary, 157
Hammond, William, 157-58
Harbage, Alfred, 51, 71, 89
Harvey, Robert, 48, 50, 53
Hawkins, Francis, 160
Hayne, William, 9
Hectors, or False Challenge, The, 190
Heminges, William, 53
Henrietta Maria, Queen of England, 66, 70, 85, 89
Herbert, Sir Henry, 49, 63, 73, 89
Herbert, Lucy, 50
Herbert, Philip. *See* Pembroke, Philip Herbert, 4th Earl of
Herbert, William, 177
Herrick, Robert, 157
Heywood, Thomas, 154
High Holborn. *See* Holborn
Hill, George, 16, 150, 156

Histriomastix, 93
Holborn, 2, 46, 47, 140. *See also* London
Holland, Henry Rich, 1st Earl of, 41, 50, 117, 118
Honoria and Mammon, 184
Honour and Riches, 100-01, 184
Horae Vacivae, 160
Howarth, R. G., 99, 116, 147, 149
Howel, James, 87
Humorous Courtier, The, 57, 65
Hunter, Joseph, 156
Hutchinson, Christopher. *See* Beeston, Christopher
Hyde, Bernard, 156-57
Hyde, Edward. *See* Clarendon, Edward Hyde, 1st Earl of
Hyde Park, 55, 56, 60, 64, 118, 147

Imposture, The, 59, 140-41
Independents, 139
Inner Temple, 53. *See also* Inns of Court
Inns of Court: as university, 10; influence, 43; education at, 43-45; students, 44, 45; writers, 44-45; entertainment at, 45; liberties of London, 45-46, 140; inhabitants near, 46; masque of (*Triumph of Peace*), 48, 92, 93-97
Irish gentry, 115-16
Ives, Simon, 93

"JVC". *See* Cane, John Vincent
Jackson, John, 126
James I, King of England, 85, 91-92
Jenkins, Philip, 197
Jermyn, Henry, 71, 98
Jones, Inigo, 67, 86, 91-93
Jonson, Ben, 47, 49, 55, 65, 66, 67, 86, 91-93, 144
Jordan, Thomas, 119, 125-26
Jovial Crew, 72
Just Italian, The, 67

Katherine Hall, Cambridge, 10, 11
Kempe, George. *See* Kempt, George
Kempt, George, 194-95
Kildare, George Fitzgerald, 16th Earl of, 115, 117
Killigrew, Thomas, 120, 196
King and the Subject, The, 63
King's Men, 65, 67, 69, 140, 192. *See also* Blackfriars

La Danse Macabre or Deaths Duel, 160
Lackenby, John, 181-82
Lacrymae Cantabrigienses, 18
Lady of Pleasure, The, 57, 60, 62, 118, 146
Lang(s)ton, Francis, 178-79
Latinam Linguam. See Via ad Latinam Linguam

Laud, William, Archbishop of Canterbury, 12, 97, 115, 141-42
Lawes, William, 93
Leech, Clifford, 67
Lefkowitz, Murray, 94
Lenton, Francis, 44
Lessons and Exercises Out of Cicero ad Atticum, 46
Liber Eleccionum, 20
Lincoln's Inn, 93. *See also* Inns of Court
Locke, Matthew, 184
London: at end of 16th c., 1-3; surrounding areas, 1, 2, 140, 150, 181; Holborn, 2, 46, 47, 140; Great Fire, 3, 182, 199; Puritanism in, 139, 142, 143-44; political changes, 139, 150; anti-Catholic agitation, 143
Londonderry Plantation, 116
Longleat Papers, 94
Look to the Lady, 120
"Love for Enjoying," 89
Love Tricks, or, The Schoole of Complement, 42, 47, 99
Love Will Finde Out the Way. See The Constant Maid
Lovelace, Lord Richard, of Hurley, 117-18
Lovelace, Richard (poet), 157, 158
Love's Cruelty, 50-51, 128
Love's Welcome at Bolsover, 93
Lover's Melancholy, The, 48, 49, 59, 65

Loving Enemie, 190
Lowndes, Richard, 193

Mad Couple Well Matched, A, 65
Maid of Honour, The, 61
Maid's Revenge, The, 47, 128, 140
Manductio, 193
Manners, Francis. *See* Rutland, Francis Manners, 6th Earl of
Markham, Gervase, 147
Markham, Gilbert, 147
Markham, W., 126
Marshall, W., 193
Marston, John, 43, 55
Marston Moor, 146
Massinger, Philip, 49, 50, 53, 57, 60-63, 65, 66, 67, 69, 70, 87, 140
Mathew, Tobie, 54, 98
May, Thomas, 16, 47, 49-50, 53, 87, 155, 179
Memorials of Bulstrode Whitelocke, 93
Merchant Taylors' School, 8-9, 12
Mercurius Bellicus, 161
Mercurius Britannicus, 101, 161
Mercurius Politicus, 188
Mervyn, James, 127
Middle Temple, 43, 94. *See also* Inns of Court
Middleton, Thomas, 55
Mompesson, Sir Giles, 61
Montague, Walter, 88

Moseley, Humphrey, 157, 185
Mountnorris, Francis Annesly, Lord, 115
Moyle, Walter, Esq., 191
Mulcaster, Richard, 8
Muses' Looking Glass, The, 52
Mynne, Anne. *See* Calvert, Lady Anne

Nethercot, Arthur H., 71
New Way to Pay Old Debts, A, 60, 61-62
Newark-on-Trent, 145-46
Newcastle Circle, 147-49; mentioned, 144-56 *passim*
Newcastle, William Cavendish, Earl (later Marquis) of, 48, 86, 93, 97, 144-47, 149, 193
News from Plymouth, 70
Newton, Marie, 3
Nightingale, Sir Thomas, Baronet, 190-91
Ninth Whelp, 113
Nottinghamshire, 147, 149. *See also* Roman Catholics

Oblivion, Act of, mentioned, 195
Ogilby, John, 113-14, 118-19, 124, 178, 184-85, 189
"On a black Ribband," 151-52
Opportunity, The, 16, 120, 123, 129
Order of the Black Ribbon, 161
Orgel, Stephen, 91

Ormonde, Elizabeth Butler (Preston), Countess of, 116
Ormonde, James Butler, 12th Earl and 1st Duke of, 116-17, 127
Osborne, Henry, Esq., 128
Owen, Richard, 16, 129
Oxford University, 12-13

Papists. *See* Roman Catholics
Parliamentarians, 145-46; mentioned, 139, 150, 155
Patronage and publishing, 86. *See also* Patrons
Patrons: 49, 180; court, 71; Catholic, 97, 98, 99-100, 100-01. *See also* Shirley, James
Paulet, William, 186-87
Pawlet, Lady Jane, Marchioness of Westminster, 97, 186
Pawlet(t), William. *See* Paulet, William
Pembroke, Philip Herbert, 4th Earl of, 41, 73, 87, 171, 177
Pembroke, William Herbert, 3rd Earl of, 177
Percy, Lucy. *See* Carlisle, Lucy Herbert, Countess of
Perry, William, 119
Phillips, Edward, 179
Phoenix Theatre. *See* Cockpit Theatre
Pickel, Margaret B., 85
Picture, The, 53, 61

Plague, 114, 182
Platonic love, 67, 70-71, 87-88, 88-89
Platonic Lovers, The, 56, 88
Politician, The, 119, 190, 191
Politique Father, The, 188
Porter, Charles, 128
Porter, Endymion, 50, 51, 52, 71, 128, 129
Porter, George, 128
Poulton, Mary, 183, 198, 199
Poulton, Richard, 183, 198
Powell, Edward, 155-56
Praeludium, 52
Presbyterians, 139
Prestwich, Edmund, 190
Private Memoirs of Sir Kenelm Digby, The, 51
Professional dramatists, 54, 60, 65-66, 74-75, 87
Prynne, William, 93
Puritans, 13-15, 65-66, 89, 139, 141, 142, 143, 150, 179

Queene of Arragon, or Cleodora, The, 50
Queen's Men, 65, 119, 125, 192. *See also* Acting companies; Theatres

Randolph, Thomas, 52-53, 60, 66, 69
Raworth, John, 123
Recusants, 142, 143, 145. *See also* Roman Catholics

Red Bull Theatre, 67, 68, 69, 119, 125. *See also* Acting companies; Theatres
"Register of Friends," 157
Reimer, Andrew, 192
Rich, Henry. *See* Holland, Henry Rich, 1st Earl of
Rivers, John (Augustine), 160
Robbins, William, 119
Robinson, Humphrey, 185
Roman Actor, The, 50, 61, 65, 66
Roman Catholics, 141, 143, 156, 160, 190, 194-95, 198; and education, 14-15, 195; in the Civil Wars, 96-97, 144- 45; in Ireland, 114-15; in Nottinghamshire, 147, 149. *See also* Shirley, James
Rosania, or Love's Victory. See Doubtful Heir, The
Rose Alley, 46, 47, 150. *See also* Holborn; London
Royal Master, The, 115, 119, 122-23
Royalists, 13, 14, 96-97, 139, 145-46, 147-49, 179, 195-96
Rudiments of Grammar, The, 193
Rutland, Francis Manners, 6th Earl of, 97, 98-99
Rutland, Elizabeth, Countess of, 88

Sachell, Standerdine. *See* Shirley, Standerdine
St. Albans, 17, 18, 22, 23, 41
St. Albans, Archdeaconry of, 17, 18, 19, 21-25 *passim*
St. Albans Grammar School, 18, 19-20, 20-21, 42
St. Andrews, Holborn, Parish of, 46, 47, 150-51
St. Bride's, Parish of, 178, 182, 183-84
St. Clare, Christopher of. *See* Coleman, Walter
St. Giles, Cripplegate, 41, 43
St. Giles in the Fields, Parish of, 140, 202
St. John's College, Oxford, 10
St. Mary Woolchurch, Haw, Parish of, 3
St. Patrick for Ireland, 119, 121-22, 123, 192
Salisbury Court Theatre, 52, 54-55, 72, 73. *See also* Theatres
Saltmarsh, Edward, 178
Schoole of Complement, The. See Love Tricks
Serger, Richard, 123
Shakespeare, William, 47
Shepherd's Paradise, The, 88
Sheppard, Samuel, 196
Sherburne, Edward, 47, 157, 158-59, 178
Shirley, Christopher, 198, 201
Shirley, Lady Dorothy (Devereux), 7, 99-100
Shirley, E. P., 6, 7

Shirley, Elizabeth, 18, 19, 151, 152-53, 201
Shirley, Frances, 182-84, 201
Shirley, Henry (dramatist), 7
Shirley, Sir Henry, 7, 99
Shirley, James: family background, 3-8; baptism and birthplace of, 3; portrait and engravings of, 6, 12, 100, 193; education at Merchant Taylors' School, 8-12; employment for scrivener, 11; at Oxford University, 11-12, 13; study at Cambridge University, 10, 11; and clerical studies, 13, 18; university influences, 13-14, 16-17; literary motto, 15; early university friendships, 15-16; and subscription oath, 17; ordination, 17; study for M.A., 17-18; connection with Archdeaconry of St. Albans, 17-18, 21, 22-23, 24; marriage to Elizabeth Gilmet, 18, 19; as curate, 19; children, 19, 41, 46, 140, 194, 198, 201; and headmastership of St. Albans Grammar School, 19-21; license to teach, 22; Catholicism, 23, 50, 101-03, 149, 160-61, 183, 190, 194-96; early preaching, 24; move to Cripplegate, London, 41; years in Holborn, London, 43, 46-47, 149-50; Gray's Inn influence, 45-46; admission to Gray's Inn, 48; and John Ford, 49; commendatory verses to friends, 53, 124, 160-61, 189-90; relationship to theatre audience, 56-60, 64, 67; compared with Massinger and Brome, 60-65; the theatre wars, 65-72; Platonic love, 89; made valet to Queen, 86; Cavalier taste, 90; comment on middle class, 90; theme of love and honor, 90; recusant, 101, 149; move to Ireland, 113, 114; patrons in Ireland, 117-18; prologues and epilogues for plays in Ireland, 119; plays produced in Ireland, 119-20, 121-22; publishers, 123-24, 178, 180-81, 192, 193; Catholic friends in Ireland, 124-25, 126, 127; return from Ireland, 129; Irish audience, 130; residence in St. Giles in the Fields, London, 140, 151; playwright for King's Men, 140; political plays, 141-42; Newark in the Civil Wars, 145-46, 148-49; Newcastle circle, 147-49; return to London,

149; Stanley coterie, 151-52, 154-62; Latin grammars 158-59, 161, 177, 181,193; Beaumont and Fletcher Folio, 160; commendatory verses on *Via ad Latinam Linguam,* 178-80; residence in St. Bride's parish, 178, 196; Committee for Compounding, 182; marriage to Frances Blackburne, 182-83; will, 180, 183, 197-98; publication of *Six New Plays,* 185; occasional works, 193; later years as schoolmaster, 193-94; Bill of Uniformity, 194; travel abroad, 194; reputation of, 196- 97; death and burial, 201-02

—masques: at Court, 85, 87-88; importance of, 91; Jonsonian, 91-93; as masque writer, 94-95; *Contention of Ajax and Ulysses for the Armour of Achilles, The,* 192-93; *Cupid and Death,* 184-85; *Honoria and Mammon,* 184; *Contention for Honour and Riches, A,* 100-01, 184; *Triumph of Beauty, The,* 154; *Triumph of Peace, The,* 48, 93-97

—patrons, acknowledged: Henry Rich, Earl of Holland, 41, 50, 117, 118; Lady Diana (Tufton) Curson, 41, 99; William Cavendish, Earl of Newcastle, 48, 86, 93, 97, 144-47, 149; Thomas Stanley, 89, 154-55, 157-58, 159, 161-62; Sir Edward Golding, 97, 100-01, 184; Francis Manners, 6th Earl of Rutland, 97, 98-99; Thomas Wentworth, Earl of Strafford, 115; George Fitzgerald, 16th Earl of Kildare, 115, 117; Sir Robert Bolles, 186; Sir Thomas Nightingale, Baronet, 190-91; Walter Moyle, Esq., 191. *See also* plays; poetry

—plays: dedications of, 7, 16, 50-51, 98, 99, 101, 117, 118, 128, 129, 140, 142-43, 144, 156, 158, 159, 177, 186, 190-91; licensing of early plays, 41-42, 47; criticism of manners in, 42; sources, 47-48, 120; Cockpit Theatre, 47-48; comedies of London life, 55-56; prologues to, 58-60, 59-60, 140-41, 142, 144; comedy of manners, 74-75; in Ireland, 119,

140; for King's Men, 140-41; last plays, 141; ownership lists, 196; *Ball, The,* 55, 62-64, 89; *Bird in a Cage, The,* 93, 101; *Brothers, The,* 158-59, 188; *Cardinal, The,* 141-42, 161, 185-86; *Changes, or Love in a Maze,* 7, 99; *Constant Maid, The,* 119, 123, 192; *Coronation, The,* 120; *Court Secret, The,* 142-43, 185, 187; *Doubtful Heir, The,* 56, 119-20, 187; *Duke's Mistress, The,* 59-60; *Example, The,* 58; *Gamester, The,* 89-91, 121; *Gentleman of Venice, The,* 119, 121, 190-91; *Grateful Servant, The,* 50, 66, 67-68, 69, 72, 98; *Humorous Courtier, The,* 57, 65; *Hyde Park,* 55, 56, 60, 64, 118, 147; *Imposture, The,* 59, 140-41; *Lady of Pleasure, The,* 57, 60, 62, 118, 146; *Look to the Lady,* 120; *Love Tricks, or, The Schoole of Complement,* 42, 47, 99; *Love Will Finde Out the Way. See Constant Maid, The; Love's Cruelty,* 50-51, 128; *Maid's Revenge, The,* 47, 128, 140; *Opportunity, The,* 16, 120, 123, 129; *Politician, The,* 119, 190, 191; *Politique Father, The,* 188; *Rosania, or Love's Victory. See Doubtful Heir, The; Royal Master, The,* 115, 117, 119, 122-23; *St. Patrick for Ireland,* 119, 121-22, 123, 192; *Sisters, The,* 142, 144, 186; *Tragedy of St. Albans, The,* 120; *Traitor, The,* 54, 144, 160; *Wedding, The,* 22, 47, 48, 50, 51, 65; *Young Admiral, The,* 49, 118, 186

—poetry: early poetry, 15, 23-24; *Poems,* commendatory verses, 16, 50, 155-56; occasional poems, 18, 160; Platonic love poetry, 89; poems to patrons, 115, 159; prologues and epilogues in *Poems,* 119; political poetry, 143-44; Civil War poems, 147-48, 151-54; publication of *Poems,* 149; poems in manuscript, 152-53, 157; dedication of *Poems,* 155-56; last poems, 197; "Common-Wealth of Birds, The," 147-48; Dirge, 153-54, 193; "Echo and Narcissus," 15, 100; "Epithalamium," 89,

159; "Friendship," 159; "Goodnight, The," 152; "Love for Enjoying," 89; "On a black Ribband," 151-52; "Songe, A," 143-44; "To His Mistris Confined," 89; "To Odelia," 151; "To the Painter preparing to draw M.M.H.," 157; "Vpon the Death of G.D. Engineere," 147; Vpon M:E:S: Epitaph," 152-53; "Vpon Scarlet and blush coloured Ribbands," 148
Shirley, James ("the younger"), 201
Shirley, James, Sr., 3, 4-5, 8
Shirley, James, Jr., 201
Shirley, John, 46
Shirley, Katherine *als*. Chetwin, Chatwyn, 5, 6
Shirley, Lawrinda, 198
Shirley, Marie, 19
Shirley, Mary, 46, 198
Shirley, Mathias, 41, 194, 201
Shirley, Michael, 140
Shirley, Sarah, 201
Shirley, Standerdine *als*. Sachell, 145, 150, 191, 198, 201
Shirley, Thomas, 4, 6, 46
Shirley (Sharlie, Shorley), William, 3-4, 7-8
Short Treatise Against Stage-Playes, A, 66
Sisters, The, 142, 144, 186
Six New Plays, 185

Smith, W., 125
Somerset House, Queen's Chapel, 97
"Songe, A," 143-44
Speed, Samuel, 192
Stanley Coterie, 151, 157-59, 160-62, 178
Stanley, Thomas, 89, 151-52, 154-55, 157, 158, 159, 160-62, 178, 181, 188, 193
Stanley, Venetia, 51
Stapleton, Robert, 52, 53, 69, 98
Stayner, Sir Richard, 194
Stemmata Shirleiana, 6
Stevenson, Allan H., 113, 123, 125
Stone, Lawrence, 86
Stow, John, 4
Strafford, Thomas Wentworth, Earl of, 113, 114-16, 143
Strafford, William Wentworth, 2nd Earl of, 187-88
Strong, Roy, 91
Sturges, Robert, 198, 199
Subscription, Oath of, 17
Suckling, Sir John, 66, 70, 71-72, 73, 98, 120
Survey of London, 4

"T.B." *See* Bird, Theophilus
T.I. *See* Jordan, Thomas
Taylor, Aline M., 100
Temple of Love, The, 88
Thanet, Earl of. *See* Tufton, Diana and Mary

Theatres: audience of, 56-60, 66-67, 121-22; private theatres, location of, 140; Cockpit, 42, 43, 54-55, 65, 67, 69, 72, 73, 94; closing of, 52, 141; Blackfriars, 49, 65, 72, 94, 140; Salisbury Court, 52, 72, 73; Red Bull, 67, 68, 69; Werburgh St., 119
Theatrum Poetarum, 179
'Tis Pity She's a Whore, 49
"To His Mistris Confined," 89
"To Odelia," 151
"To the Painter preparing to draw M.M.H.," 157
Tragedy of Albovine, King of the Lombards, The, 49, 70
Tragedy of the Cruelle Warre, The, 96-97
Tragedy of St. Albans, The, 120
Traitor, The, 54, 144, 160
Tresham, William, Esq., 97, 99
Tribe of Ben, 66
Triumph of Beauty, 154
Triumph of Peace, 48, 93-97
Tuckyr, Francis, 155
Tufton, Lady Diana (Curson), 41, 99, 148
Tufton, Lady Mary (Bishop), 99, 148
Twing, Albertus, 194

Uniformity, BIll of, 194
"Upon a Gentlewoman that died of a Fever," 23-24

Via ad Latinam Linguam, 158, 161, 177, 178-80, 181
Villiers, George. *See* Buckingham, George Villiers, Duke of
Volpone, 65
"Vpon the Death of G. D. Engineere," 147
"Vpon M:E:S: Epitaph," 152-53
"Vpon Scarlet and blush coloured Ribbands," 148
"Vppon Sr. G:Ca:Ladie:Ep," 23

W.A. *See* Habington, William
Wainwright, John, 194, 195
Walton, Izaac, 54, 200
Warter, John, 200
Warwick, Philip, 87
Webbe, Joseph, 46
Webster, John, 141
Wedding, The, 22, 47, 48, 50, 51, 65
Weeding of Covent Garden, The, 55
Weekes, Richard, 119
Wentworth, Thomas. *See* Strafford, Thomas Wentworth, Earl of
Wentworth, William. *See* Strafford, William Wentworth, 2nd Earl of
Werburgh St. Theatre, 119
Wertheim, Albert, 146
Whitaker, Richard, 123, 180, 192

Whitaker, Thomas, 180
Whitehead, Elizabeth, 201
Whitford, David, 181, 189
Whitfriars Precinct, 181, 183.
 See also London
Wood, Anthony à, 3, 11-12, 41,
 46, 144, 150, 155, 158,
 181, 201-02
Wright, Major, 190

Young Admiral, The, 49, 118,
 186
*Young Gallants Whirligigg: or
 Youths Reakes, The,* 44
Youths Behaviour, 160

QU

N

(

Q